HUNGER FOR HOLINESS

THIRSTY FOR GOD

GROWING YOUR GIFTS

by Stephen Gaukroger

Christian Focus Publications

© Stephen Gaukroger 2001

ISBN 1-85792-535-1

This edition first published in 2001 by Christian Foucs Publications,
Geanies House, Fearn, Ross-shire, Scotland, Great Britain, IV20 1TW

www.christianfocus.com

Printed and bound in Scotland by Omnia, Bishopbriggs, Glasgow

Cover design by Owen Daily

Scripture quotations are from the Holy Bible, New International
Version. Copyright © 1973, 1978, 1984 International Bible Society.
Published by Hodder and Stoughton.

The song on page 83 is copyright © 1987
Mercy Publishing/Thankyou Music,
1 St Anne's Road, Eastbourne, East Sussex, BN21 3UN, UK

Hunger for
Holiness

Malachi: A call to commitment today

Contents

1 A God committed to his people..................................7

2 Worship that is worthy...............................16

3 A faithful representative...........................29

4 Commitment in personal relationships...................43

5 A passion for justice..............................57

6 Integrity with money...............................69

7 A new freedom...................................78

8 Refuse to be average..............................85

1

A God Committed To His People

One winter's night, a cold, exhausted tramp was found in the streets by the Salvation Army. Two of their officers half walked, half carried him back to their hostel. They sat him down on a bed, gave him a towel and some soap and suggested he might like to have a wash. Looking in on him ten minutes later, he was still sitting there, huddled up, too exhausted to move.

So they lifted him gently and carried him to the bathroom where they helped him wash. Then they took him back to the bed and tucked him in.

It's OK for God to tell us that we need to be spiritually clean, but we need help to get to that point.

Even when he's given us the soap and towel, we still don't know how to go about cleaning up our act. So he comes alongside us and works with us to bring about the results he wants to see.

God encourages our holiness

In the Boston Public Library in America there is a huge painting of all the 'minor prophets', by John Sargent. On the far right of the painting is Malachi. It's a brilliant portrayal of him, because it manages to capture all three of the main themes of the Book of Malachi: affirmation, confrontation and anticipation.

Like the child who needs to be helped and encouraged to do what his father asks him, we can be sure of God's total involvement in all that he asks of us. As we look at the ins and outs of commitment to God in today's world, we'll discover how he helps us achieve this: he affirms his love for us; he confronts us over things that are wrong in our lives; and he reveals to us the big picture of his activity in the world, so spurring us on to bring ourselves more fully under his rule.

Affirmation

A first glance at Malachi in the Boston painting reveals a smiling, warm-natured man. As you walk past, Malachi gazes down on you benevolently, affirmingly. Affirmation was something the Israelites badly needed at the time when Malachi brought God's word to them.

In 597 BC Jerusalem was beseiged by the Babylonians. The king and many of the important officials were captured and taken away to Babylon, and the Babylonians put a puppet king in place in Jerusalem. But eleven years later, the Babylonians decided to finish the job they had started. They came back to Jerusalem in force and completely demolished it. The massacre of its citizens was appalling and those who escaped the sword were taken into captivity in Babylon.

Seventy years passed. Babylon was itself over-powered by the Persian king, Cyrus, but he made it possible for the Israelites to go back home to their ruined towns and villages. Later, under the leadership of Zerubbabel, the temple was rebuilt and, in 458 BC, many more Jews returned to Ezra the priest. In 445 BC Nehemiah returned from Persia and took charge of the rebuilding of the walls of Jerusalem.

But then, in about 433 BC, Nehemiah was recalled to Persia, and the people's confidence began to waver. True, the people were now back from exile, but the great promises of blessing that had been made to them by prophets like Isaiah didn't seem to be materializing. The people became depressed and discouraged. 'Didn't God say he would bless us once we got back here?' they asked, '... but it doesn't look like there's much going for us at the moment ...'

'Didn't God say ...?' is classic 'Satan talk'. In the very first temptation in the Garden of Eden, Satan sowed seeds of doubt in the couple's mind. 'Did God really say that ...?' he asked. 'Did he really mean that you weren't supposed to do that ...?' Nagging doubts, fears and questions began to erode the people's commitment to the God who had brought them back from exile. But God's first word to them through Malachi is one of love and assurance. 'I love you and I am going to fulfil my promises to you; I will never fail you.' It is important for us to know that God's first word to us is the same. Before anything else, he loves us. When we're going through discouraging times, whether individually or as a church, he wants us to know he's going to keep his promises to us. They are as immovable as Ben Nevis and more secure than any guarantee you could get anywhere in the world. God has never failed anyone yet, and he is not going to start now! He loves us too much for that.

Confrontation

If you look back at that picture of Malachi on the wall of the Boston Library, you may see another expression. On closer examination, the prophet isn't quite as happy as you first thought. His brow is furrowed and he looks, well, a bit concerned.

There's a strength and determination behind God's love. Underlying his words of affirmation, 'Yes, I love you, my people,' is a deep concern for our holiness: '...and here's the reason why some things are going wrong in your life, your society, your culture. Get these principles right, and you'll be able to receive my blessing in those areas.'

We need to be confronted again today by God's holy word, individually, and as church congregations, so that our lives can be brought into line with his plans for us.

A few years ago our church spent some weeks looking at what the Bible says about social action. People are not just souls with ears, but living human beings with all sorts of physical, social and emotional needs, all of which matter to God. As we thought together about this we realised that we had to act on what God was saying in his word. We thought seriously about employing a full-time social worker – and did so. Soon we had two, linked with Spurgeon's Childcare Project. Now the church has a social service which is respected and valued by the local secular social service organizations. When we listen, God will speak and direct our plans.

Anticipation

There's a third feature of the Boston painting. All the other prophets seem to be looking outwards, into the world, as it were. But Malachi is looking forward, straining to catch a glimpse of the future. The Book of Malachi is the last book in the Old Testament, and Malachi was the last prophet the Jews had until the coming of John the Baptist. The picture shows him looking forward to the coming of Christ, when God's promises would be fulfilled.

Malachi knew that much of the pain and suffering of God's people could not be resolved without a major intervention of God himself. So he looked forward to the day when God would affirm his love so clearly that the people would have no doubts about it at all. He also saw that this would mean the clearing out for good of all the people's unholiness, guilt and failure. He looked forward to the 'Day of the Lord' when, with God's help, his people would be made completely holy.

God often uses these three things – affirmation, confrontation and anticipation – to help us move on in our ministry, work, or the way we live our lives. When I was a student at Spurgeon's College, a church in Dallas invited me to go over there for a year's placement. At first I felt a tremendous sense of excitement, privilege and thrill. It was great to feel so affirmed and needed! But then people began to confront me with my motives. Was this going to be just a 'year out' before the 'real' work? Was it a cheap way of seeing the USA? What was I going to be able to give to that church? And then I began to ask questions too. What if God has got something *here*, in England, for me to do? Would I be missing out on doing his work here by disappearing off to America?

But then I found that, as I talked through all these doubts and questions with my father, I felt a growing sense of anticipation about the prospect of going to the States. He helped me see that there were lots of things I could learn, some things I could contribute, and that the call was one I should accept.

With the help of friends and family, God had moved me through these stages of affirmation, confrontation and anticipation, to the point where I was sure that the move was the right and good one to make.

God affirms his love

> An oracle: The word of the LORD to Israel through Malachi.
> 'I have loved you,' says the LORD.
> 'But you ask, "How have you loved us?"'
> 'Was not Esau Jacob's brother?' the LORD says, 'Yet I have loved Jacob, but Esau I have hated, and I have turned his mountains into a wasteland and left his inheritance to the desert jackals.'
> Edom may say, 'Though we have been crushed, we will rebuild the ruins.'
> But this is what the LORD Almighty says: 'They may build but I will demolish. They will be called The Wicked Land, a people always under the wrath of the LORD. You will see it with your own eyes and say, 'Great is the LORD – even beyond the borders of Israel!' *Malachi 1: 1-5*

Esau and Jacob were the two sons of Isaac, but the names were later given to the two nations that descended from them. Because of their origins the nations were really 'brother nations', but there was never anything but hostility between them. The nation descended from Jacob ended up living in the land of Israel, while those descended from Esau settled in the land of Edom, to the south-east of Israel.

God's love for Israel

Because God's people are disheartened and discouraged after their national defeat and long period in exile, he reminds them of one thing: 'I love you.' And he adds, 'What's more, if you look back through your past you can see the proof of that! Think of all the times you've been wayward, rebellious, and gone off on your own without me. Even so, I've never stopped loving you! I had to shout pretty loud to get you to hear my warnings - your exile wasn't just an accident! But I've brought you back from there, too. I didn't forget about you for one moment; I've never stopped loving you.'

The Edomites, by contrast, had a history of all-out rebellion against God. Israel's history was an up-and-down one, but Edom's seemed to be just down-and-down. To Israel, the thing that had been like a kick in the teeth to them was the way the Edomites acted when Israel was invaded and overpowered by the Babylonians. It seems that the Edomites just stood around watching. They didn't lift a finger to help as they saw their blood-brothers dragged off in chains to captivity, tortured and mutilated. They didn't even raise a squeak of protest on their behalf. In fact, they went one stage worse than doing nothing. The evidence suggests that they cheered on the invaders and gleefully helped them haul the Israelites off to Babylonia.

Israel had been totally devastated by that. It was like a man breaking off all contact with his brother when he hears he's on trial for a robbery; or like a husband walking out on his wife when he discovers she has cancer. Israel felt betrayed, abandoned, hopeless and totally helpless.

Yet God says, 'I know. I know all about that. I saw it all happen. I felt your anguish. I counted all your tears. I want you to know that I really hurt with you during that time. And I'm angry with Edom for their treachery, and will bring them to account for it.'

God's love for his people today

God knows the state of his people today, the church. He knows about all the arguments, divisiveness, in-fighting and the cutting way Christian people behave towards one another. He's seen the lack of power and authority in church life, and the vast numbers of people that leave it each year. He's seen how, in many of our churches, you have to backslide just to fit in! As the people of God together, we're far from God's ideal of what it is to be his people. Even so he says to us, 'I love you. I loved you enough, even knowing of all this failure and error, to send my Son to die for you. And I will not rest until you are holy, the true image of my Son.'

Something remarkable happened when God got involved in Jacob's life. Jacob's name meant 'deceiver' or 'cheat', but God told him all that was to change. And to prove it he gave Jacob a new name, Israel. It was as though God said, 'With my love and guidance, you'll become a different person. It may take time to show, but I'll be changing you from the inside out. I take you for my own; I'm committed to you, and will never let you go.'

Individually too, we are his people. When we're discouraged we need to hear God's words of love and care again. Just as he said to Israel, he says to us, 'I've seen the way your commitment to me goes up and down like a yo-yo. I've seen the way that sometimes you're on fire for me, and sometimes you're freezing cold. But I love you.' He's seen our ups and downs, the good and the bad, and longs to reach out to us with his love and care.

You may be feeling that life's burdens are intolerable right now, and that no one understands what you're going through. That may be true – your situation is unique to you. But God knows what's happening to you, he understands how you feel, and he cares about you more than you can ever grasp. Even if there is fault on your part, that doesn't stop him loving you. He never turns his back on us and says, 'Oh well, then, that's it, isn't it? If you can't do what I say, don't expect to hear from me again!' To prove that he will never say that, he's given us the history of his people, Israel. And that shows us very clearly that God's love is persistent. It never fails. It never stops. It never gives up on us.

Many people have found that in the times of their deepest distress, God gives them a special assurance of his love surrounding and upholding them. A pastor was phoned up one day by a young mum telling him the good news that her second baby had been born. 'God's given me a very special baby,' she said. 'Wonderful!' the pastor replied. 'Yes,' she went on, 'he's only got one hand.' Though the shock that she and her husband felt continued to work its way through, God had taken the edge off their deep disappointment. He had given them a clear assurance that this wasn't a mistake – but that he was trusting them with the special care of this special child.

God is in control

It's all very well having a God who loves us, but is he really able to do anything for us? The question that still bothers people today is as old as the hills: 'If God is so loving, why doesn't he do something about the state of the world? Because he's not powerful enough! Or perhaps he is powerful enough, but he doesn't really love us that much to be bothered. No way can God be both loving and powerful!'

Malachi gives a different picture. In his little book of just four chapters he refers to God as 'the LORD of hosts' twenty-five times. It's his favourite name for God: the Lord Almighty, the Lord of the hosts of heaven; Lord of the sun, the moon and all the stars, the planets and everything in the whole of creation. He made it; he's in control of it.

It's great to hear that, but it's sometimes very difficult to believe that God is even interested in what goes on out there in the world, let alone in control of it in some way. We know how he's changed our lives as individuals and how he works with us as a church, but it's harder to read the papers and watch the news on TV and to keep hold of the fact that God is Lord of the whole earth. We're brainwashed by the media into thinking that the ultimate destiny of the planet hangs on the foreign policy of America, or on which third-world countries have nuclear weapons, or on how quickly we can clean up the polluted environment. Yet God's word to Israel was, 'You will see it with your own eyes and say, "Great is the LORD – even beyond the borders of Israel!"' No politician, army general or terrorist is outside the scope of God's authority. He is Lord of all the earth, in control of events, people and rulers far beyond our circle of knowledge.

God's plans for his people don't stop at personal holiness. They're long-term and global! In Philippians we catch a glimpse of what the goal is to which God is working: 'that at the name of Jesus every knee should bow, in heaven and on earth and under the earth, and every tongue confess that Jesus Christ is Lord, to the glory of God the Father' (Philippians 2:10-11). Such a mighty God has the power to make us holy.

You might have the newest, space-age washing machine, that plays tunes and makes you coffee while you wait for it to do the wash; you might get the best eco-friendly washing powder and fill the machine with carefully filtered water, but if the electricity board has cut off your electricity supply, all those things won't be of much help to you.

God doesn't tell us to be holy – and leave us to flounder around getting nowhere. He gives us his powerful love, forgiveness and grace to see that we really make it.

2

Worship That is Worthy

I remember being taken to Sunday School as a child. One morning I was late, so I ran all the way and arrived breathless and dishevelled, one sock up, one down, shirt hanging out and already grubby. I must have looked a real mess. My Sunday School teacher stopped me at the door and, while she tucked my shirt in, she said, 'Stephen, we wouldn't come into the Queen's presence looking like this, would we? We're going into God's house now, so we ought to look our best, shouldn't we?'

I expect many of us had parents who said much the same to us about going to church on Sunday. Getting dressed up in your 'Sunday best' was seen as a mark of respect. But it could also degenerate into an obsession with how you looked. Church life in the 1950s and 1960s especially was obsessed with external appearance. Today if people ask how they should dress for worship, I suggest they come however they feel most comfortable. But the principle of showing respect for God and his house is one that holds good. Malachi certainly felt that not just the Jewish people, but the priests themselves, had forgotten the majesty of God and had grown dangerously slack in their approach to him:

> A son honours his father, and a servant his master. If I am a father, where is the honour due to me? If I am a master, where is the respect due to me?' says the LORD Almighty. 'It is you, O priests, who show contempt for my name.
> But you ask, "How have we shown contempt for your name?"
> You place defiled food on my altar.

But you ask, "How have we defiled you?"
By saying that the LORD's table is contemptible. When you bring blind animals for sacrifice, is that not wrong? When you sacrifice crippled or diseased animals, is that not wrong? Try offering them to your governor! Would he be pleased with you? Would he accept you?' says the LORD Almighty.
'Now implore God to be gracious to us. With such offerings from your hands, will he accept you?' – says the LORD Almighty.

Malachi 1: 6-9

Worship with respect

Malachi confronts the priests and people with two pictures from everyday life: parent and child, and master and servant.

'It's true, isn't it,' he asks, 'that parents are due respect from their children?' Mum and Dad expect little Johnny to tidy up the toys when they tell him to, or to stop bashing his little sister when they tell him that's not the right way to behave. Teenagers are told to be home by a certain time of night – trouble starts when their respect for their parents is not as strong as the pull to be out with their mates, regardless of the consequences! 'You get annoyed when your children don't respect you,' says God, 'but you're much worse than they are! If your children started treating you the same way you treat me, you'd go off the deep end!'

And then there's the boss. If you invited him and the Managing Director of your firm home for a meal, would you serve up last week's left-overs, all mixed up together? Imagine your boss's reaction if you did! You'd be lucky to have a job the next morning. 'Yet you treat me in just that way,' says God. 'Can't you see how insulting it is?'

The religious laws in the Old Testament stated that people should bring regular sacrifices to the temple, to be offered in penitence for their sin. And the animals brought were to be perfect, without any defect or blemish – no gammy hoof, bad teeth or scruffy hide. But Malachi discovered that the people were going through their herds and flocks, picking out the animals that weren't

up to much – the lame, diseased and old ones – ones they were
well rid of anyway, and bringing these instead. 'Try offering those
to your governor!' he suggests. 'See what sort of response you
get!'

'Try offering those to your boss' is a good guideline to follow.
It was probably the thought behind all those parental admonitions:
get washed, cut your nails, wear a suit, look solemn, don't talk,
walk in and out quietly.' But perhaps we've reacted so far against
that sort of approach to church that we've simply fallen off the
horse the other side. We've begun to treat worship very casually.
We don't often think about our attitude to worship, we're not too
bothered about getting there on time, and when we are there
we're perfectly happy to chat to people when other things are
going on. We pride ourselves on not being hung up on the
externals of worship, but what we've put in its place is not the
worship of a heart filled with awe and reverence, but the casual
commitment of someone who just happens to be there, relaxed
and waiting for things to get going.

So how should we approach God in worship?

Bring God your best

The point Malachi was trying to get across was that it's genuine
worship that God wants, worship from the heart – nothing less
and nothing else. A substitute for the real thing won't do. Even a
pedigree lamb or calf wouldn't have been good enough if the
person bringing it did so just for show and not out of genuine
love and reverence for God.

> 'Oh, that one of you would shut the temple doors, so
> that you would not light useless fires on my altar! I am
> not pleased with you,' says the LORD Almighty, 'and I
> will accept no offering from your hands.'
>
> *Malachi 1:10*

A staggering verse! God would actually prefer our churches
to close down and be sold off for redevelopment, than have

hypocritical, insincere worship going on there. He is not satisfied when we offer him 'rubbish' worship, the worst of our time and possessions rather than our best.

My financial training started very early in life. One important principle I was taught as I grew up was this: 'When you begin to earn, Steve, decide how much you are going to give to God. Then make sure you give it to him first, before you spend anything else, because unless you do, you'll find that the money gets spent on other things and you'll end up giving God just what's left over.' God has the right of access to my money before anyone else does.

The principle doesn't stop with money. God ought to have the best of everything we have. Often, our lowest time priority is to spend time with God. 'I'll get round to it if I have time.' So we do everything else that needs to be done, and fit God in to the last few moments of the day. Usually, that's our 'tired' time: it's a bit too early to go to bed, but we don't really feel like doing anything much else. So God gets our left-overs.

Plan your giving

If God is going to get the best of our time, abilities and possessions, we'll need to make a definite decision to put him first. That will demand some self-discipline; not a very popular thing today:

> 'Discipline' has become a dirty word in our culture ... I know I am speaking heresy in many circles, but spontaneity is greatly overvalued. The 'spontaneous' person who shrugs off the need for discipline is like the farmer who went out to gather the eggs. As he walked across the farmyard toward the hen house, he noticed the pump was leaking. So he stopped to fix it. It needed a new washer, so he set off to the barn to get one. But on the way he saw that the hay in the hayloft needed

straightening, so he went to fetch the pitchfork. Hanging
next to the pitchfork was a broom with a broken handle.
'I must make a note to myself to buy a new broom
handle the next time I get into town' he thought ...
By now it is clear the farmer is not going to get his eggs
gathered, nor is he likely to accomplish anything else he
sets out to do. He is utterly, gloriously spontaneous,
but he is hardly free. He is, if anything, a prisoner to his
unbridled spontaneity.
The fact of the matter is that discipline is the only way
to freedom; it is the necessary context for spontaneity.

John Guest

Here are some ideas for how to go about planning what you give
to God.

 # Make an inventory of your time. 'When a person gets into the
habit of wasting time, he is sure to waste a great deal that does
not belong to him.' All the time a Christian has is God's time. Is
God getting a good deal on the time he has entrusted to our care?
Where does all the time go? Here's one way of finding out:

• Take a sheet of paper and draw two lines across it to divide
it into three parts. These parts represent 'morning', 'afternoon'
and 'evening'.

• Note down, at the side of each part, the major activities you
will be engaged in during the day, such as sleeping, eating, working,
playing with the children, housework, study, shopping, travelling,
free time, sport ... or whatever your day involves. Include an
'unaccounted for' line!

• Then, as you go through the day, note down in each part
how long you spend on each activity. If you find that a lot of
time is 'unaccounted for', do the same exercise the next day, but
specify exactly what you are doing for each fifteen-minute period
of the day. This will help you to see how your time is being spent.

• When you have done this for a few days, look over the
results and ask yourself these questions: Is the way I am spending

my time the best way to spend it? Are there things I think are important (perhaps being with the family, visiting an elderly neighbour, spending time in prayer) but that just aren't getting done? Are there things I think unimportant but that I'm spending a lot of time on?

• Now you know where your time is going, plan the next week's activities, dividing each day into 'morning, afternoon and evening' slots, and noting down what you would like to accomplish in each. As someone has said, 'We master our minutes, or we become slaves to them; we use time or it uses us.'

Make an inventory of your abilities. Do the same sort of exercise for your abilities, gifts and areas of interest. The aim is the same: to see what is being underused and what could be better used in God's service. Remember to include all the skills you use at work – often these are invaluable in the church context too.

Get the help of friends. Most of us need other people to help us when we want to stick at something or discipline ourselves. Just think of all the women (and some men) who go to *Weight Watchers*. Are they all stupid? Can't they count calories for themselves? Of course they can! It's just that they're realistic enough to know they need a bit of peer pressure to help them keep up the dieting properly.

Steve Ovett, the runner, once went through a bad patch when he became depressed and fed up with running. So he stopped training. And that might have been the end of his career had not his running partner persisted in dragging him out of bed at six o'clock each morning to go running with him. In time, the old enthusiasm returned – but the skills had been maintained by that crucial partnership.

We all need 'running partners' to help us keep up our Christian commitment. You could covenant with a friend to pray once a week about something specific, instead of watching *Eastenders*. Tell your friend about your resolve to visit that particular person once a month, or your commitment to phone so-and-so regularly over the next eight weeks, and give them permission to keep asking whether you have!

It is this sort of practical care that we need to take if the responsibilities which God has entrusted to us are going to be discharged well.

Be balanced. Don't be ruled by your diary. It's good to have free time, unplanned and unstructured, when you can relax and do whatever you want to. But remember that spontaneity can be overrated! Try to keep a balance between the two.

Catch the bigger picture

'My name will be great among the nations, from the rising to the setting of the sun. In every place incense and pure offerings will be brought to my name, because my name will be great among the nations,' says the LORD Almighty.

'But you profane it by saying of the LORD's table, "It is defiled", and of its food, "It is contemptible." And you say, "What a burden!" and you sniff at it contemptuously,' says the LORD Almighty.

'When you bring injured, crippled or diseased animals and offer them as sacrifices, should I accept them from your hands?' says the LORD. 'Cursed is the cheat who has an acceptable male in his flock and vows to give it, but then sacrifices a blemished animal to the LORD. For I am a great king', says the LORD Almighty, 'and my name is to be feared among the nations.'

Malachi 1: 11-14

A growing church

God's great promise to his people is that they are part of something that will ultimately succeed. God is going to speak powerfully to nation after nation, and the people all over the world are going to have the chance to respond to God in love and worship.

Today, because of the coming of Jesus, we see this happening in ways Malachi would never have dreamt possible; nor might we have guessed a few decades ago just how fast the Christian church would be growing in some parts of the world. In the city of Seoul in South Korea, the church led by Pastor Yonggi Cho now has about half a million members and about twenty thousand housegroups! That's mind-boggling enough. But Paul Yonggi Cho's church isn't the only one in Seoul; there are *lots* of big churches there. There's a Presbyterian Church with 50,000 members, a Baptist Church with 10,000 members, an Episcopal Church with over 25,000 members, and dozens of other churches besides. God is moving in that city. And the same sort of thing is happening in other cities all over the world. There's a revival going on in Rio de Janeiro and in some parts of the city you can go from house to house and find nothing but Christians! The sun of Christianity may appear to be setting over the countries of the West, but it is certainly rising in many countries of the two-thirds world.

The promise God gave to his people through Malachi, that 'my name will be great among the nations', was already being fulfilled in the rebuilding of the Temple and in the people's recovery from their time of exile. But these things prefigured something far more wonderful. God was assuring his people that they were part of his cosmic, eternal plan. That isn't going to be fulfilled in the next five minutes or next five years, but embraces the whole history of God's people through all ages and to the end of time. The Lord encourages us to look forward to the day when the whole world will know that Jesus Christ is Lord.

You and I may feel pretty insignificant, and our churches in the West may not be very exciting, but God is working among his people. The signs may be quiet, but they are there! I think of the captain of a Boys Brigade Company, and his wife. For many years they laboured and struggled with that group of boys, but now they can see how greatly God has used their work. Some of the church's most committed members and leaders are former members of that Boys Brigade. Or what about three single women who started a Crusader Class over twenty years ago. Now the girls they nurtured, encouraged, prayed over and gave so much of their lives to, are scattered all over the world, working as missionaries, nurses, teachers, and as leaders in the churches in which they have settled.

There's no way we, or the church, will be the losers if we give all that we are and have into his service.

A great God

I spend most of my time preaching 'Fear not' sort of sermons. Jesus was often reassuring his disciples: 'Do not be afraid, little flock, for your Father has been pleased to give you the kingdom' (Luke 12:32). When the disciples were terrified by seeing Jesus walk out to them on the lake in the middle of a storm, he wanted to reassure them: 'It is I: don't be afraid,' he said (John 6:20). And in Revelation, where John has a vision of the risen, exalted Christ, he is paralysed with fear. But Jesus reaches out to him and says, 'Do not be afraid' (Revelation 1:17). And yet, there is a right fear of the Almighty. Because he is so great, God is to be approached with awe and reverence.

In many of our churches, we seem to have lost this godly fear. We need to rediscover it. If we don't, we're going to end up with a false image of God: someone who is our friend and pal, who does things for us if we ask him to – a sort of powerful magician. We will lose the true picture of God as the Almighty Deity whom we are to worship.

In our society, it's hard to keep the right view of God in our sights. Any form of authority tends to be mocked. The authority of the police officer, teachers and the leaders in our communities is challenged in a way it hasn't been before. Subjects are joked about on Saturday evening TV in a way that would have caused a public outcry twenty years ago. The borders of acceptability grow wider, and God himself is well inside them. The danger is that, when we live in an atmosphere that ridicules and belittles all authority, we can easily absorb the same attitude ourselves and bring it with us into our relationship with God.

Check it out for yourself: do you see God as a God to be feared? The God of the Old Testament that the prophets pictured striding the mountains with power so that the whole earth quaked with his voice? Somehow, we don't seem to worship that God any more. Now he is a much more containable God, a God who can be packaged in any way we choose to define him, presented in our own image. He's a God more easily understood; a nice, kinder God; a God at our control.

To worship God in the right way we need to come to him with:

Awe: a sense of wonder, almost fear.

Adoration: our total submission to God. As we admit his greatness, and meditate on his great love for us, we free ourselves to love him. The word 'love' is one that easily becomes cheapened in a decadent society. The New Testament Christians felt they had to coin a new word for God's love – *agape*. In our day, 'adoration' conveys the depth of our love for God.

Reverence: being aware that we are in the presence of royalty. The way I like to describe reverence is 'worship on tiptoe'. It's thinking carefully about all that you do in worship, all that you say, and listening attentively for God's voice.

A God who cannot be boxed

We cannot tame God, nor mould him to suit the image we prefer. Perhaps we want to keep him in our denominational 'box' – obviously God prefers Anglicans (or Baptists, or Roman Catholics, depending on your own denomination). We need to recognize his living presence in denominations other than our own. He can burst out of our structures, plans and ideas whenever he wants to, and he doesn't need to ask our permission first!

Among evangelicals, the dividing lines today tend to run between different 'theologies' rather than between different denominations. You may be a 'charismatic', but can you see God acting in quiet, unspectacular ways in people's lives? You might be in a traditional, conservative church; are you willing to let God work there in new ways? In our theological arrogance we often want to keep God boxed into one way of relating to us and his church.

Perhaps we feel we can dictate to him how he should act in the life of someone close to us, or how he should change the attitude of the boss at work. If so, we should prepare ourselves for a surprise! He has the complete picture, not just our interpretation of events, and he will act accordingly.

Perhaps we feel despair about the state of the world. If you're an ardent campaigner for cleaner air, the laws on Sunday trading, the abolition of Third-world debts, or anything else that affects our life together on this planet, you will know what it is to be frustrated and discouraged. Even here, God can surprise us with dramatic answers to long years of prayer – some world leaders' responses to the Jubilee 2000 campaign have been encouraging, for instance.

A warning

There's a note of warning at the end of this section: 'Cursed is the cheat' – the person who cheats God out of what is rightfully his. In the Old Testament, when we read of someone being under a 'curse', it doesn't mean that God, in a fit of spite and annoyance, finds a way of getting his own back on a person who disobeys him. A curse was more a statement of a principle: 'If you persist in that course of action, then this is what will inevitably happen to you.' If we deliberately turn our backs on God, then we shall reap the fruit of that disobedience. All that God longs to give us– freedom, joy, love, peace, a worthwhile life – will be beyond our reach.

I see this time and again in people's lives. A lack of trust between marriage partners; strained relationships in the family because one member refuses to forgive and be reconciled; heart attacks brought on by the stress of covering up dishonest dealing at work; AIDS as a result of sexual promiscuity. Society is 'cursed' by these things.

The effects of consistent, prolonged disobedience can be like a curse in a person's life. They have an inner dissatisfaction and lack of fulfilment. The Christian who persists in doing what is wrong – even when they know it – will not be able to enjoy a stable, peaceful relationship with God. So the hurt and frustration go on, and produce twisted, hurting and distorted people.

We often think we can help people in this situation by changing their circumstances. But what they really need is help to come back to God in repentance. No amount of pastoral care, love or compassion is going to affect the situation of someone living in disobedience to God until that person admits her sin and chooses to release herself from the curse of her own actions.

In his book, *Spiritual Care*, Dietrich Bonhoeffer, a German theologian who died challenging the Nazi regime during the Second World War, wrote this:

> Disobedience, as well as obedience, has the power to transform a person completely. Through disobedience in a particular decision, one can falsify the whole sequence of right thinking...
>
> Disobedience comes in a variety of disguises: as superficial indifference or as the continuous creation of problems; as ascetic rigourism or as sectarianism; as the quest for novelty or as a philosophical restlessness. All that stuff is given a lot of weight pre-eminently to cover a scar in the conscience that lies hidden in the background.

Know yourself
It's important to know what God's standards are if we are to worship him faithfully. But it is also important to know ourselves. What areas of weakness are there in my life that I need to bring under God's control?

All of us have weak points, areas where we find it really hard to obey God. For many people sexual temptation is the big one. The thoughts come into our minds and we enjoy exploring them

– until it dawns on us that they're getting out of control. We shouldn't have let them in in the first place, let alone encourage them to stay. If this is an area of weakness for you, you will always need to be on your guard against giving sexual temptation a foothold in your mind. Displace it by encouraging right thoughts and loyalties to grow there instead: remember your pledge of loyalty to your husband or wife; turn your thoughts to the Lord of your life who died to make you his own, and let love for him fill your mind.

Others of us are workaholics – always working and not giving the time we should to our families, to God in prayer, to relaxing and just being human. It's a constant struggle to disentangle ourselves from the demands of work. If you are naturally conscientious, you will always find it hard to keep work inside its fences. The secret is to want God's good gifts even more! To want to spend time with him, to enjoy the kids, to discover the world he's put us in.

Others of us are basically lazy and have to be kick-started into doing anything at all. We can be really sure God is prompting us to invite our next-door neighbour to church, or to sit down and plan the family holiday, but somehow we just don't get round to it. It is crucial to admit this tendency to ourselves, and to plan ways to fight against it. Get the help of a friend – someone with whom you can share your plans and who will keep asking whether you've put them into practice yet!

William Temple defined worship as 'bringing all that we know of ourselves to all that we know of God.' That means the weak patches of our characters as well as the good bits. Once we allow God's holiness and greatness to probe every area of our lives, he can begin to heal and restore them, change our perspective and our priorities, and help us to worship him with the respect and love he is due.

A Faithful Representative

John Stott, an Anglican minister well known for his writing and teaching, was once asked a question about his devotional life. 'When you get down on your knees and pray to God, how do you feel about your relationship with him? What happens to you?' He answered:

> When I kneel and close my eyes, it's like finding myself against a brick wall. For quite some time as I pray and read the Bible, I feel as if I'm blindly groping my way along this wall, desperately trying to find some way into God's presence. For a while, it's just terrible! I feel as if I'm just going through the motions of prayer. But suddenly I get to a point, after a while of praying and praising and reading the Scriptures, where it's as though my hand comes on the door handle of a huge door; it swings open in front of me and I burst through into a glorious sunshine beyond. At that point, I know I'm in the presence of God.

The door into God's presence

John Stott says that it takes time to find the door into God's presence, and that the key to unlock it is the key of fixing his mind, will and spirit on the one goal of hearing God. It means getting to the point of saying, 'Lord, I want to hear from you, and I'm now ready to receive whatever you have to say.' Stott adds that until he does reach that point everything else he says is just empty words because he's not really ready to accept what God wants to say to him.

We can read our Bibles and pray every day, hear the word of God expounded each week, go to Christian conferences every year and hear more of God's word taught there. But we can still hold ourselves back from God – not letting him into our emotions, spirits, minds and wills for him to change them. Malachi had this to say to some people who must have known God's word inside out – the priests – yet their spirits were not willing to come under its authority:

'And now this admonition is for you, O priests. If you do not listen, and if you do not set your heart to honour my name,' says the LORD Almighty, 'I will send a curse upon you, and I will curse your blessings. Yes, I have already cursed them, because you have not set your heart to honour me.

'Because of you I will rebuke your descendants; I will spread on your faces the offal from your festival sacrifices, and you will be carried off with it. And you will know that I have sent you this admonition so that my covenant with Levi may continue,' says the LORD Almighty.

'My covenant was with him, a covenant of life and peace, and I gave them to him; this called for reverence and he revered me and stood in awe of my name. True instruction was in his mouth and nothing false was found on his lips. He walked with me in peace and uprightness, and turned many from sin.

'For the lips of a priest ought to preserve knowledge, and from his mouth men should seek instruction – because he is the messenger of the LORD Almighty. But you have turned from the way and by your teaching have caused many to stumble; you have violated the covenant with Levi,' says the LORD Almighty. 'So I have caused you to be despised and humiliated before all the people, because you

have not followed my ways but have shown partiality in
matters of the law.'   *Malachi 2: 1-9*

The admonition that Malachi brings to the priests is a devastating
one. There is no cruder, more violent language against priests and
their shallow religiosity anywhere in the minor prophets. He takes
them by the scruff of the neck, shakes them up and says, 'There's
absolutely no integrity about the way you carry out your duties as
priests! You say all the right words and do all the right things
outwardly, but in your hearts you despise me and couldn't care
less about my people!'

Priests of the New Covenant

The tabloids love it when they can get hold of a story of a 'naughty
vicar' and splash the sordid details all over their front pages. People
still feel particularly cheated when someone they have trusted
betrays that trust or takes advantage of their position of
responsibility. Recently, the media spotlight has not been so much
on church ministers as on parents and teachers who abuse the
trust of the children in their care. Many people have felt the same
sort of outrage and cynicism over the one or two doctors who
abuse the system and breach patients' trust.

This sort of hypocrisy sickens: people posing as good, upright
and trustworthy, while all the time fleecing those who take them
at their word. So when we see their come-uppance, we're glad.
'Great! They're getting the hammering they deserve! Isn't it good
that they're being criticised – those 'holy men'?'

It's easy to point the finger. But we are the priests of the new
covenant. All who live this side of the cross, by faith in Christ, are
called to pray for others, and to set an example of holy living.
Malachi's words to the priests of his day don't apply just to those
'in holy orders' but to all who call themselves Christians.

Unity of word and action

Part of a prayer of confession in a recent service during the Week

of Prayer for Christian Unity, went like this:
    We acknowledge that in many ways
        our lives lack unity.
    Between the ideals and the pressures
        there is compromise.
    Between the dreams and the realities
        there are frustrations.

    Between the belief and the expression
        there is misunderstanding and conflict.
    And so we turn to you to unite us.

    Lord, to whom else could we go?
        You alone have the words of eternal life.
    As we centre our lives on you,
        melt our divisions and make us one.

Malachi takes the same idea of a divided people, but applies it to the life of the individual. It's not just relationships with others that are fragmented and cold, but within ourselves there are divided loyalties, different aims and desires, all pulling us in different directions.

I have known dozens of Christians who made a commitment to Christ many years ago and who now read their Bibles, pray, and think their spiritual act is together. But in reality they have never come to the point of saying, 'God, I really will do what you tell me to do. I will bring my life in line with what your word says: in what I think, in what I desire, in what I do.'

Malachi's plea is for integrity: full integration of the body, mind, will and emotions in God's service. Integrity means 'oneness': being the same in what we do as in what we say. The things we say on Sunday at church are to be worked out in the way we behave on Monday at work.

Suppose you were talking with a Christian friend at work about what you were doing on Sunday. Then a non-Christian colleague comes along and joins in the conversation. I guess the topic would change very quickly! Of course, it may have to; the non-Christian may not understand a word of what we're on about. But it's often easier to be one sort of person with our Christian friends, and another with our non-Christian friends – a person we think will be more acceptable to them.

One of the tragedies affecting the Renewal movement in this country is that some people have simply taken on the language of renewal without its reality. In the last twenty years we have learnt to talk about the Holy Spirit; to say, 'Yes, Holy Spirit, come and fill my life,' but for many of us, that's as far as it has gone. Our vocabulary has changed, but the holiness of our lives hasn't. Let's not just talk about being filled with the Holy Spirit, but *be* filled with him. Let us not just talk about how important it is to be holy, but *be* holy as the people of God.

When I was an impressionable young teenager I was made paranoid about holiness of life by a speaker at a youth conference. He read two verses from Luke's Gospel, which say: 'There is nothing concealed that will not be disclosed, or hidden that will not be made known. What you have said in the dark will be heard in the daylight, and what you have whispered in the ear in the inner rooms will be proclaimed from the roofs' (Luke 12: 2-3).

Then he looked round at this crowd of insecure, guilt-ridden young Christians and said, 'One day, everything you have ever done that was wrong is going to be shouted from the roof tops!' We were terrified! 'Oh no!' I groaned; 'my parents will find out!'

Now I realize that the speaker's interpretation of those verses was completely wrong. They were actually given by Jesus to his disciples as a word of encouragement and comfort as they put up with the taunts and ridicule of the powerful Pharisees. 'Don't worry,' Jesus says, 'You may have to watch what you say about me now, but the day is coming when you'll be able to shout the gospel from the roof tops: it won't be suppressed any more.'

I believe far more harm than good came out of that speaker's misinterpretation of those verses. Many young people suffered a sort of holy paranoia for years after. We were kept in line spiritually through sheer stark fear that one day everyone would know exactly what we'd been up to and what we'd said and done. The prospect still haunts me! All the things I shouted and screamed at the kids last night; the snide thing I said to my wife when she burnt the dinner – all that on a big screen in front of the congregation in five minutes' time for everyone to see!

But if he can't tell us anything about what those verses in Luke mean, that youth speaker can tell us something about the nature of integrity. Our lives are to be more and more transparent; less and less clouded by pretence.

Setting the pace

Malachi lived in a confusing time. It was difficult to know for sure what was right and what was wrong. The whole of their society was only just emerging from total devastation; surely it was natural that the leaders and the people didn't really know what God expected of them? The lives of the Jewish people were messy and chaotic, through circumstances beyond their control.

There's a difference between an outwardly chaotic life and an inwardly chaotic one. You may be going through the most messy of circumstances. Perhaps a house move, job change, something intensely unsettling like the break up of a relationship. The lives of the Jewish people were messy and chaotic in this sense: their broken-down buildings had to be rebuilt and their social structures had to be put back on a stable footing. Yet even though the Temple had been rebuilt, they let their inner spiritual lives stay in a mess. The priests were going through all the right motions but, underneath, they couldn't care less about the God they were supposed to be doing it all for.

The hypocrisy of the Jewish leaders spread to the rest of the people like an infectious disease: 'You have turned from the way and by your teaching have caused many to stumble' (Malachi 2:8). If you are in a leadership position – whether on the shop floor, in the office or in church life – remember that the people you lead will grow to absorb and reflect your own way of thinking and behaving. If they think you're hypocritical and insincere, they'll be wary of you and become devious in the way they relate to you and one another. If you always know best and won't listen to any other opinions, the people in your care will soon see it's no use trying to talk about anything with you. So they'll wither, grow apathetic, go somewhere else, or stay and become a pain in the neck! In church life, it's a rare person who can live consistently beyond the low spiritual standards of his or her spiritual leaders.

I feel the pain of any challenge to my integrity. And that's because the accusation is often right – at least in part. None of us are completely whole people, wholly integrated. All our lives we'll be doing God's work from mixed motives, without total commitment, with plenty of selfishness and pride mixed in. But Malachi reminds me that wilful and deliberate internal disunity is a disease that will gradually destroy my spiritual health and, as a leader, will put in jeopardy the spiritual health of the people in my care.

Lives that bless others

When the reviews of Julia Roberts' performance in *Pretty Woman* dripped with her praise, she made a supersonic bound forward in her film career. But suppose a member of the Cabinet did something that was warmly praised by his rival in the Opposition; that praise would be more like a millstone round his neck! Receiving praise from the wrong people can mean the kiss of death to a person's hopes and plans!

Malachi warns the priests that, in the same way, their blessings on the people will be worse than useless. 'I will curse your blessings,' God tells them. 'Yes, I have already cursed them, because you have not set your heart to honour me' (Malachi 2:2). In blessing the people, the priests were saying, 'Lord, please give them all the things you've given me.' From now on, says God, that will be asking for trouble in a big way! Someone blessed by one of those priests could count on a future as secure and blessed as the Pope's would be if he were hailed by 'Teflon Don', the godfather of the mafia, as a close friend and confidante!

As priests of the new covenant, how can we make sure our lives are a blessing to others and not a curse?

 # Bless by your words. There are other priestly ways of blessing people than saying, 'God bless you!' As a priest of the new covenant, make sure that all you say is a true reflection of the mind of God. Hasty, bitter and angry words can cut far more deeply than we think they can, and can leave a person wounded for years. By contrast, God deals with us gently and kindly. He encourages us and builds us up, helping us to grow strong in those areas where we are weak. The cumulative effect of his words to us is blessing. Our words also should encourage and affirm others.

 # Bless by your actions. You don't need to raise your arms over a congregation, or make the sign of the cross, to give people a priestly blessing! We bless others by doing kind things for them, sacrificing our time and energy on their behalf.

 # Bless consistently. The test of a good pastor or preacher is consistency. Can he care for his flock, or preach consistently, no matter how he's feeling? The same goes for a priest. In whatever situation we're in we should be looking for ways to bring blessing to others. Keep the question in the forefront of your mind: 'How can I bless the people I meet today?' That applies especially to our families. We all hear stories of pastors or priests who bless their congregations on a Sunday morning, then go home and are miserable, domineering or sulky with their families. A priest of the new covenant should always be asking, 'how can I be a blessing today to my wife/husband, children, neighbour?'

Lives that mirror God's purity

The priests that Malachi saw prided themselves on their special position. They expected people to treat them with respect and receive with gratefulness any kind words they might utter. But Malachi challenged all that. 'You think that all you touch turns to gold? In fact, all you touch is doomed to destruction. You don't purify people by being with them, you defile them in God's sight!'

> Because of you I will rebuke your descendants; I will spread on your faces the offal from your festival sacrifices, and you will be carried off with it.   *Malachi 2:3*

When the priests offered a sacrifice, they were to remove all the animal's innards or offal, because it was considered to be 'unclean', offensive to God. Then the innards were taken right outside the inhabited area of town and dumped in the rubbish pit.

> 'Yet,' says God, 'you might as well be offering me nothing but offal on those sacrifices. Everything you do is horrible, offensive and loathsome as the most unclean thing you could offer me. That's what I think of your spiritual leadership, of your lack of integrity. It stinks! It's unclean! You think you are getting rid of the ceremonial uncleanness by taking away the innards and burning them, but you're not, because the uncleanness is inside you.'

Nowhere in the Old Testament is there another such damning condemnation of empty religiosity.

In Malachi's day the Jewish people boasted that God had given his Law to *them*, not to anyone else, and that their God was greater than anyone else's. But the nations around simply looked and scoffed and said, 'Then why aren't you *keeping* his Law, especially if he's such a great and powerful God?'

People outside the church expect to find integrity inside it. They're always hearing the church talk about morals, ethical standards and values, so when they look inside they expect to see men and women who say what they mean and mean what they say. But if they look hard, they'll probably find Christians cheating on their Income Tax, or leading immoral sexual lives and generally seeming no different from anyone else. As long as there is a gap between what we profess and what we do, the world will say, 'So what?' to our faith. Those outside the church can often spot our lack of integrity more quickly than our Christian friends can. We can fool our friends because they already trust us. Someone who doesn't have any reason for trusting us needs to have proof of our integrity before he will.

In a survey I conducted a few years ago to find out the questions and feelings non-Christians had about Christians and the church, the comment I heard most often was: 'Well I don't want to be a Christian; I know one and his behaviour is lousy!' Hypocrisy is the number one problem for non-Christians; a lack of integrity in the lives of God's people.

Every so often we need to give ourselves a spiritual MOT. Here are some things to check over:

Is everything above board? We need to live truthful lives, not just in what we say, but in how we justify our actions. 'It'll be all right if I take just a few sheets of paper from the office without paying; after all, I worked through part of my lunch hour today.' Or, 'I might as well stay at a five star hotel on this business trip; if I didn't, and claimed for the expense anyway, the firm would pay up!' Self-justification is very deceptive. There is often more than one way of looking at a situation. Many of the dilemmas we find ourselves in are not easy to untangle, and the right way to act is not always clear. But we should hear warning bells when we realize we're trying to justify our actions to ourselves. The chances are that they're not entirely above board.

Develop a guilty conscience. Two men ran a tailoring business. One day their young assistant was left in charge of the shop while one partner was out and the other worked in the back

room. A wealthy lady came in to collect a new blouse she had ordered. After she had paid for it and gone, the young assistant suddenly realized she'd paid for her £49.99 blouse with a £100 note instead of a £50 note – but he'd only given her change for £50.

Thinking he should run after her and hand over the rest of her change, he dashed first into the back room and said to his boss: 'Look! That lady gave me a £100 note, but I only gave her change for £50! What should I do?' His boss thought for a while then said, 'Well, the moral issue is a straightforward one: do I tell my partner, or do the two of us share the extra between ourselves?'

Whose moral standards are we following – the Bible's or those of the people with whom we live day by day? Like a set of bad scales, our conscience can gradually get inaccurate and needs to be readjusted along biblical lines.

How do I react when people ask probing questions? Suppose your house group leader announced that she was going to tail you for a week, coming to work with you each day and wandering about in your house in the evenings. Would there be things you wanted to hide from her? Things you'd rather she didn't know about? When people start getting close to us, either by being around or by asking probing questions, our reactions may tell us something about the integrity of our lifestyle. If we quickly feel 'got at' it may be a sign of an uneasy conscience.

A faithful representative
In the middle of the report of the priests' base behaviour, Malachi sets a gem: a lovely description of the life of a man or woman of God, when that life faithfully reflects God's character.

'Levi ... revered me and stood in awe of my name. True instruction was in his mouth and nothing false was found

on his lips. He walked with me in peace and uprightness,
and turned many from sin.'   *Malachi 2:5-6*

I guess we'd all like to have that epitaph on our tomb-stones!
Levi was one of the sons of Jacob, and it was his male descendants
who were called by God to be priests for the rest of the people
of Israel. The description Malachi gives here is of a typical Levite
early on in Israel's history, when they were still taking their priestly
tasks seriously. It shows us a person who tells the truth about
things of God, who doesn't lie or cheat, manipulate or deceive.
He is transparently honest and open, and lives life in company
with God. Any who are like him are his true descendants.

All Christian believers are called to be priests in the work of
Christ, offering spiritual worship and sacrifices of praise and
obedience (see 1 Peter 2: 4-12). We are the contemporary
descendants of Levi, and our lives should match the description
given of him.

The picture is of someone who gently but firmly gets involved
in the life of the many people around and, among other things,
'turns many from sin'. A recent survey about muggings on the
streets of New York revealed that nine muggings out of ten happen
while other people looked on and did nothing about it. And an
article in *The Times* in January 1992, headlined '750 police attacked
in ten days', read:

'"The public should be more willing to help police who are
attacked", the Association of Chief Police Officers said yesterday
as it released figures showing that nearly 750 officers were attacked
over Christmas and the New Year ...'

The association, which represents chief constables, said: 'We
don't want to put anyone at risk but all too often many officers
report that when they are struggling with an offender in the street,
members of the public just stand there and look on when some
modest gesture of physical support might be all that is needed.'

We don't want to get involved. 'That's somebody else's
problem.' 'He's paid to do that.' 'I may get dragged into the whole

business.' We are becoming increasingly isolated from one another in society, running from the safety of our nuclear-family houses to the security of the office, and back again, talking to as few people in between as possible. All kinds of sociological pressures push us into this way of living.

It's so easy to drink in the spirit of the age. When we see the neighbour's son getting increasingly involved in some harmful activity, or hear one neighbour's bitchy comments about another, we pray for them, of course. But we also prefer to let them go their own way than take the risky step of 'interfering'. And we justify that by telling ourselves, 'They don't want me to get involved; they'll think I'm just a nosey busybody.'

The godly priest is defined as one who does get involved; not in a pushy way, but by being bothered about how others behave, and drawing them back from the brink of wrong with love and compassion.

Getting involved without getting people's backs up

When we are concerned about someone, how can we get involved without getting their backs up? Here are some suggestions:

Speak with genuine humility. Don't assume you are speaking with the voice of God; it is possible that your perception of the situation might be wrong! An arrogant approach will very quickly alienate people but a gentle, humble approach may help to draw them out: 'I don't want to interfere but it seems to me that ...' 'Please tell me if my perception is all wrong, but it appears to me that ...'

Write to the person concerned. That gives them more time to weigh up what you are saying, and gives you more time to choose your words carefully. You can also be more subtle, simply hinting at an area where you think there may be problems. Perhaps a couple seem to be drifting apart; you could broach it by writing something like: 'If John's long hours at work ever are a problem, I'd be happy to do what I can ...' Open up the possibility for communication.

\# *Invite the person round for coffee,* so that you create a 'natural' time for talking.

\# *Cultivate your friendships deliberately,* both inside and outside the church. Get to know people increasingly well, and don't stay content with superficial levels of friendship.

\# *Let people know that the church as a whole is a place of refuge and resource. You* might not be the person your next door neighbour wants to unburden herself to, but she may be prepared to find someone else at church with whom she'll feel happier to do so.

\# *Live an approachable lifestyle.* Take the long way round to the shops if it means you're likely to see more people to speak to. Allow extra time for those 'chance' conversations in Sainsburys or Tescos. Be around, be visible. Of course, it's not always possible to live like this; the pressures of work don't allow it. In that case, schedule into your diary planned times of 'slack', when you can be available to others without feeling guilty about the work that's not getting done.

\# *If your church has just one service on a Sunday, use the rest of the day constructively to build up friendships and get to know your neighbours.* Invite them round for the evening, or invite out for the afternoon that new couple from the church. Our time and our homes are gifts from God to use in building up his kingdom. Let's use them!

4

Commitment in Personal Relationships

Jewish tradition would have us believe that the problem of unfaithfulness in marriage is one that has plagued us from the dawn of time. Whenever Adam was late back home, the story goes, Eve counted his ribs to make sure God hadn't made another woman out of them!

Malachi, too, speaks of marriage and faithfulness in the context of creation – the creation of the people of Israel:

> Have we not all one Father? Did not one God create us? Why do we profane the covenant of our fathers by breaking faith with one another?
> Judah has broken faith. A detestable thing has been committed in Israel and in Jerusalem: Judah has desecrated the sanctuary the LORD loves, by marrying the daughter of a foreign god. As for the man who does this, whoever he may be, may the LORD cut him off from the tents of Jacob – even though he brings offerings to the LORD Almighty.
>
> *Malachi 2:10-12*

Malachi is confronting the people with the fact that they have broken their covenant of commitment to him. God sees our decision to follow him and commit ourselves to him as being as binding and exclusive as a marriage covenant. And when we turn away from that commitment, it is as painful to him as adultery. He says that the Israelites, who once faithfully pledged themselves to him as their only God, have forgotten all about him and are taken up instead with 'the daughter of a foreign god.' All their time, concern and interests are directed towards everything but God.

Married to Christ

In the New Testament, Paul speaks of Christians being the bride of Christ (Ephesians 5: 25-27). When you became a Christian, you gave your life to Christ. He came to live inside you and the two of you became one. The divine life of God joined itself with your spirit, and a sort of supernatural oneness took place. God came to live inside you – the new, number one relationship in your life. It is a unique relationship between God and you. An abbot called Symeon, who lived in the tenth century, described the wonder of it like this:

> He was suddenly completely there,
> united with me in an ineffable manner,
> joined to me in an unspeakable way
> and immersed in me without mixing
> as the fire melds one with the iron,
> and the light with the crystal.
> And he made me as though I were all fire.
> And he showed me myself as light
> and I became that which before I saw
> and I had contemplated only from afar.
> I do not know how to express to you
> the paradox of this manner.
> For I was unable to know
> and I still now do not know
> how he entered, how he united himself with me ...
> Nevertheless, having become one being,
> I and he to whom he was united,
> how shall I call myself?
> God, having two natures, is one person;
> he has made me a double being.

When we live as if God is just one among many relationships that we have, or even act as if he's not there at all, we're living a divorce; we're divorcing God. Some of us divorce him from our daily lives, not thinking of him from one week to the next. Some of us divorce him from our sexual lives – not allowing him any say in what happens there. Or perhaps we divorce him from our moral and ethical life – what goes on at work, for instance. Some of us divorce him from everything apart from the religious bit. We keep him wrapped up in a box and stick a label on it that says: 'For Sunday morning, Sunday night and house-group night only. Do not let out at any other time!' And we'll only release God into our lives on those occasions. That's like keeping your spouse locked up; perhaps allowing him or her to use the bathroom and the bedroom, but not any other room in the house.

God calls us back to a full marriage relationship with himself, to be completely and utterly faithful to him. Only then, when God is fully involved in every aspect of our life, will our behaviour as Christians be filled with integrity.

It's easy to think that ministers, pastors and other people in full-time Christian work don't have this problem. After all, they spend all their time reading the Bible or praying, preaching or counselling, don't they? But even for those of us in that sort of work, our marriage to Christ has to be maintained. Unless I *invite* God into every situation, he won't be there, despite the fact that I may be going through the religious exercises. I can counsel someone and leave God completely out of it by not inviting his Spirit and his word to cast light on the problem. I can even read the Bible without inviting God to speak with me through it. You might find me at nine o'clock on a Sunday morning, frantically leafing through Malachi chapter 2 and saying, 'Lord, you must have *something* to say out of this!' That's just using God to get a sermon or talk; studying the Bible for its own sake, rather than to hear what God has to say to me.

Perhaps you teach a class at school, work in a factory or office, travel a lot in the car or deal with people – whatever your situation, if God is divorced from it there will be a lack of integrity in your life. You are married to Christ. So, day by day, invite him into every aspect of your life, so that he becomes fully part of it.

Marriage within the context of faith

The Jews had done something which brought real problems in their relationship with God. Many of them had married people from another culture and race. Now that in itself is not a problem. It can be very enriching. The Bible gives examples of good, God-honouring marriages between people of different races and cultures. The problem with the marriages that Malachi saw as he looked around was that the Jews had married people who had no commitment to God. Those people had brought their own 'gods' into the marriage. They had different priorities and moral standards, and certainly didn't try to live their lives according to what God wanted.

That still happens today. A young Christian woman falls in love with a nice, kind, good-looking guy – who's not a Christian. So what? Does it matter? As long as he's happy for her to carry on going to church, isn't it all right? And anyway, won't she be able to have a good influence on him, and bring him to faith in Christ, too.

But isn't it a bit underhand to marry someone hoping to convert him or her? We feel hypocritical if we invite someone to an evangelistic service at church without first telling them what's going to happen. It doesn't seem any better to marry someone with the aim of converting him after?

Many young Christian women, feeling the pressure to get married, have gone ahead with marriage to a non-Christian. The years that follow are not always as happy as they had hoped for. Here is a letter written by one such woman to a younger girl in her church:

I watched you tonight; I wished for an opportunity to talk with you. I watched your beautiful face as you sang and worshipped. You reminded me of myself seven years ago. And then, after church, I watched you as you got into that car with a boy who does not know God. Oh yes, he was at church tonight. He even went to the altar and shed a few tears. I am sure you would not accept the idea that for him this is just a means to an end.

Seven years ago I was in your shoes. I had known God since my early teens, and had grown up under God-anointed preaching and teaching. I didn't lack boyfriends or dates, as is so often the case with Christian girls in churches where the girls outnumber the boys. Some very consecrated, wonderful young men came my way. But Satan, who watches diligently and waits patiently to ensnare a soul, saw me one day as I was lukewarm. Oh, I was still going to church and doing all the right things outwardly. But I had never really had that special moment with God when his will and mine were made one.

I met him at work. And before long, without anyone else knowing it, I felt I couldn't live without him. He knew about genuine Christianity, and when he went to church with me, he went to the altar and cried. And so I married him, while my family and those who loved me wept and agonised.

It was just six months after, that I realized my soul was in danger and that I needed a special touch from God. I prayed through, and got a grip on God. Then the battle began. No, he wasn't going to church any more. I can count on my fingers the number of times he's been during the last seven years. Before I married him, the thought of living without him was unbearable. 'How lonely I would be!' I thought. But now I know what real loneliness is, and I'd like to tell you about it.

Loneliness is receiving a blessing from God and going home to a man you can't share it with. He isn't interested; he's watching television. Loneliness is going to a church social alone and watching the young couples enjoy God's blessings together. You can go alone or stay at home alone; he has other interests.

Loneliness is feeling the urgency of Christ's coming and knowing the one you love most on earth is not ready, and shows no signs of caring.

Loneliness is seeing two children born and knowing that if your influence is to outweigh his it will be a miracle.

Loneliness is going to a General Conference and seeing young couples everywhere who are truly one and dedicated to God's work. And there goes the young man who loved you once and wanted to marry you. He's preaching the gospel now, and has never married. Oh, God! Help me! I mustn't think of it.

Loneliness is lying awake struggling with the suspicion that he's unfaithful. Then comes the unbelievable pain of knowing for sure. He doesn't care if I know. She even calls me on the phone. After a time, he makes an effort to break it off. I vow to do everything humanly possible to keep this marriage together. I will love him more and pray for him more. Seven years of my life are involved in this. There's a little girl and a little boy!

Loneliness is now. My children and I will go home to a dark, empty apartment that will be my home until the lawyer says it's all over. I, who have always been afraid to stay alone, now welcome the peace and solitude. As I look in the mirror I see that seven years haven't changed my face so much. But inside I am old, and something that was alive once and was beautiful is now dead.

Of course, this is not an unusual story. The remarkable thing about it is that I am still living for God. I am thankful for my family and their prayers of intercession for me!

Oh, I am praying for you, Christian girl. Please believe me when I tell you that no matter how wonderful he is – you cannot build a happy life upon disobedience to God's word. You see, no matter what the future holds for me, I have missed his perfect will for my life. I will never stop paying for breaking a commandment of God's.

Don't let it happen to you.

The Bible is clear in its teaching on marriage between Christians and non-Christians:

> Do not be yoked together with unbelievers. For what do righteousness and wickedness have in common? Or what fellowship can light have with darkness? What harmony is there between Christ and Belial? What does a believer have in common with an unbeliever? What agreement is there between the temple of God and idols? For we are the temple of the living God.
>
> *2 Corinthians 6: 14-16*

Marriage is the most intimate relationship anyone can have with another person – the physical relationship combined with a lifelong commitment to that person. So the Bible teaches that a Christian's marriage partner must also be someone in whom Christ lives, and who puts Christ first.

This is a principle with an incredible cost, but it is part of the total cost of discipleship. For young women in particular, who in most areas of the UK still outnumber the men in our churches, the cost is very great. It is for all of us, and especially those in leadership in churches, to make sure that church is a place where singles are welcomed as single people, and helped to take a full part in church life. Churches can sometimes feel as if they're designed only for couples or children, making single people feel different and excluded.

If you are a single Christian, and feel the pull of marriage to a non-Christian, what can you do to help yourself?

\# Tell God about it, and say exactly how you feel. The first need is to be totally frank with yourself and him about the temptations you struggle with and the fears you face. When we are honest with God, we open the door for him to get to work in that situation.

\# Share your feelings with a mature Christian of your own sex, whom you trust and get on well with. Ask him or her to support you in sticking to what you know to be right. It will need to be someone who will pray for you and with you regularly - try to meet with him or her once a week for a short time of chat and prayer together. Perhaps you could widen the focus of your prayers together to include others in similar situations or going through other struggles.

\# Allow Christ to take first priority in your life. You will need to be determined that he alone is going to rule in your life, even above your own wishes, desires and fears.

\# Find out where the single Christians meet. If there isn't any one place or group, suggest to your church leaders that you start one.

\# Remember that your choices in this area of life don't affect just you. You can guarantee that the younger girls and guys in the church will be watching your every move with avid interest! That can be intensely annoying, but it does mean that, whether you like it or not, you are being a role model for them. You are giving them a living demonstration, by what you do, of what it means to be a Christian.

Remember that God wants the best for you. The Lord who gave up his life for you isn't going to stand idly by while you suffer torments. Don't lose faith that he has good plans for your life.

What if you are already in the difficult position of being married to someone who is not a Christian, and perhaps not at all sympathetic to your faith either? Your commitment to him (and it usually is 'him') is precious, and something God can use for his good. So:

\# Continue to be committed to him. The fact that he's not a Christian doesn't give you the right to walk out on him.

\# Love him. When this is hard, ask for God's love to fill you. Ask to be able to see him in the light of God's great love for him.

\# Pray for him. And encourage a few close Christian friends to pray for him, too, without making him feel the victim of a Christian campaign! It may take many years for him to come to know and love the Lord Jesus, so stick at it. God will honour your resolution.

Faithfulness within marriage

All through this chapter of Malachi, the ideas of faithfulness to God and faithfulness to other people are intertwined. It seems you cannot have one without the other:

> Another thing you do: You flood the LORD's altar with tears. You weep and wail because he no longer pays attention to your offerings or accepts them with pleasure from your hands. You ask, "Why?" It is because the LORD is acting as the witness between you and the wife of your youth, because you have broken faith with her, though she is your partner, the wife of your marriage covenant.
>
> Has not the LORD made them one? In flesh and spirit they are his. And why one? Because he was seeking godly offspring. So guard yourself in your spirit, and do not break faith with the wife of your youth.
>
> 'I hate divorce,' says the LORD God of Israel, 'and I hate a man's covering himself with violence as well as with his garment,' says the LORD Almighty.
>
> So guard yourself in your spirit, and do not break faith.'
>
> *Malachi 2: 13-16*

In Malachi's day Jewish men were guilty of divorcing their wives very casually and easily. Women, of course, were rarely in a position to divorce their husbands in that society. Some rabbis taught that if a woman put too much salt on her husband's lunch, he could divorce her. I can't see many marriages lasting longer than the honeymoon on that basis! One rabbi claimed that, 'If you see a woman who pleases your eye more, you may divorce your first wife.' But others like Malachi disagreed and said that attitude was a complete denial of what God taught in his law. 'The wife of your youth was given to you in covenant by God,' they said. 'That covenant must not be broken.'

In Matthew's Gospel, Jesus said that divorce could be allowed on one ground only, something he called 'uncleanness' or 'unchastity'. But it's very hard to know exactly what he meant by the term he used. In any case, he taught that divorce is the very last resort, and insisted strongly that it was not what God wanted. (Matthew 5: 31-32).

'I hate divorce,' says God. The word is very strong – God loathes and detests divorce. But he *does not hate people who have been divorced.* It's vital to get that clear. If you have suffered the pain of divorce, you'll understand why God hates it. He hates to see people in pain. He knows the dislocation it brings to the human psyche. He knows all about the social problems it brings when a person to whom you have been committed is wrenched away from you.

God sees the social fabric of society being torn to shreds. Teachers today can count on the fingers of one hand the number of children in their classes who still live with both natural parents. And God understands the terrible loneliness of having to raise children on your own. He knows the anguish and hell of having someone you trusted and gave your life to no longer on the scene. It's worse than losing a limb. The agony of divorce rests in your soul and grips you to the point of tears, and you feel so lost and alone in a hostile world. That's why God hates divorce.

If you have been through a divorce or separation, or are going through it now, God wants you to know that he hates what has happened to you with an almighty, divine hatred. *But he doesn't hate you one little bit.* When Jesus started his ministry, he quoted the prophet Isaiah, who spoke powerfully about God's desire to rebuild lives that have been broken and ruined, like cities that have been attacked and had their walls broken to pieces:

> The Spirit of the Sovereign LORD is on me,
>   because the LORD has anointed me
>   to preach good news to the poor.
> He has sent me to bind up the broken-hearted,
>   to proclaim freedom for the captives,
>   and release from darkness for the prisoners,
> to proclaim the year of the LORD's favour
>   and the day of vengeance of our God,
> to comfort all who mourn,
>   and provide for those who grieve in Zion -
> to bestow on them a crown of beauty
>   instead of ashes,
> the oil of gladness
>   instead of mourning,
> and a garment of praise
>   instead of a spirit of despair.
> They will be called oaks of righteousness,
>   a planting of the LORD
>   for the display of his splendour.
> They will rebuild the ancient ruins
>   and restore the places long devastated.
>   *Isaiah 61: 1-4*

God longs to rebuild and restore those who have been devastated through divorce. That couldn't be clearer. And there are ways we can help in that process:

\# Have confidence in God. He doesn't reject you, and divorce isn't the unforgiveable sin. God takes us from where we are – not from where we ought to be – and leads us on into the future.

\# Looking back over your past, there may be a point at which you need to be repentant for your part in what went wrong. Share this with one of your church leaders so that they can help you.

\# Forgive others. Even if those who have wronged us do not want our forgiveness, it is important to be sure that we hold no bitterness against them. Again, if you find you've been hanging on to feelings of anger and bitterness, talk and pray that through with one of the church leaders.

Maintaining the commitment

Our society has trivialised love. When people go to marriage counsellors after eighteen months of marriage and say, 'We're not in love any more,' what they mean is, 'He/she doesn't make me feel gooey inside any more.' *Of course* they're no longer in love in that sense! I don't know of one married couple who could honestly say that they're always 'in love' with each other in that warm, sentimental-glow sense. If we're honest, there have probably been many times this week when we have felt pretty unloving towards our partner – something they did or didn't do – again; a cutting word that was spoken, a broken promise.

Did you know that married couples speak to each other in code? In our household, the code goes something like this:

Me: How are you?
(Meaning : I think I've blown it again.)

Jan: Fine.
(Meaning: Awful. And it's all your fault!)

Me: Do you want to talk about it?

(Meaning: Well at least *I'm* making
   an effort to be grown up!)

Jan: No.
   (Meaning: Yes.)

Or take this example:

Jan: Steve, will you take the rubbish out,
   please?
   (Meaning: Now before the dust cart
   comes.)

Me: Yes, of course. (Meaning: Yes, of
   course; perhaps this afternoon.)

Another common variation on this one is:

Me: Don't worry about the washing up.
   (Meaning: I suppose it's my turn again.)

Jan: Oh, are you happy to do it, then?
   (Meaning: Great! If Steve does that
   now, I can get on with preparing for
   tonight's dinner party.)

Me: Yes, that's fine. Leave it to me.
   (Meaning: I'll do it tomorrow morning.)

Let's be realistic. That gooey sort of love doesn't last. Real love
is a deep and faithful commitment to a person that persists in
spite of the coded ways we talk and relate to each other. So what
can we do to help maintain that commitment?

Work at it! Marriage is jolly hard work. Staying happily married isn't something that just happens – unlike falling in love.

Put your marriage relationship before every other relationship – including your relationship with your work.

If you or your partner are under stress and it's telling on your marriage, don't delay in getting others to pray with you and for you.

If your church offers an opportunity from time to time for partners to renew their marriage vows, take it! If your church doesn't do this, you could suggest to the leaders that it might be helpful to do so. Even if the church doesn't have a public service for couples to do this, dig out the order of service of your wedding, and go over the promises you made then. You can renew them on your own before God, and ask him to help you keep them.

5

A Passion For Justice

'A trail-blazing burglar broke into a vast mansion on millionaires'row in June 1982 at Bel Air, Los Angeles. While on a sack-filling tour of this palatial structure, he went through the ballroom into the hall, down the escalators to the single-lane swimming arbour, up to the library across the dining-room, out of the annexe and into the conservatory containing sixty-three varieties of tropical plants and a cageful of sulphur-crested parrots.

Deciding that now was the time to make a quick exit, he went back through the dining-room, up to the gymnasium, across the indoor tennis-court, down a spiral staircase to an enclosed patio with synchronized fountains, out of the cocktail lounge, through junior's sound-proofed drum studio and back into the roomful of increasingly excited parrots who normally see nobody from one day to the next.

Panicking slightly, he ran back towards the library, through the swing doors into a gallery containing the early works of Jackson Pollock, out through the kitchen across a jacuzzi enclosure and up two flights of stairs, at which point he became hysterical, ran outside along the balcony around the circular corridors, up more stairs, down the landing into the master bedroom and woke up the owners to ask them how to get out.

In order to spare him further distress, they arranged for a local policeman to escort him from the premises.' (From *The Return of Heroic Failures* by Stephen Pile, Harmondsworth: Penguin 1989.)

Most of us have a strong sense of justice, and are delighted when a wrongdoer gets caught. Children have a very keen sense of justice. 'Its not fair!' is the wail of outrage and despair often heard among them as they play. That sense of justice persists into adult life and is the key to our making sense of life at all. If there was no punishment for doing wrong, or reward for doing right, there could be no order in society and, in the end, no purpose to life at all. When it seems that evil people are being allowed to get away with their crimes, and that the innocent and defenceless are suffering ever greater wrongs, we want to know why. What are the police up to? What are the courts doing about it? And why is God letting them get away with it?

A just God?

It was an issue that bothered the people of Malachi's day. They had all but given up on God. 'He's obviously not interested,' they said. 'He doesn't see or hear what's going on. He probably doesn't care any more – unless he's on the side of those with power.' And then God spoke to them through Malachi:

> You have wearied the LORD with your words.
> 'How have we wearied him?' you ask.
> By saying, 'All who do evil are good in the eyes of the
> LORD, and he is pleased with them'
> or 'Where is the God of justice?'
> *Malachi 2:17*

'What's the use of doing good when those who do bad get away with it? We do good and nothing happens; we do bad and nothing happens. It doesn't seem to make any difference at all to God!' This was the nearest a Jew of Malachi's day could get to atheism. Asking, 'Where is the God of justice, who is supposed to be putting things right?' is the next best thing to saying, 'If there isn't a God of justice, there isn't a God at all.' Twentieth-century man tends to ask a slightly different question : 'If there is a God, how come there's all this suffering?' That is the problem that makes us doubt the existence of God.

Throughout the Bible we find people looking at the injustices around them in the world and saying 'It's not fair!' And as we look round the world today we see evil world rulers, rampant terrorism, and terrible poverty and starvation as a result of evil people deliberately refusing food, clothing and water to their fellow creatures. Hundreds of thousands of people live and die in refugee camps in the most appalling conditions, because governments refuse to agree. Seeing all this we cry out to God to do something, to make things right.

But side by side with the demands from people in the Bible to know what God thinks he's doing, there is also a strong affirmation that God will one day sort it all out. In the King James' Version of the Bible, Psalm 37 begins, 'Fret not thyself because of evildoers.' And it goes on to say that evildoers will not go on getting away with it. They will get their just deserts. The God of all the world will see that right is seen to be right and wrong is seen to be wrong. It may have to wait until that great day at the end of time when all of us stand in front of the Almighty God and he finally says, 'Enough is enough.' Then all wrongs will finally be righted.

A people called to bring justice
Now, though, God calls his people to start doing what they can to bring about justice. Many of the things we have come to regard as our 'rights' today were won for us by the hard work of committed Christians. William Wilberforce and John Newton struggled politically and prayerfully to bring about the banning of the slave trade in this country, so ending a horrible form of injustice. Lord Shaftesbury campaigned year after year for the reduction of children's working hours in the mills, factories and pits of Britain when it was newly industrialized. God calls his people to be his agents of justice

on earth. He does establish his righteousness when his body takes it seriously and does something about it.

To some extent we are culpable as a church world-wide for the lack of justice in the world today. If we were the church God intended us to be, his justice would reign in a way we would find simply incredible. But even if we were doing all we are supposed to, there would still be loose ends to be tied up, and they will be tied up on that great Day when Jesus comes again. This is exactly what Malachi was saying to the people of his day, speaking of the first and second comings of Christ almost as though they rolled into one:

> 'See, I will send my messenger, who will prepare the way before me. Then suddenly the LORD you are seeking will come to his temple; the messenger of the covenant, whom you desire, will come,' says the LORD Almighty.
>
> *Malachi 3:1*

Prepare the ground

Throughout the Old Testament there is constant reference to a messenger who will come immediately before the Lord himself comes. The messenger will prepare people to receive him. Isaiah writes:

> Prepare the way for the LORD;
> make straight in the wilderness
>   a highway for our God.
> Every valley shall be raised up,
>   every mountain and hill made low;
> the rough ground shall become level,
>   the rugged places a plain.
>
> *Isaiah 40: 3-4*

It's a lovely picture of huge, cavernous valleys being filled in with earth and great mountain ranges being levelled flat so that when the King comes he neither has to go on massive detours into the valleys nor struggle over huge mountains. He can go straight to his people.

The classic example of the messenger who fulfils this prophecy is John the Baptist, who was the forerunner of Jesus. When he started preaching to the needy people in the first-century world he said, 'I am not the Christ but am sent ahead of him' (John 3:28). He said he wasn't worthy even to untie the shoelaces of the one who was to come after him.

John was the wild man of the first century. A man who lived in the desert and fed on locusts and honey, and would leap out from boulders when people came down to the Jordan to do their weekly wash, and shout out, 'Repent!' Of course, they would be most upset at having their weekly laundry disturbed in this way, and they got a little frightened of him too. But John became a curiosity:

'What are you going to do today?'

'Well, we thought we'd go to see what John is up to. It's quite a good show really, if you get there early enough; but he'll be saying all sorts of things we don't understand.'

Great crowds would gather day after day and John would say, 'Someone holy and mighty is coming soon. Repent of your sins now, before it is too late. Change your minds and change your behaviour.' One day he saw a figure walking down towards the river and he pointed to him. As the huge crowd turned to look, John said, 'Look, the Lamb of God, who takes away the sin of the world.' Almost immediately, John recedes from the stage. From then on the Gospels take up the story of Jesus.

John was a forerunner, a preparer of the ground. God calls us, too, to prepare the ground for him so that he can move smoothly into people's lives. We can prepare the ground in two main ways.

In preaching and teaching.
As we listen to God's word, week by week, it can help us to clear away the debris in our lives so that God has a clear pathway in. When we leave church thinking, 'I needed that this morning; that

really spoke to me,' that's great! But it is only the ground being cleared. We then need to act on what we have heard and invite the King to come into our lives along that clear pathway. Many people who hear preaching, or read books or even the Bible, never get to the stage of welcoming in the King. They have got as far as the ground-clearing but their lives have not been materially changed.

By prayer.

Even Jesus did not act in his ministry without preparing the ground first. He said, ' The Son can do nothing by himself; he can do only what he sees his Father doing' (John 5:19). He first looked for what God was already doing in people's lives, then he operated on the strength of what he saw. Jesus deliberately limited himself to working where the ground had been prepared. That has implications for us.

It has implications particularly for prayer, especially when we are involved in any sort of counselling ministry. When we are talking with others, it is important to be praying too, listening to what God is saying to them and discerning what he is doing in their lives. Otherwise we'll simply be coming out with our own good ideas. When we listen to what God is saying to these people, and hear it in our spirits, we can pray for those people in line with God's will for them. Then we can be sure of our prayers being effective.

One reason why the Pentecostal revival happened, in the first decade of last century, was that the ground had been prepared. It didn't just happen by God saying, 'Let there be revival!' People had been meeting for months and years before to fast, pray and seek God, and it was on the basis of that preparation that the Holy Spirit came, and what we know as the modern Pentecostal movement sprang out of it.

It is a principle that works in our own lives too. When we are prepared spiritually, when we have prayed and perhaps fasted, the Lord comes in a special way. Occasionally he will surprise us when we are unprepared, but generally speaking God acts when there is a prepared heart to act into.

Welcome in the King

The problem with so many of us is that we are too busy for God, and see his coming into our lives as an intrusion rather than as a visit from a dear friend that we have been looking forward to for ages. A hymn by Isaac Watts, that we sometimes sing at Christmas, says:

> Joy to the world, the Lord is come;
>   Let earth receive her King!
> Let every heart prepare him room
>   And heaven and nature sing.

When we prepare him room in our hearts, he will come in and live there.

If Aunt Esmerelda is coming for the weekend, or the grandparents are going to be around or some other visitors are coming, you've got to do something with the spare room! You hurry around, get the sheets out, air the room and make sure the cobwebs don't look too obvious. And what about the meals? What food do you need to get in? We do a lot of planning.

If special guests are coming we do even more – searching through the cupboards for the serviettes that must be here somewhere. We dust down the best china that hasn't been used since the day after we were married, and all the special things start to come out.

I remember the day Janet came out of hospital having given birth to Bethany. I had festooned the front of the house with toilet paper and various other things, spelling out, 'Welcome home, mother and baby'; 'We love you'; and all those kind of things. As Jan got out of the car, with the three-day old baby in her arms, she was terribly excited to come home to all this slightly soggy toilet paper! Well, maybe it was the feeling that she was loved and that I wanted her back home, that pleased her, rather than the amateur decorations!

God wants us to prepare for the coming of a very special guest, himself. Yet most of us go through our Christian lives fairly unprepared, and if we have an encounter with the living God at all, it's a haphazard, chance event. We may happen to bump into him in the street of our life – a casual contact in the passing busyness of everyday concerns, rather than a welcome into a home lovingly prepared for him.

A God who refines and purifies

God's coming into our lives may be welcomed by us, but it may not be an altogether comfortable experience:

> But who can endure the day of his coming? Who can stand when he appears? For he will be like a refiner's fire or a launderer's soap. He will sit as a refiner and purifier of silver; he will purify the Levites and refine them like gold and silver.
>
> Then the LORD will have men who will bring offerings in righteousness, and the offerings of Judah and Jerusalem will be acceptable to the LORD, as in days gone by, as in former years.
> *Malachi 3: 2-4*

Gold and silver were refined in furnaces so that any impurities were 'boiled away' and all that was left was the pure silver or gold. Launderer's soap wasn't so much a fourth-century BC Camay, as a bleaching agent. It was a whitener used to make dirty, grimy material gleaming white again. A fourth-century BC commercial for launderer's soap would show a stunning difference between the 'before' and 'after' look of the clothes being whitened!

In the same way, the coming of the Lord to his people would involve the purging away of all that was wrong in them, and the purifying of all that was right and good. It was a process that would be aimed particularly at the Levites, the priests and teachers of the Law.

Jesus was that purifier, the Lord who came to his temple and found the priests of his day full of impurities and corruption. When he spoke in public to the Pharisees, Jesus didn't mince his words. Here was no gentle, warm glow to make them feel comfortable, but a blaze of fire that was intended to sift the evil from the good: 'You are hypocrites! You put massive burdens on people when God didn't put those burdens on them. You claim extortionate amounts of the tithe for yourselves instead of releasing it so that the people can be cared for properly. You say to people, "Don't bother to spend your money in looking after your elderly relatives, give it to us instead and God will take care of them." You are like tombs that look lovely and white on the outside, but inside are full of stinking rotten matter!' (See Matthew 23)

And when Jesus comes the second time, to bring to an end the world as we know it, he will do precisely the same thing. Soon after his harsh words to the Pharisees, Matthew records Jesus talking about the end of the time, when the 'sheep' will be separated from the 'goats.' The good from the worthless.

The work of the Holy Spirit

This refining work is also the role of the Holy Spirit. John writes that, when the Holy Spirit comes, 'he will convict the world of guilt in regard to sin and righteousness and judgment' (John 16:8). That's why he's called the 'holy' Spirit, not the 'power' Spirit or the 'love' Spirit, or the 'joy' Spirit, even though he gives his love, joy and power. When he comes into our lives he convicts us of our sin, and that is why any experience of the Holy Spirit – be it called Baptism, the Fullness or the Filling – which does not involve an experience of our own sinfulness and unworthiness, is rarely a genuine experience. The Holy Spirit cannot come without his holiness. He is like the launderer's soap and the refiner's fire which burns away the rubbish in our lives.

How easy it is for us to be thrown! To have our backs put out, or be offended, or react in an immature, childish way. We are easily thrown by changes just in our routine! We sometimes think we've got it all together, spiritually, that we're walking with God. But then someone makes a critical comment which we take ever so personally, and suddenly we're moody and immature children again. Why? Because there is still enough grot in our lives for the devil to get his hooks into. God's job is to refine us to get rid of all the mud that clings to us, so that when the devil throws his grappling irons towards us, his little hooks just slide off again. There should be no mud or dirt in our lives for them to grip hold of. But as long as we are unrefined the devil's claws have got something to grip into.

And then he starts to churn us up emotionally, because when we are churned up emotionally we act irrationally and say things we don't mean. With just a bit of stirring, the devil can make us blow everything up out of proportion, and then his work of wreaking havoc in our lives is straightforward. That's why we need to have all the dirt refined out of us. We are called to be holy.

There's the lovely hymn which traces the struggle we have in releasing our grip on our 'rights', and the unholy things we want to cling on to, and handing them over to God instead. The line at the end of verse one goes, 'More of self and less of thee,' and then the very last line of the hymn is, 'None of self and all of thee.' It is a little like the caterpillar and the butterfly where, in a sense, the caterpillar has to die in order to release the butterfly. That which is worldly and corrupting in us has to die before Christ can be fully formed in us instead.

God is the judge of society

When the Lord returns again, it is not just individuals who will be judged, but society as a whole:

'So I will come near to you for judgment. I will be quick
to testify against sorcerers, adulterers and perjurers, against
those who defraud labourers of their wages, who oppress
the widows and the fatherless, and deprive aliens of justice,
but do not fear me,' says the LORD Almighty.

Malachi 3:5

When God says that he will be 'quick' to judge, he doesn't mean
he's going to make a snap decision. The word used is an unusual
Hebrew word that also conveys the meaning 'expert'. How can
'quick' mean the same as 'expert'? Well, it's not as silly as it first
sounds.

If you went out to your car now, looked at it and found you
had a flat tyre, you'd probably try to get it pumped up again.
Suppose you couldn't, because it was too badly damaged? You'd
need to change it. And for that, you need the right tools. Someone
who has got the right tools and has done the job many times is
going to change it much more quickly than someone with none
of the tools or skills! If you stand around, kick the wheel and try
to get the nuts off with your finger nails, it will take you an age to
get the wheel changed! An expert does the job quickly.

A few years ago, Jan and I went to the Ideal Home Exhibition
in London. We wandered around and saw a number of
demonstrations of things that the home 'Should Not Be Without'.
One of them was an amazing grater. All you did was to rub your
salad vegetables up and down on it, and the shreds would magically
appear, beautifully designed and artistically arranged. It was
amazing, and was an absolute bargain! So we bought one. After
we got home we enthusiastically had a go with the new toy – but
nothing like the magnificent salads appeared! It took hours of
practice before anything like the right shapes began to emerge.

An expert produces things quickly. God is quick to judge
because he is the expert. He knows all about the people he is
judging. He is quick, not because he is casual, or unthinking or
superficial, but because he has perfect knowledge.

Four areas of judgment

Malachi warns that every area of life is going to be examined by God. The examples he gives represent the four major areas:

Its spiritual life. Everything that is corrupt spiritually will be judged: the 'sorcerers', the occult and the misleading.

Its moral life. Those who by immorality wreak havoc in society, breaking up homes and destroying the security of children, will be judged.

Its ethical life. 'Perjurers' are those who bend the truth in order to make others think they are better than they are. All lies, deception and deceit will be judged.

Its social justice. How does our society treat its poor? What provision does it make for them? How does it care for the sick, the mentally ill, the disabled? What are we doing about the scourge of unemployment? Where is justice and fairness in our life together as a society? These are questions that God will ask of us and our leaders.

Stepping into the refiner's fire

The Lord calls us to step into the refiner's fire. If we are to be able to call society back to God's standards of holiness and justice, we must first allow his Holy Spirit to work in us. We have to be willing to let go of those areas of impurity in our lives, deliberately turning our backs on them and renouncing them. And we need to let the Holy Spirit fully into every corner of our hearts, to shine his spotlight onto the dirt that remains and to purge it out. And then we need both to speak out in society, and to act, working to clear out the evils we find and to put positive alternatives in their place.

6

Integrity with money

Pastor: You say you can't give to the church because you owe everybody else. Don't you feel that you owe the Lord something? *Church member:* Yes, of course I do. But he isn't pushing me like the others!

At a social event one man told another: 'I've met you before but I can't place you. Or perhaps you just look like someone I see around a lot. I can't place him but I know I don't like him. Isn't that strange? He's someone I resent – but I can't think who he is. Isn't that odd?'

The other man answered, 'Nothing strange about it! It's me you've seen a lot and I know why you resent me. For two years I used to pass the collection plate round in church!'

Money is a tricky subject to talk about publicly, especially from the pulpit. Give just one sermon a year on our financial responsibilities to the church, and people resent it and say, 'The church is always asking for money!' God introduced the subject of money to his people in a very different way:

'I the LORD do not change. So you, O descendants of Jacob, are not destroyed. Ever since the time of your forefathers you have turned away from my decrees and have not kept them. Return to me, and I will return to you,' says the LORD Almighty.
But you ask, 'How are we to return?'

Malachi 3: 6-7

The ultimate Securicor

Time and again the Israelites broke their covenant with God. Yet
he remained faithful to them. Despite the punishments he sent
their way, he never gave up on them. He held open the invitation
to return to him, to restore their relationship with him of love
and trust.

Because God does not change, we have a marvellous security
as Christians. If we have given our lives to Jesus Christ and he has
come to live inside us, we form part of the great Kingdom of
God that cannot be shaken because it is ruled by a King who will
never change and whose power will never be diminished. He is
the ultimate Securicor.

It is good to know that in our volatile world. As we look at
the TV or read the papers, we see the moods of international
politics fluctuating, and learn to accept that major changes in the
political geography of the world can take place overnight. It can
be frightening to think about. Yet the Christian can have the inner
certainty that the God who holds us in the hollow of his hand will
not change. 'Jesus Christ is the same yesterday, today and for
ever' (Hebrews 13:8). Because of that, you and I can face the
future with confidence.

What is true on the international scale is also true on the personal
scale. I suspect that most of us are affected by our moods, to a
greater or lesser extent. The state of our digestive system can
determine the way we react to an innocent question someone
asks us. Whether or not we enjoyed breakfast can affect our mood
for the rest of the day. If someone cuts us up when we're driving,
it can make us irritable and grouchy. God has none of those
mood swings, but is steady and constant, always ready to receive
us. So when we come to him in the evening and say, 'Lord, I
want to talk about my day,' he doesn't say, 'Keep it to yourself!
You think *your* day was bad? You should have seen *mine*! I've had
another uprising in the Middle East to deal with, a famine going
on in Africa, some delicate negotiations to oversee in the White
House ...' God may be grieved by what is happening in the world,

but he isn't thrown by it. He doesn't get moody or fed up but is constantly available to the searching believer. The fault is on our side. It is we who are praising the Lord one minute, and the next being down in the dumps, wanting nothing to do with the other Christians! In God is total security and reliability.

'So', he asks 'what's holding you back from me? Why don't you trust me?'

'Holding back?' his people ask in amazement. 'We're not holding back from you!'

'Yes you are,' he replies. 'The proof of the fact that you don't trust me is that you won't trust me with your money. In fact, not only do you not trust me with your money, you're actually defrauding me of what is rightfully mine!'

'Will a man rob God? Yet you rob me.
'But you ask, 'How do we rob you?'
'In tithes and offerings. You are under a curse – the whole nation of you – because you are robbing me. Bring the whole tithe into the storehouse, that there may be food in my house. Test me in this," says the LORD Almighty, "and see if I will not throw open the floodgates of heaven and pour out so much blessing that you will not have room enough for it. I will prevent pests from devouring your crops, and the vines in your fields will not cast their fruit,"says the LORD Almighty. 'Then all the nations will call you blessed, for yours will be a delightful land', says the LORD Almighty.

Malachi 3: 8-12

The word translated 'rob' means 'plunder'. It's a very strong accusation. It's the idea of coshing a Securicor guard on the head when he's loading money out of the bank into a van. It means taking by force what is not yours.

Yet there is another side to the picture. 'Will a man rob God?' asks the Lord. 'Don't be so ridiculous,' comes the reply. You might as well suggest to an ant that it gets a little black mask with two eye-holes, tucks a cosh under one leg and a torch under another, and creeps up on an elephant to mug it. Even though he bashes away at the elephant's big toe, the elephant won't even know he's there. 'And can insignificant, puny human beings plunder the God of the universe?' asks Malachi.

There is a barb in his question. It might be impossible, but the Israelites are certainly trying it on! In two ways they are defrauding God of what is rightfully his.

Value people above money

Their culture was materialistic, as is ours, with a sick attitude to money. At a conservative estimate, about 50million pounds is gambled away each year on the Grand National – and that's only the officially placed bets. What could 50million pounds achieve if all those people chose to put their betting money to a different cause? What sort of society is it that can encourage that amount to be squandered, while at the same time saying that little can be done about the lack of housing and health care?

One night I had the dubious privilege of walking the floors of the casino in Monte Carlo. Wandering around the tables, I saw gambler after gambler throw dice to the end of a table, or bet on the spin of a wheel. I saw people playing cards and losing hundreds of francs. The whole atmosphere of the place is depressing and heavy. It's supposed to be fun! It was anything but that. I left very depressed about the kind of world that encourages such incredible waste, and encourages people to believe that trying to get something for nothing is the way to spend their leisure time.

The Grand National and the Casino are simply indicators of the grasping spirit that wants more and more, and that regards the needs of the poor, alienated and suffering as far less important than a few moments' thrill at watching the horses or spinning the wheel.

Malachi condemns the people of God for an attitude to money that is basically unhealthy.

In our society it is easy to think that giving to charity has increased over recent years because of the efforts of 'Children in Need' or 'Red Nose Day' or various other TV appeals. But if you read the annual report and accounts of some long-standing missionary societies and Christian agencies, you will discover that what has happened is simply that the amount of money they receive has decreased in corresponding measure to the amount the newer ones have netted. The overall level of giving in this country hasn't really changed very much.

We need to watch it in the church, too. Although we can criticise the nation, the spirit of the age fills the Church of Jesus. Our attitude to money becomes warped, and our priorities become increasingly materialistic and decreasingly those of the Kingdom of God. It is easy to be robbed of a sense of the Kingdom at work, actively and successfully in the world, by a cultural system that values money and things more highly than people.

Value God above money

Malachi's second call was to a rethink of the value they put on God. His accusation was that they were not keeping the law on tithing, that is, committing to God one tenth of all their income, whether financial or in kind with wheat and corn. Because the tithe was not being paid, there was no way the priests and other temple staff could carry out their jobs properly. The priests were not allowed to own their own land, so they were dependent on the people supplying the basic necessities of life for them. Because the money wasn't there, the priests' families were going hungry and the whole temple 'system' was under pressure. 'That can't be right,' says Malachi. 'How come you've got money to spend on all sorts of things that you want, but God's house remains impoverished, empty and weak?'

God's work through the church

Here we are, 2400 years later, and still the work of the Kingdom of God is hindered through lack of finances! Ask anyone involved in evangelism – Christian publishers, broadcasters and missionaries – and you will hear the same story: 'Barring a miracle, we are not going to make the budget again this year.' Sometimes missionary societies don't get the vision right, and that is why the money isn't provided for their work. But nine times out of ten their vision is right, their goals for development and ministry are sound, but they cannot go in to take the ground because God's people, on whom they rely, are not giving as they should be.

I had the privilege, while I was in Monte Carlo, of talking to Christians who have set up a broadcasting station there. Many of them had been thrown out of old-style Communist countries or had escaped under threat of death, or had suffered torture for their faith. Yet as they walked through the streets of Monte Carlo and looked up at the opulent buildings and glamorous sights, they could honestly say it had no appeal for them. Their faith in the Lord was so rich that material things seemed utterly worthless in comparison.

Our own priorities

When John Wesley went to Oxford as a student in the early years of the eighteenth century, he lived on twenty-eight pounds a year. It would be pretty difficult to do that now! But at one point his salary was doubled and he still lived on twenty-eight pounds a year – he gave the rest away. In about the twentieth year of his ministry, his writing and the patronage he was gaining meant that he was receiving an annual income of thousands of pounds. Yet he still lived on just twenty-eight pounds a year.

Admittedly, he didn't have a problem with inflation in those days. Yet it was still a remarkable commitment.

Today, our finances are much more complicated. We have family responsibilities and pressures, and the practicalities of insurance and mortgages. But the principle is still a crucial one to hold on to: we rob God and we rob his kingdom if we are not generous supporters of his work.

What can we do about this accusation?

Assess what money you *need*, and be clear about what are really unnecessary luxuries that you could go without.

Do you know what wastage is? Wastage is what someone else spends their money on! It's never something I spend *my* money on! I can say to Janet, 'For goodness' sake! Not another dress? I mean, you had one last year!' I can make her feel incredibly worldly for buying new clothes or cosmetics. 'Do you really need to give money to that wretched Avon lady?! It's just so worldly!' Of course, the money I spend on books is easy to justify. That's 'spiritual'!

God is calling us to look at the way we are using our *own* finances and resources, not anyone else's, and to ask ourselves, 'Is that really right?'

Aim to give a tenth of your income to the work of the church. A tithe was a tenth – that was what the people owed God. A gift to God was anything in excess of that sum. People differ today about whether that is still the sum Christians should be giving, but I have always found it a good guideline.

Trust God. 'Test me in this,' says the Lord, 'and see if I will not open the floodgates of heaven and pour out so much blessing that you will not have room enough for it.' Now I have heard people talk about giving and tithing as though it is a direct equation: give 'x' amount to God and he will give you 'x' plus 'y' in return. Giving on that basis ceases to be the duty or love gift it was meant to be and turns into a mercenary, commercial deal instead. It is simply an unbiblical approach to money. I give because God tells me to give; blessing is the result of obedience.

I know of many couples who were once in a real mess financially. Then they talked and prayed together about it and they decided that, for the first time in their married lives, they would give a tithe. God would have first claim on their money, then they would prioritise how to spend what was left. And these

couples would affirm that God has never let them down. They
have been able to meet their needs, despite giving away that amount.
God has honoured their commitment and their desire to use their
money responsibly.

\# God doesn't demand that we give beyond our means. We
need to be sensitive to his Spirit, to give as we feel we ought to,
taking into account the responsibility he has also given us to feed,
clothe and care for our families.

The resolve to act

> Then those who feared the LORD talked with each other,
> and theLORD listened and heard. A scroll of remembrance
> was written in his presence concerning those who feared
> the LORD and honoured his name.
>
>   'They will be mine' says the LORD Almighty, 'in the day
> when I make up my treasured possession. I will spare
> them, just as in compassion a man spares his son who serves
> him. And you will again see the distinction between the
> righteous and the wicked, between those who serve God
> and those who do not.'   *Malachi 3: 16-18*

The need to listen

After Malachi's challenge to the priests and people, they decided
they needed to do something about it. 'Those who feared the
Lord' held a meeting and discussed what it would involve to put
things right, and how they should go about it.

If God has been speaking to you through the words of
Malachi, as you have read them in this book, don't dismiss his
voice. Share your thoughts with other Christian friends and ask
for their reactions to what you think God is saying to you. Then
go on to what the people of Malachi's day did next: action!

The resolve to act

You may have been challenged about one or more of the areas we have looked at so far in this book: your worship, your representation of God as his priest, your personal relationships, the part you are playing in bringing about a more just society, or your use of your money and things. Look back over those chapters that concerned you most, and decide now exactly what you are going to do to put things right. Prayerfully, draw up a plan of action for yourself. Then share your decisions with a friend and ask for his or her prayer support and practical encouragement to stick to it.

The affirmation of God

We noticed at the beginning of Malachi that God does not condemn for long before bringing renewed affirmation of his people and his love for them. That comes out again here. First, God affirms that his people are totally secure with him; he never changes. Then he challenges them to take him up on that and entrust themselves and their money to him. Now again he wants them to know that they are his treasured possession. Whether or not they have much in the way of this world's goods, they are themselves of great value to God. Despite their failures in the past, he will see that they get into heaven, not just sliding in at the back, but being borne in with triumph as the crown jewels!

God knows our situation. He knows that life gets rough and dispiriting. He knows that it is a struggle for us to keep putting him first. He takes note when Christians go without for years, in order to provide for others. He knows when they clothe others and go about badly dressed themselves. He knows when they are providing the means for others to be housed, yet suffering poor housing themselves. One day, all of that will be recompensed in heaven. Those who love the Lord and choose to identify with him here in his poverty will be received by him as honoured guests at the feast at the end of time.

7

A New Freedom

I remember a time when I was in the States. I had just said goodbye to Jan and was about to drive to the airport to go on a trip to Israel. On the way to the airport I called in at my apartment to pick up one or two things – I thought I might need the odd shirt for a fortnight away. But the moment I stepped inside I developed the most awful pain in my side, so bad that I couldn't even stand. Fortunately, my future mother-in-law was there, and we phoned a doctor friend in the church to get some advice.

'Yes,' he said, 'It sounds bad. Drive into the surgery.' And he put the phone down, without telling us where the surgery was! So I frantically looked through the church membership list to try to find out if his office was listed. It was. So, grasping a map and this huge, twenty-thousand-member list, I climbed into the front seat next to Jan's mum. As she drove, I sat hunched over in pain, giving directions: 'It's left here, right here...' We went right the way round north Dallas. At last we arrived – and the first thing they wanted to know was how I was going to pay! Well, things got sorted out in the end. The pain was diagnosed as kidney stones and I got some helpful treatment.

For the whole of that journey I was desperate to get there! All the time I'd been thinking, '*Surely* it must be just here! Just round the next corner ... it *must* be!' In America the blocks are numbered, so you can tell when you're getting near your destination. Say you have to get to block 20, and you're now at block 40. You count every block: '39, 38, 37 ...we're getting there! 27, 26 ... not far to go now !'

This was the sort of longing desperation that the Old Testament prophets felt for 'the day of the Lord', the day when he would come and sort out the mess the world had got into. It was a day Malachi longed for too:

> 'Surely the day is coming; it will burn like a furnace. All the arrogant and every evildoer will be stubble, and that day that is coming will set them on fire,' says the LORD Almighty. 'Not a root or branch will be left to them. But for you who revere my name, the sun of righteousness will rise with healing in its wings. And you will go out and leap like calves released from the stall. Then you will trample down the wicked; they will be ashes under the soles of your feet on the day when I do these things,' says the LORD Almighty.
>
> *Malachi 4: 1-3*

'Surely the day is coming,' says Malachi, 'when God will at last intervene, and the world's pain, injustice and corruption will be dealt with!'

Longing for fulfilment

It is a longing we share today. When Malachi and the other prophets spoke of the day of the Lord, they saw two times compressed into one – the time when Jesus first came to this earth, and the day when he will return a second time. They longed for two things to happen: the law of God to become a part of his people, 'written on their hearts' as Jeremiah had put it, and they longed for all society's rottenness to get sorted out.

When Jesus came, these two longings began to be fulfilled. He came to give us his Holy Spirit. That means we can truly begin to think, feel and act like Jesus himself. And it also means we can begin to do some of his purifying work, acting as salt and light in society.

I sometimes have the opportunity of counselling many non-Christians at big events. On one occasion, after a seminar called

Agnostics Anonymous, one man came up to me and said, 'I'm really enjoying it here but, tell me, how do I know this Jesus?' He asked me while we were with a group of people, so I said that if he would give me ten minutes on his own I would answer him.

We met again the next day. He was a research scientist in his middle age, and we spent about an hour talking about all the questions of the universe and the God who made the world. He saw that the Christian view made sense of all this so, after a while asked, 'What are we waiting for?' 'Well, nothing,' I replied. So we went back to his chalet and sat on his bed with his wife, and we prayed that he would come to know Jesus as Saviour and Lord. He looked up from that prayer, his face transformed, and said something like, 'Now I know! My wife has been a Christian for ten years, and I've been to church with her every Sunday morning because she wanted me to go with her. But now I have stopped longing to know what on earth it was she had; now I know for myself!' For him, the frustrating time of waiting and puzzling was over.

It's not just people like this man who wait and wonder what it's all about. Many of us Christians come to church Sunday by Sunday and sit in on the worship, but we may be feeling, 'When is it going to feel real for me? When am I really going to know this Jesus?' Perhaps you have been a Christian for many years and have been longing to be filled with the power of the Holy Spirit, but don't quite know how to 'get hold' of it. You may be saying to yourself, 'Surely the day is coming when God will bless me?' Yes, he wants to come to bless you and fulfil your longings to know him better.

In the coming of Jesus, the prophets' time of waiting was over. And for all of us our time of waiting will be over when he returns for the second time.

The cutting edge

There are some people who are not looking forward to that day. Ham and chicken pie sounds very nice, but not if you're a pig or a chicken! Whether we look forward to that day or not depends on our vantage point. If we're the kind of person Malachi mentions first, ' the arrogant and every evildoer', the day of the Lord will be our judgment day. But if we're a different sort of person, that day can hold no fear for us: 'But for you who revere my name, the sun of righteousness will rise with healing in its wings.'

All evil and all evil people will be as stubble in the fire, on that day. This is the cutting edge to the Old Testament message which we sometimes miss or try to soften in current Christian teaching. We tell people about God's love for them, and about how Jesus will give them peace and forgiveness if they come to him. We tell them how he will bring them into a new family and give them his Holy Spirit. All that is true, but the flip side of that coin, of which the prophets constantly remind us, is that God's holiness means that he is angry against sin.

God is not just a God of love. He is also a God of righteous anger. Far too often we allow people to get away with a caricature of Jesus as gentle and mild, going around being nice to children and widows, caring for those who were sick, and raising dead people back to life again. Of course he did do that. But he also strode into the temple in anger and overturned the tables of the money changers, pushing off the piles of money, scattering the pigeons, sheep and goats that were in the courtyard, and driving out the traders with a whip! Jesus was passionately loving, but also strongly angry against sin. The gospel is news of God's love. But its cutting edge is the news of God's judgment.

Freedom and healing

'The sun of righteousness will rise with healing in its wings.' For centuries, people have believed that the sun's rays have healing properties. We now know it to be true, that vital vitamins are made in our skin only by the rays of the sun. There's something depressing about being shut up inside, perhaps having to study for exams, when the sun is shining brightly outside and the weather is warm and inviting.

From darkness to light

Malachi pictures the coming of the Lord as breaking into the dark cells of our lives and of our world, and letting us out into the warmth, freedom and sunshine. He uses a lovely picture of a calf that has been confined to a stall during the winter months and is longing to go out into the fields to see the spring. Suddenly the day comes when the door is unlocked and the calf is free to rush out into the sunlight, to gambol and dance around the field.

The revelation of Jesus brings the same sort of joyful and healing freedom to us. When we come to know him for the first time as adults, the contrast between the darkness and the sunlight is particularly strong – we have so much more of life behind us to contrast with the present.

From chains to freedom

The coming of the Lord into our lives brings us freedom from the chains that have bound us in the past. I once met a man who was confined to a wheelchair. One day he came to know Jesus for himself. He wasn't physically healed, but he was as free as any person can possibly be – all his bitterness and anger was released in prayer, and a freedom came into his life that you could almost touch. Looking at him still in his wheelchair you might say, 'That man's not free!' But he would call you a liar, because the greatest freedom of all had come to him – freedom from inner guilt and pain. It was marvellous to see him! He was just like a young child all over again. It was as if he had discovered a new lease of life, clapping at everything – even at the wrong time – warm and enthusiastic. Everything was new and fresh. Everything had suddenly become just great for him.

There is an old hymn which says, 'Something lives in every hue, Christless eyes have never seen.' The language may be a bit old-fashioned, but it contains a lot of truth. When that man had his eyes opened to Jesus and had his bitterness washed away, something did live in every situation that he had never seen before. The world was richer, brighter, fuller. He was free for the first time.

From fear to confidence

Yet many of us have been like that calf, leaping out of the stall with great joy – only to hit our hoof on a stone and twist it. We've lost our nerve, hobbled back to the stable and never ventured out again. So now, when we look at the enthusiasm and joy of other young Christians discovering Christ for the first time, we say, Eeyore-like, 'Oh, that's just a stage they'll grow out of.'

The Lord wants to turn our fear and doubt into confidence. We all need to have our characters changed, and the Lord works with us to help us become like Christ – more loving, caring, holy, honest. But many of us also need to have our personalities changed by the Lord too. We need to be healed of the damage of past hurts, which have made us afraid and doubtful of our own abilities. The experiences and condemning words that have left us feeling failures and no-hopers need to be seen for the lies they are. In their place, God wants us to see ourselves in our true light, that is as he sees us. And that is as his precious, loved children. There's a song by D J Butler which describes this process of healing and change that happens as we come out of the stable and into the sunlight:

> I will change your name.
> You shall no longer be called
> Wounded, outcast,
> Lonely or afraid.
> I will change your name.
> Your new name shall be:
> Confidence, joyfulness,
> Overcoming one,
> Faithfulness, friend of God,
> One who seeks My face.

God is looking through the stable door at you and saying, 'I've got a great list of things out here for you to explore and enjoy! Unlock the door and let the glorious light shine in, and come out to me and enjoy the freedom I want to give you!'

Freedom from sin and evil

Part and parcel of our complete freedom at the end of time will be the destruction of all that is evil, and the wiping out of all our sinful traits. The stones that twist our ankles now will be gone then. It won't be possible to run out of the stall only to find ourselves charged by a mad bull! The world will be a place of total safety: '"you will trample down the wicked; they will be ashes under the soles of your feet on the day when I do these things," says the Lord Almighty.'

The Old Testament writers aren't squeamish about evil, the way we tend to be today. The psalmists in particular didn't beat about the bush when they spoke about evil people:

'Lord, get 'em! Lord, smash 'em up! I hate them, because they hate you!' Today we're much more sophisticated, far nicer: 'Lord, convict them!'

At least the Old Testament writers had a strong hatred of evil. They saw in the raw the devastation it brought to people's lives. We need to watch that we don't tolerate sin too easily today, pooh-poohing it, treating it lightly or making excuses for it. The Lord himself does not treat it lightly. One day he will make an end of Satan, the serpent, and all his wiles. The evil influence which Satan and the powers of darkness exert over the earth now will one day be gone for ever.

There will be a new heaven and a new earth, in which only goodness and righteousness shall reign. Then we and the whole creation will be truly free for the first time, and go leaping into the new, open and clean world 'like calves released from the stall.'

8

Refuse to be average

Benjamin Disraeli said, 'As a general rule, the most successful man in life is the man who has the best information.' He was only partly right. The best information isn't much use unless you act on it!

At the end of Spring Harvest, I sometimes think that there has been just too much information for some folk to take in. It's a case of information overload. What am I going to do with all those notes? Now that I've been to my forty-fifth seminar in a week, how am I going to be able to use all the information I've gleaned? It would take a good six months to put one tenth of it into practice– and the next six months to prepare for next Spring Harvest!

Grow in what you know

If we are to be successful in our Christian lives, we need to make our knowledge real by living it out. 'Remember!' says Malachi. 'Don't gain new insights and knowledge just to forget it all again. Grow in what you know. Refuse to be average!'

> 'Remember the law of my servant Moses, the decrees and laws I gave him at Horeb for all Israel.'   *Malachi 4:4*

This is a kind of summary of the message of all the prophets. Their task was to point people back to the laws and teaching God had given them through Moses at the outset of their life together as a nation. 'Remember' is also the key word throughout the book of Deuteronomy. It occurs there about twelve times, always at major points in the people's experience of God. They were to take to heart the things that they learnt at those times, and not let the lessons slip from their minds.

Malachi reminds the people that the day of the Lord is coming. 'In view of that,' he asks them, 'how do you think you ought to be living now?' The obvious answer is, 'In a way which will please him.'

When we feel we are not growing as Christians, the problem is often not that we need to discover new truths, but that we need to act on the old truths. Yes, we do need new experiences of God, but we need to enter into the joy of the old experiences as well.

Sometimes we can hear too much preaching and read too many Christian books! We can try to take in too much new information before we have properly digested what we have already heard and read. Perhaps we have known some biblical truths for years, but are still not living in the light of them. We need to grow in what we know, by putting it into practice.

Start in your own family

The difference that Jesus makes in our lives should be seen most clearly in the way we live with those closest to us, our families:

> 'See, I will send you the prophet Elijah before that great
> and dreadful day of theLord comes. He will turn the hearts
> of the fathers to their children, and the hearts of the children
> to their fathers; or else I will come and strike the land with
> a curse.'   *Malachi 4: 5-6*

Most commentators think the mention of Elijah is a reference to the ministry of John the Baptist. God's messengers – whether Elijah, John the Baptist, Jesus himself or us as Jesus' disciples – have a crucial job to do: that of healing and renewing family bonds. When Jesus comes into our lives, with all his purity, power and healing, it should make a difference to our families.

The most crucial way he will do that is to help us 'turn our hearts towards our children.'

We need to give time to our families, both 'quality' and 'quantity' time. Some of us are so busy with work or church that our husbands, wives or children don't get what they need either from us or from the Lord.

My experience of family life as a leader is probably fairly typical of other leaders' lives. I spend at least twenty minutes a day at home, snatching something to eat before running out to do some more counselling or speaking. Once, a while ago when Bethany was little, I was sitting reading my Bible, trying to prepare for a talk, and with my coat on ready to go. Bethany came up to me and pulled the edges of my coat. 'Coat off!' she said. 'I can't take my coat off; I'm not staying!' I explained. So then she asked, 'Daddy reading Bible?' 'Yes.' 'Daddy put Bible away!' Frantically, I said, 'No! I can't do that!' So she took the Bible, closed it and put it on one side. Then she gave me *Jane goes to Noddyland,* or something like that, and said, 'Daddy read this!' So I read it to her – at about a hundred miles an hour – and rushed out to my engagement.

What are we teaching our children about God by the amount of time we spend with them? Are they growing up to hate the Bible for keeping them away from Mummy or Daddy? Are they developing a deep resentment against the church because all their other friends are out at the seaside on a Sunday morning and they're struck in a dreary old building for hours on end? Are they learning to resent people coming into our house because they take up all Mum and Dad's time and mean no bedtime story? We need to be very careful that we are not always too busy for our children, but make their well-being our priority.

Part of the secret is to work to God's timetable rather than our own. If our children need us to minister to them – or just to go for a walk with them or play with them – we should see that as God's work, every bit as much as preaching to one thousand people. God's values are not always the same as ours! We might think it is better to spend ten hours preparing a sermon; God might think it would be time far better spent taking the family out for the day.

We want our children's hearts to be turned towards us, don't we? There's usually not too much trouble with the younger ones, but it's when they reach the impossibly awkward teenage years that we fear they are turning away from us. One mother ruefully confided to me, 'My daughter's at the teenage rebellion stage.' 'What's so unusual about that?' I asked. 'Well' she said, 'she's only six!' If we want our children's hearts to be turned towards us, and to our Lord, what are we doing to turn our hearts towards them?

The only alternative

The last verse of Malachi, the last book of the Old Testament, is devastating: ' ... or else I will come and strike the land with a curse.' This is not God being vindictive and angry. It is, rather, God pointing out the only possible alternative to living his way. We will not be able to avoid bringing sorrow and trouble on ourselves. The unspoken message is, 'Come-back to me.' A stark way to end the Old Testament.

Yet if we look on to the last verses in the New Testament, we have the same sense of expectation, the same warnings of the alternative, and the same invitation to return to the Lord:

'Behold, I am coming soon! My reward is with me, and I will give to everyone according to what he has done ...

'Blessed are those who wash their robes, that they may have the right to the tree of life and may go through the gates into the city. Outside are the dogs, those who practise magic arts, the sexually immoral, the murderers, the idolaters and everyone who loves and practises falsehood....

'I, Jesus, have sent my angel to give you this testimony for the churches ...'

The Spirit and the bride say, "Come!" And let him who hears say, "Come!" Whoever is thirsty, let him come; and whoever wishes, let him take the free gift of the water of life.'   *Revelation 22: 12-17*

The Lord holds out two alternatives to us: life or death, judgment or grace. Let us choose life!

Thirsty for God

The Sermon on the Mount

Contents

1 A new approach to life 95

2 A new thirst for God 108

3 Salt and light..120

4 Playing by the rules.....................................135

5 Pure in heart..149

6 A transparent life.......................................160

7 Handling the pressure....................................178

8 Ultimate commitment....................................190

9 Sound judgment 200

10 Persistence 209

11 Building on solid ground 220

1

A New Approach to Life

I would like to be able to write the best sermon in the history of the world but I am not sure that I am capable of doing that! So instead, I have written about the best sermon in the history of the world – the Sermon on the Mountain.

Matthew chapters 5, 6, and 7 are at the heart of the teaching of Jesus. As Jesus preached this sermon, something very interesting happened. At the beginning of chapter 5 we read, 'His disciples came to him, and he began to teach them.' But if we look on to the end of chapter 7 we find that, 'when Jesus had finished saying these things, the crowds were amazed at his teaching.' The disciples were the first to come, but by the time the sermon ended there were crowds of people listening, riveted by what he was saying about himself and the kingdom of God. As news of Jesus' teaching spread, so more people arrived to hear him.

There were crowds of people hungry for the word of God, their spirits were thirsty for something that would really satisfy. And there are many people today with the same hunger and thirst. There's a lovely illustration here of how the church can help people find the living bread and water they are looking for. As you and I spend time with Jesus, perhaps together with other Christians, hearing his word and letting it change us, there will be others hard on our heels, wanting to hear it too.

Impossible stuff?
When G K Chesterton first read the Sermon on the Mount he said, 'This is impossible stuff!' I'm glad he recognised that. Without

the Holy Spirit living in our lives its teaching simply cannot be lived out.

> Now when [Jesus] saw the crowds, he went up on a mountainside and sat down. His disciples came to him, and he began to teach them, saying:
> 'Blessed are the poor in spirit,
>   for theirs is the kingdom of heaven.
> Blessed are those who mourn,
>   for they will be comforted.
> Blessed are the meek,
>   for they will inherit the earth.
> Blessed are those who hunger and thirst for righteousness,
>   for they will be filled.
> Blessed are the merciful,
>   for they will be shown mercy.
> Blessed are the pure in heart,
>   for they will see God.
> Blessed are the peacemakers,
>   for they will be called sons of God.
> Blessed are those who are persecuted
> because of righteousness
>   for theirs is the kingdom of heaven.'
>   Matthew 5:1-10

It is important to note right at the start that Jesus' teaching here does not describe the way to become a Christian. Keeping the beatitudes will not earn us salvation, any more than keeping the ten commandments will. Rather, these sayings give a description of life in the kingdom of God; the way kingdom people, who are already converted, are meant to behave. They describe the totally new approach to life and to God that comes with conversion. Our natures undergo a radical change when we are redeemed from the power of sin over us. In Jesus we have become 'new creations' (2 Cor. 5:17).

The beatitudes are all about new attitudes working themselves out in new behaviour. They are the 'be-attitudes'– attitudes about being. They are all very practical – we should be-merciful and be-pure and be-peacemakers. If these attitudes are deep in our hearts, our behaviour will be that of God's children. It won't be 'impossible stuff' because it will simply be a matter of living in a way that fits our new nature.

A Lifestyle for today?
Yet, this does *seem* an impossible way to live in today's cut-throat world. It might have been all right for Christians in the first century – people who knew Jesus first hand. But don't the pressures and demands of life today call for a very different sort of response?

I don't think so. In fact, when you think about the principles and values by which most people live today, I can imagine nothing more effective than the complete contrast of a life being lived according to the principles that Jesus set out.

Contrast this set of 'twentieth- century beatitudes' with those we have just read:

> Blessed are the pushers,
>> for they get on in the world.
> Blessed are they who complain,
>> for they get their way in the end.
> Blessed are the blasé,
>> for they never worry over their own sins.
> Blessed are the slavedrivers,
>> for they get results.
> Blessed are the knowledgeable,
>> for they know their way around.
> Blessed are the troublemakers,
>> for they make people notice them.   JB Phillips

Well, you probably have some sympathies with that list! And all of us know people whom they describe perfectly. But there would also have been plenty of people in Jesus' day who would vote in favour of those principles rather than Jesus'.

The political situation

People in the first century who heard this teaching of Jesus were living under enormous stress. Israel at that time was like one big pressure cooker. The heat was on the Jewish people as they found themselves living under Roman occupation. They responded in four basic ways, just as we today respond to our own country's political structures and processes.

Firstly, there was the revolutionary response. The motto of one of the violently anti-Roman Zealot groups was, 'Let their blood be spilt in the streets.' Revolution would right all wrongs. They saw that the whole system was sick, full of oppression and injustice, and they wanted to get rid of it once and for all. Revolution was the only way to do that.

Then there were the escapists. A group called the Essenes felt that the problem was with the whole of society. The whole thing was so corrupt that there was no way it could be reformed. So they hived off to the desert and lived in their own community. They wanted nothing to do with the world. All it could do was contaminate them, so they separated themselves from it and left it to its own devices.

Thirdly, there were the compromisers – people like Matthew who took a job with the Roman occupying army and collected their taxes for them. The compromisers didn't think they could change anything and decided it was safest to 'play the system'. But they were seen as traitors by the other Jews.

Fourthly, there was the response of abdicating responsibility. This was the fall-back position of almost everyone in the ancient world. Basically, they had given up. 'How can we compete with this massive Roman army of occupation? It's just too much for us!' So their day-to-day lives were characterized by a kind of stoic acceptance: 'Well, this is all there is – what can we do about it?'

You will see these four attitudes in evidence during any general election campaign today. There are always a number of fringe parties who say that the election makes not one bean of difference – because the great revolution is coming soon and all these 'jumped up' politicians pretending to know what they're talking about will disappear overnight. And there are the escapists, who say they won't have anything to do with it; the kind of Christian who washes his hands of 'the whole rotten business', isn't going to vote, isn't going to listen, doesn't want to know anything about it. 'No one has got the answer,' they say. Thirdly, it is easy to settle for compromise. 'Maybe that policy isn't very fair, but I don't suppose anyone has come up with anything much better – and anyway, it won't really affect me.' We can get so sucked into the world's way of thinking that we haven't a distinctive voice any more. Perhaps the most common response today, though, is apathy – abdication of responsibility. Whatever result comes out of a general election you can be certain that thousands of people entitled to vote didn't do so. They simply couldn't be bothered.

It was to people very much like ourselves, with the same sort of scepticism, cynicism and idealism, that Jesus brought this teaching. It is just as appropriate today as it was back in the first century.

The voice of the church

Where were the Jews' religious leaders in all the people's turmoil – the equivalent of our national church leaders today? What help and guidance did they offer the people? Well, the Pharisees had locked up their faith in a traditionalism that simply had no power to address the issues of the day. They had nothing to contribute because they had not thought through the way God's people should interact with society and its political processes. They kept themselves largely separate from it, waiting for God to step in and change things for them, miraculously.

How does the church of Jesus in this country compare today? We are called to point people to the alternative values of the kingdom of God, by the way we live out its principles now. It is a kingdom that is already 'up and running' – it knows no beginning because it originated in the eternal God, and will know no end because Jesus' second coming will take it into eternity. Jesus' teaching in the Sermon on the Mount shows how we are to influence the kingdoms of this world for good, by the way we season them with the values of the kingdom of God. We cannot just sit back and wait for God to work a miracle – perhaps to make all politicians Christian, just and truthful overnight! Nor can we wash our hands of involvement in society because we dismiss the possibility of non-Christians doing anything really worthwhile. Jesus calls us to change our own attitudes first, by the power of his Spirit within us, and then to let the influence of God's kingdom values flow out from us to change and help our wider society.

Empty hands

When we are living for Jesus alone, our approach to life, its ups and downs, meaning and purpose, will alter out of all recognition. Our understanding of ourselves is the first thing to change, as we see ourselves for the first time from God's perspective:

> Blessed are the poor in spirit,
> for theirs is the kingdom of heaven.

Over the years I have talked with many people before they have become Christians. Some of them find the decision a real struggle because they come to Jesus wanting to bring so much. They are so full of themselves: 'If I became a Christian, my word! I have this degree or that, this talent or that, I'm good at this or that; see how much I can bring to God! Wouldn't he be pleased!' Others have said, quite blatantly, 'I'd be quite a catch for God, wouldn't I?' And I've had to respond, 'Not really; no more than anyone else, because we can only receive all that God wants to give us if we come to him aware of our need of him. We need to come with empty hands.'

Augustus Toplady wrote a famous hymn which contains the lines, 'Nothing in my hands I bring, simply to thy cross I cling.' This is poverty of spirit; knowing that 'nothing good lives in me', as Paul said (Rom. 7:18). It's those who recognize their poverty before God who will be blessed, says Jesus, because only they are really able to receive from him.

The basis of our Christian life has nothing to do with what we can bring God, but everything to do with what he brings us. It's not, 'blessed are the greatly skilled; blessed are the degree-holders.'

Rather, blessed are those who come to God and say, 'Lord, I've nothing to bring to this arrangement – it's all on your side. All I bring with me is my sin, guilt, shame and failure, and I am asking in return for your life and love to fill me'.

It's a very one-sided operation! And it is vital that we realize this. After our conversion, the growth pattern in our Christian lives is dictated by our ability to recognize our continuing poverty of spirit. However baptized with the Spirit we are, however filled with his authority, however mature or spiritually gifted, unless we can see that without Jesus himself we are poverty stricken, arrogance and pride will soon settle into our lives.

There is a danger that, as we go on in our Christian lives, we can sometimes become arrogant. It's the feeling that, basically, we are better than others because God has used us or gifted us. We need to remember that we are made acceptable to God only because of what Jesus has done for us, not for anything we have done for God. The ground at the foot of the Cross is level. We are all equal there. We are all equally desperate, hungry for the Saviour to reach and fill us. D.T.Niles, a famous missionary theologian, said that, when it comes down to it, evangelism is simply a matter of 'one beggar telling another where to find bread.'

There is an opposite danger too: we can become discouraged and dispirited because we don't seem able to live up to all that we think God asks of us. But Jesus says to us, 'It doesn't matter that you can't live a perfect life. Come with empty hands to me and

let me clothe you with my perfection.' There's a song which puts
it well:

> I am covered over with the robe of righteousness
> that Jesus gives to me – gives to me;
> I am covered over with the precious blood of Jesus
> and he lives in me – lives in me.
>
> What a joy it is to know
> my heavenly Father loves me so –
> he gives to me my Jesus;
> when he looks at me he sees
> not what I used to be,
> but he sees Jesus.'

The Cheam Fellowship

Special benefits

When we live in the kingdom, living totally for Jesus, our approach
to suffering will change, and we will discover some special benefits
for his followers:

> Blessed are those who mourn,
> for they will be comforted.

There is a special place in the kingdom for those who are
hurting. The word Matthew uses is a general word meaning 'those
who suffer pain and hurt'. He does not just mean 'mourn' as in
'bereaved'.

There is a story about an Indian woman who lived in a small
village. Disaster after disaster struck her life. Eventually she went
to the wise man of the village and said, 'I am broken and crushed.
I have lost my husband and my son through illness and now I
have no home at all. Life is so unfair, I want the gods to take it all
away and give me a fresh start.' The wise man replied, 'All right.

Collect a bowlful of fruits from all your neighbours. But you may only take a fruit from them if no tragedy has struck their household. So the woman went round the village as she was told, and came back with an empty bowl. Then she understood that suffering, tragedy and pain, in different measures and in different degrees, fall into every human life.

As Christians we are not exempt from this, the common lot of humanity. This is not a very popular thing to teach. Most people prefer to be told that if they come to know Jesus he will bring them joy and happiness, and every moment will be filled with a blissful awareness of his presence. Like the sad Indian woman, we all prefer a god who will wave a magic wand and release us from trouble and suffering. Jesus didn't promise this at all. In fact he promised the opposite. He warned that we are actually *adding* to our problems by becoming his disciples, because we are entering into spiritual conflicts too.

So why does Jesus say that those who mourn and suffer are 'happy' or blessed? Because he will be there with us in all our suffering, mourning, pain and hurt. He will not leave us to mourn and suffer on our own. Throughout his life Jesus showed that his concern was for the hurting, the destitute, powerless, the physically and emotionally crippled, lame and blind. Those who commit themselves to Jesus will have the special benefits of his life and strengthening. They will know they are infinitely precious to him and that he is able to turn all these difficulties into good. If you are hurting, whether through bereavement, pain or some other loss, the Jesus that we worship in our kingdom is specially sensitive to your needs; he loves you.

There is another way, too, in which kingdom people find special benefits in their suffering. Just as Jesus turned his focus outwards, to bring compassion and care to those who mourned, so his followers learn to minister in the same way to one another. The Christian community is designed to be a place of comfort and healing for those who are distressed. 'Love each other as I have loved you', Jesus said (John 15:12).

A life under control

When we live in the kingdom, the way we treat ourselves will change. We will be concerned to train and discipline ourselves in order to be able to do the work Jesus set before us – that of reclaiming the world for him:

> Blessed are the meek,
> for they will inherit the earth.

In the French version of Matthew's Gospel, the word 'meek' is translated 'debonair'. It's an interesting reflection on the gentlemanly nature of the word. The Greek carries the idea of being 'tamed'; blessed are those who are tamed, under control.

If, like me, you're not particularly keen on dogs but tend to visit quite a few people, you will know what it's like to go into a house with a dog which keeps you constantly on edge. You sit on the edge of the settee or chair, looking out for it, imagining that at any moment it will be going for your throat! And you worry that if you move suddenly, even to shake your host's hand, you will find your arm bitten off at the elbow by a dog that is over-protective towards its master! Or you'll knock on the door, praying that the dog's out, only to hear a huge barking noise as it comes racing to the door. 'This is going to be another of "those" visits,' you groan.

Yet other people you visit may also have a dog but you haven't even known it's been there! It's not that it's locked up somewhere; it's just under control. When the owner says 'Sit!' it sits! That home is a much more peaceful place than one dominated by an animal that is simply out of control.

The same is true, to some extent, of our children, in that they, too, need to be 'tamed'. James Dobson, a doctor with many years of experience in working with children and families, writes of the need to shape a child's will without breaking his or her spirit. He speaks of this as bringing to bear a 'taming' influence on them. We've all been in homes where the children behave really badly. It's simply no fun to be there because the children are allowed to dominate everything. Their behaviour rules the whole household. Once you leave you breathe a sigh of relief!

Jesus' disciples are expected to have 'tamed' themselves, to have themselves under the control of the Holy Spirit. William Butler Yeates defined civilization as 'an exercise in self-restraint'. This self-restraint is to characterize citizens of the kingdom of God, too. Perhaps we need to be more careful about thinking *before* we respond to someone who goads us, or to hold back from instantly objecting, being angry or striking out. It is easy to 'open mouth and insert foot'! If we are aware of difficult situations that regularly crop up, or know that a particular person always winds us up, perhaps we could develop the habit of taking a moment to pray about our attitude and response before speaking. We should not be out of control but under God's control.

We need this self-discipline and training in order to be quick to hear the prompting of the Holy Spirit as he tells us how to respond in a given situation, or makes us aware of needs we can meet, or calls us to pray. Without self-discipline, no war is won!

Releasing our grip on rights
When we live in the kingdom, we will develop a new approach to other people:

> Blessed are the merciful,
> for they will be shown mercy.

There is lovely gentleness in the word 'mercy'. In New Testament times it was usually used in the context of gladiatorial combat in the public arena. After a fierce and bloody fight a man lies prone on the ground, with a gladiator standing over him holding a sword or spear to his throat. The gladiator would look up to Caesar for the final word and if Caesar gave the 'thumbs up' sign the man would be allowed to live. If it was 'thumbs down' the man was to die. Perhaps the defeated combatant would cry out for mercy, and sometimes Caesar would stand up and say that, yes, he could go free.

Throughout the New Testament, 'mercy' speaks of a lack of revenge, the decision not to get my own back. In *The Merchant of Venice*, Shylock the Jew was determined to get all that he was entitled to from an agreement made with the merchant, Antonio. If Antonio could not repay by the set date the money borrowed from Shylock, he would forfeit literally a pound of his flesh. When it came to judgment, Shylock would not give an inch. He demanded justice. The judge urges him to show mercy, eloquently describing its true nature.

> 'The quality of mercy is not strain'd,
> It droppeth as the gentle rain from heaven
> Upon the place beneath: It is twice blest;
> It blesseth him that gives and him that takes:
> 'Tis mightiest in the mightiest: it becomes
> The throned monarch better than his crown
> His sceptre shows the force of temporal power,
> The attribute to awe and majesty,
> Wherein doth sit the dread and fear of kings;
> But mercy is above this sceptred sway;
> It is enthroned in the hearts of kings,
> It is an attribute to God himself;
> And earthly power doth then show likest God's
> When mercy seasons justice. Therefore, Jew,
> Though justice be thy plea, consider this,
> That, in the course of justice, none of us
> Should see salvation: we do pray for mercy;
> And that same prayer doth teach us all to render
> The deeds of mercy.'
>
> *The Merchant of Venice, Act 4 scene I*

Mercy is the opposite of the Shylock complex, the 'pound of flesh', 'pay me back' attitude.

How do you react when you have been snubbed and hurt by someone? Though we may not physically fight back, we usually want revenge! We are glad the person who made life difficult for us at work is overlooked for a promotion. We are secretly gleeful when a neighbour who has harassed us doesn't get the limelight he wanted, or doesn't succeed at something or his children get a reputation for being troublemakers at school.

Revenge is taken in more subtle ways in the twenty-first century than it once was. We no longer go round to someone's house and burn it down, but revenge is no less alive in the human heart. It is the desire to see other people openly put in the wrong, so that we appear to be justified. But we know that is not the way we are justified. Our justification comes about only through God's mercy. And in recognition of that, God calls those he has justified to show that same mercy and compassion to others.

2

A New Thirst for God

Longing for holiness

Another big change that happens in us when we come to know Jesus as Saviour and Lord is that our whole attitude to God changes. We can't get enough of him! And his concerns will become burning concerns for us:

> Blessed are those who hunger and thirst for righteousness, for they will be filled.

Every time the phrase 'hunger and thirst' is used in the New Testament, it is used in the sense of hungering and thirsting for *some* of something – some of that bread, some of that wine. Except here. This is the only place in which it means, 'hunger and thirst for *all of it*' – not *some* bread, *some* wine, *some* anything else, but *all* of it.

I don't want just some – I thirst for all of it, to have it all in my life. If we are going to get anywhere in our discipleship, we must be filled with *all* of God's resources, not just a modicum or small amount of them.

Isn't that just like us as human beings – to be satisfied with a little, when God offers us a lot? Let's not be the sort of Christians who have had some of God's blessing but who will not cross the line of faith to receive more. There is still a wealth of things to experience beyond that which we already know. So let us ask God to awaken in us that hunger and thirst to be totally righteous and holy.

When the children come in at tea time and say, 'Mum, I'm starving!' we know they're not really. Probably not many of us have been at starvation point, desperate for food. The gnawing, aching hunger found in Ethiopia or the Sudan doesn't come in a week. It comes over months and years of having next to nothing. The desperation of that gnawing, empty pain is what God looks for in our spirits. Perhaps some of us are not more filled by God's presence, and not more fully anointed by his power, because our desire for it is only superficial. There can be a covering of complacency over our spirits; we are happy as things are. God longs for people who are desperate for himself, so that he can fill them with his Spirit.

Being single-minded

Our thirst for God will spur us on to seek him out, to spend time with him, to discover what he wants done in his world and to figure out how we can fit into those plans:

> Blessed are the pure in heart,
> for they will see God.

Purity is something we usually associate with the sexual aspect of our lives. Traditionally, a bride's wedding dress is white to signify her virginity. But the context here is much bigger. Jesus is talking about a purity or singleness of aim, being single-minded, doggedly pursuing a single goal without being deflected from it.

The goal Jesus speaks of is that of 'seeing God' – of bending all our efforts to know God and be known by him. The person who sets his heart on this will pursue God relentlessly! Knowing God will be the most important thing in his life and he will let nothing deflect him from seeking him out, talking to him, listening to him, growing in love and knowledge of him, and wanting to carry out his will. And Jesus assures us that if this is our aim, and we pursue it single-mindedly, we shall not be disappointed: 'they will see God'.

If we were all to start 'pursuing' God in this way, many of our churches would be revolutionized! House groups, worship services, decision-making meetings would all be transformed because we would have one common aim: to know God and make him known to others.

If we are honest with ourselves, we know that it is often other motives which drive us and make us decide for or against a particular course of action. Sometimes we are hurt by a cutting remark and our primary aim is to set the record straight. So we speak out in our own defence – and generally manage to 'do down' the person who dared to slight us. Or we feel we have been overlooked for some role in the church fellowship that we wanted, so we volunteer for another task – not genuinely out of a desire to see God's work done, but out of our need for recognition. And suddenly we find we are out of sorts with the world, with ourselves and with God.

We need to question our motives from time to time. But a word of warning: questioning ourselves too often and too carefully is a sure way to madness! We can never really get to the bottom of our motives; and because of our fallenness our motives will always, to some extent, be mixed. But we can usually become aware, without too much probing, of times when we are acting out of hurt, jealousy or fear. That's the time to be open with our brothers and sisters in Jesus and to let them minister to those needs. Then we will be more free to set our sights on achieving things for God's sake, rather than for our own. And, more importantly, we will be free to *be* the people he intended us to be, people who find their security in their *relationship* with him, rather than in *doing* things for him; people who are single-minded in their devotion to him.

Simon Stylites was a Christian who lived in Syria between about AD390 and 459. He wanted to be utterly pure in his devotion to God so, in order to prevent anything deflecting him from pursuing that goal single-mindedly, he lived in the desert on a twelve-foot square platform at the top of a tall pillar. He lived there for about thirty-five years. He may have achieved some good but living like that was not what Jesus meant by being 'pure in heart'.

I know some Christians who misinterpret Jesus' words, though, in much the same way as Simon Stylites did. They think that being single-minded for God means that their lives should be dominated by 'religious' activity. They feel very uncomfortable about letting their children play for too long, or about wanting a lie-in on Saturday morning, going out for a meal, watching a video or playing a game of some kind. As soon as the thought comes that one of those activities would be rather nice, a little voice inside rebukes them: 'Tut, tut ... this isn't exactly being single-minded for God, is it? I mean, how will sitting here watching Walt Disney achieve anything for the kingdom?'

Some years ago, when I was in the middle of preparing a sermon, there was a knock at my study door, and I yelled out, 'Come in!' Nothing happened. So I yelled again, 'Come in!' Still nothing happened. That really annoyed me. It was so frustrating to be interrupted in the middle of prayer and study by some idiot – a deaf idiot at that, I thought. (It just shows how unspiritual we can be when we are being spiritual!) So I threw down my Bible, leapt out of the chair and ran round to the door wondering why this person didn't come in. I pulled the door open – and it was Bethany, my small daughter. 'Daddy, come in the house,' she said, 'No!' I replied. Then I thought, 'Now, Stephen...' and took myself in hand and gave myself a talking-to for a minute. Then I invited Bethany into the study and spent a little time with her. I showed her some of the books as we walked round it and then I took her into the house and did spend some time playing with her. I was badly in need of a reminder that spirituality isn't always about high-powered stuff like praying!

Jesus' call to true spirituality is not a call to spend every minute of the day seeking God in prayer and reading the Bible. It *is* a call to make God the number one priority in our lives, and when that happens all these other things – watching films, going out, as well as prayer and Bible reading – will fall into place. When our overall

aim in life is to please God and serve him, we'll soon discover
that there are actually many, many ways in which he wants us to
work that out in practice. God loves it when we spend time with
our families! He is honoured when we are caring for them, enjoying
their company and being happy with then. And we'll find that he
provides us with the time for recreation and relaxation, as well as
for the hard work needed in the kingdom of God.

Positive action

Our discovery that God is the thirst-quenching source of all that
is best and most real in life will make us want to share him with
others. We will want our friends and neighbours to know, too,
what it is to be at peace with God and with one another:

> Blessed are the peacemakers,
> for they will be called sons of God.

I think this beatitude is one we can easily misread. We can
think it says, 'Blessed are the peace lovers'. It doesn't! It is speaking
of something much more active and positive. Peace*makers*
positively bring peace where trouble would be the natural state.
Peacemaking calls for hard work, patience and a sympathetic
understanding of the grievances of the warring parties.
Peacemakers long to see a unity of purpose and unity of activity
among God's people. The idea behind the word is of those who
'make two into one'.

Again, this desire to bring about peace and harmony will mark
out the Christian as someone different, because by nature we are
all trouble-makers! Some of us love confrontation and conflict.
We thrive on a good argument and love to tie someone up in
verbal knots. We love it when there is a public disagreement
followed by a good ding-dong argument. The tense atmosphere
and distraught looks make for a good bit of real live drama! You
might even feel specially gifted to take on the role of devil's
advocate whenever there is a discussion in progress. At the office,

at the house group, at the school parents' evening, you've always got to disagree.

Well, sometimes this is necessary; there are occasions when we do need to speak out and it is right that people should feel uncomfortable with what we are saying. But we need also to watch that we are not doing so simply because we like to be noticed, or want to show off our gift with words. To build people up is much harder than knocking them down. To make peace between two people who are suspicious, wary, or downright hateful of each other calls for a genuine commitment to the good of others. We will enable others to develop a respect for and unity with each other only at the cost of our own wishes and comfort.

We have already noted that peacelovers are not the same as peacemakers. Many people are afraid of conflict. They don't even like to disagree with someone, no matter how politely. Often, this is because conflict was handled badly in their family when they were children. As a child they would learn the signs of mother's temper brewing, and would scarper before the storm broke. Or, if they weren't able to get away, they would make themselves as small and unnoticeable as possible in order to try to avoid being hurt when she lashed out in frustration and anger. So now, when they sense disagreement in the air, all their instincts tell them to run or freeze – at the very least to keep the peace at any price. And now they avoid talking about contentious subjects. But avoiding subjects that cause conflict, glossing over them or not letting people be heard, does not make for peace. It just prolongs for more years the agonies of untruthfulness, fear and unreality.

Peacemaking can only happen when two conflicting sides are brought out clearly into the open, and are encouraged to listen to each other fully. Sometimes we need to find healing and reconciliation for the emotional conflicts within ourselves before we can handle being in the presence of others in conflict. These hidden sources of our own fears need to be unearthed, brought to the surface and dealt with. This takes courage and a determination to

enter into the fullness of the salvation Jesus has won for us–
wholeness of mind and emotions, as well as of spirit. If this is
your situation, your role as a peacemaker will be won only at a
high personal cost, but will be all the more effective because of
the additional insights and empathy your own struggles will give
you.

Peacemakers are not content to let two Christians maintain a
frosty, but polite, relationship. After the opening up of Eastern
Europe in 1989, Lawrence Eagleburger, the American
Under-Secretary of State, commented on a radio programme:
'One of the nice things about the cold war was that it was a time
of stable relationships among the great powers.' 'Cold war', no
matter how stable, isn't true peace, whether conducted between
nations or individuals! The peace the Bible speaks of is not just an
absence of conflict, but denotes a wholeness and healthiness of
relationship. We are selling ourselves and each other short if we
do not have the courage to live with the untidiness of growing,
developing relationships.

God is good at creating things out of chaos. He calls us to go
out of our way to *make* peace wherever there has been conflict,
hurt, coldness or simply silence.

A radicalism that offends

Each of these 'beatitudes' captures an attitude that is different to
those we normally come across, either in the way we relate to
other people, or in the way we relate to God. In fact, the two are
always linked. That is seen very clearly in the last of the beatitudes:

> 'Blessed are you when people insult you, persecute you and
> falsely say all kinds of evil against you because of me. Rejoice
> and be glad, because great is your reward in heaven, for in the
> same way they persecuted the prophets who were before you'
> (Matt. 5:11-12).

Our world is under the influence of 'the ruler of the kingdom of the air, the spirit who is now at work in those who are disobedient' (Eph. 2:2). Because of his influence in people's personal lives and in social and political structures, the whole tide of human thought and opinion is flowing his way. But when people meet Christ and surrender themselves to his will and his control, he turns them around to face the other direction. Slap bang into the oncoming tidal wave. Each of the beatitudes highlights an area of struggle, where the person who follows Jesus will find herself in conflict with the views of people around. But this struggle is proof of the reality of her faith.

Two misunderstandings

There are two common misunderstandings of persecution, or of what Jesus elsewhere calls, 'taking up your cross' (Matt. 16:24).

The first is the idea that whenever anything goes wrong I am being subjected to spiritual 'attack'. I might wake up with a headache, the kids are being atrocious, the boss at work is impossible, and when I run out at the end of the day, anxious to catch the early train home, I trip over something and fall flat on my face in a puddle. We all have days like that – it is part of being human! It is not likely to be anything more sinister.

The second misconception is to think we are being persecuted for being Christians when in fact we are being persecuted simply for being prigs. It's important to understand the difference! Some of us are so 'holier than thou' about our Christian faith that people are put off by our attitude, not by Christianity itself. If we go around with our noses stuck in the air, unwilling to get involved with them simply as people, we will find ourselves ostracized. This is not being persecuted for righteousness, it is simply being persecuted (and deservedly so)!

The real thing

The persecution Jesus meant is that which comes with being identified with his revolutionary new kingdom, and all that it stands for.

It is not something we know much about in the west, where it is understood that, within reason, we tolerate other people's beliefs. This attitude of tolerance was itself established largely through Christian concern and pressure for minority groups. Yet every country goes through times of hostility to Christianity. British Christians have been through them, winning the peace we now enjoy; and times of persecution will come again.

Persecution is very much part and parcel of Christian discipleship for many people in other parts of our world. Jesus seemed to regard persecution almost as synonymous with discipleship, because his disciples will find themselves swimming against the tide of their society's values and beliefs. What's more, having been 'born again' we no longer belong to this world or feel at home in it in the same way as before. We are essentially strangers here, foreigners – and we know how foreigners are generally treated by the indigenous population!

There is a hard question here which we need to face. If Christianity really is a radical call to be different, to be changed by the power of a living God who is totally involved in the world of the twenty-first century, why do we not experience more persecution in the west? I think it is largely because we have hidden the radical nature of the Christian faith behind a veneer of respectability. We have been more concerned to be acceptable to society at large than to be faithful to our Lord. So we have lost our cutting edge. We tell people what 'the church' says on this issue or that, and our national church bodies spend more and more time debating, discussing, and 'making statements'. It is much less comfortable, much more divisive, shocking and offensive to tell people what *Jesus* taught, and to stick by that. If we did this we can be sure that the theologians who are wheeled on to radio and television programmes to comment on moral or ethical issues would be the first to condemn our naivety!

Are we prepared to face the ignominy of being considered simplistic? A bit fanatical? In today's culture the 'wise' person is deemed to be the one who accepts that truth is something no human can claim to have, so it is sheer bigotry that leads a person to evaluate one religion or creed against another. Christians involved in higher education, the media or the arts, are perhaps at the raw edge of persecution today. Their careers may suffer; they will certainly be regarded as simplistic and foolish – or that biggest of all crimes, intolerant – if they make it known that they are committed to Christ. The moral and ethical values that we must take on board as a result of this commitment run directly counter to much of the thinking of the powerful and influential in our country today.

Some questions

Here are some questions that we need to ask ourselves, also asking God to help us see if we are living as he wants us to, or if there is something we have missed:

- How many of the people you work with, live next door to, meet when shopping, know that you are a Christian?
- As far as you can tell, what do they think it means to be a Christian? How accurate is their impression?
- How far are you helping to give them a true impression of Christianity, by what you say, do, and what is important to you, and how might you be hindering them in their understanding?
- How far does your life display the revolutionary nature of contact with Jesus Christ? Perhaps one of the reasons why we are not persecuted is that we have not yet grappled with what it really means to know Jesus. Go back over Jesus' teaching in these early verses of Matthew 5 and ask yourself how far you are putting it into practice. Where do you think changes are called for?

Blessed?

You may well be feeling the sting of persecution already. You may be made the butt of jokes at work because of your faith. You may have been passed over for promotion because you are not prepared to do the shady deals expected of you. You may have lost a job because you believed your church and family commitments are more important than working on Sunday. Or at home, you may find it hard to live consistently as a Christian if your husband or wife is hostile to your faith. Other family members too can bring to bear their own, subtle forms of persecution. You may find you are not really accepted by the wider family, because of your Christian faith. Perhaps they always treat you as something a bit 'odd' or weird – they don't really let you in to the family circle and relationships between you are cold. That can be a very hard and lonely sort of persecution.

So why did Jesus say we are *blessed*, or happy, when this happens to us? Well, these are some very good reasons!

We are blessed because we are experiencing the same things that Jesus did. Jesus said that 'no servant is greater than his master' (John 13:16), and that if people hated him, they would not be too keen on his followers either. It is a real privilege to be able to follow in the footsteps of someone we love. We want to know what our daughter's first day at her new school felt like. Parents who lost sons in the Gulf war or a train crash want to go there, to know a little bit of what it felt like to be there. It gives them a link with their dead son. It's something of the same with us – we want to identify as fully as we can with Jesus, and so we are happy when we can identify with his sufferings as well as his joy.

We are blessed because persecution proves we are living out the full implications of the Christian faith. If we were not being effective in our witness and ministry, Satan wouldn't bother us and other people wouldn't feel threatened by our example. When persecution does come, don't let Satan's attacks get you down. Ask Jesus for his protection and keep your eyes on him. And when other people make life hard for you, don't hold it against them. That is your chance to show them what true Christian love is really all about!

We are blessed because we will hear Jesus' 'well done'. We are not only rewarded now, in that our knowledge of Jesus is deepened through persecution, but we will receive a 'great ... reward in heaven'. If you are being disadvantaged today because you are a Christian, be sure that the Lord has got saved up for you the splendours of heaven, the like of which you simply can't imagine!

3

Salt and Light

There's a lot of talk today about environmental pollution. Many people are very worried about it. But there's more than one way to pollute the place you live in. Someone has pointed out: 'You are the environment in which other people have to live!' Other people have to live with our anxiety, grumpiness and outbursts of temper, just as they have to breathe the air around them. What sort of environment are we creating as Christians? One that's slowly poisoning the people around us, or one that's helping them to become healthier and stronger, spiritually?

Jesus calls us to be healthy influences to the people we meet day by day. Our lives are to have an effect; and to do that, they need to be different. I was talking with an industrial chaplain the other day, and he commented that the men he works with change their behaviour when he's around. Just the fact that he's there, and they know he's a Christian, makes them behave differently. Another friend of mine said, 'It's funny, but now I'm working full time in this office, people don't swear anything like as much as they used to.'

To explain how we are meant to influence society Jesus took the images of salt and light. The Romans believed that salt was the purest thing there was, because it was made by the combined work of the sun and sea. Both salt and light can only do their jobs effectively if each is being fully itself. If salt 'loses its saltiness' – something that happened to an inferior sort of salt in Palestine, if it was left around for too long without being used – it loses its effectiveness. And the instant light gets tangled up with a bit of darkness – well, we have an indistinct half-light that's pretty lethal to drivers on the motorway! Jesus said:

> 'You are the salt of the earth. But if the salt loses its saltiness, how can it be made salty again? It is no longer good for anything, except to be thrown out and trampled by men. You are the light of the world. A city on a hill cannot be hidden. Neither do people light a lamp and put it under a bowl. Instead they put it on its stand, and it gives light to everyone in the house.
> In the same way, let your light shine before men, that they may see your good deeds and praise your Father in heaven' (Matt. 5:13-16).

In many countries, salt is still one of the essentials of life. It was certainly essential in first-century Palestine: it was the most basic medicine, used for dressing wounds and stopping the spread of infection; and it was used to preserve foods, especially meat which would otherwise go off very quickly in the hot climate.

Stop the rot!
Donald Bloesch writes: 'We are called not to be the honey of the world but the salt of the earth. Salt stings on an open wound, but it also saves one from gangrene' *(Theological notebook, vol 1).*

Whether in healing or in preserving, salt is used to 'stop the rot'. In the same way, the church is called to be the preserver of values and standards in society, to prevent it from becoming so corrupt that it's useless.

What are some of the 'rots' in today's society that Jesus is calling us to work against?

The corruption of values
Margaret Thatcher will go down in history as the Prime Minister who campaigned for a return to 'Victorian values'. Now *I* certainly don't want to get back to Victorian values – to the days when you

couldn't talk about table 'legs', for instance, and had to call them 'limbs' instead in case you offended anybody! Preserving values is not about going back to the Victorian era, but about going back to the Bible. The values Jesus calls us to preserve are God's values.

Many people today think there are no absolute values; we just make them up as we go along depending on what seems right for a particular society at any one time. Most of the time, 'civilized' people will make up rules that are generally good for people and are vaguely 'moral', or so we think. But the Bible tells us something very different: that there are some values that are absolute; they never change. They are the values that God holds, and that his people commit themselves to live by. We are to call our community and our world back to these absolute, unchanging values.

Many of the problems society faces today are here because we have ignored and abused God's laws. The results are predictable. If we think we can alter the law of gravity, so leap off a building hoping to land softly 100 feet below, we'll be disappointed! Pain will definitely be the result! If we break God's laws for living, pain in society results. It has done down the ages of history; it continues to do so today, because God's values are right for society.

The breakdown of family life

In a zoo, the lions, elephants, zebras and monkeys are all kept in separate enclosures. If they were all allowed to go wherever they wanted to, there would soon be disaster! At least, there soon wouldn't be any zebras, and the monkeys might not last too long either! God's laws build a strong fence around family life, not in order to make it restrictive and boring, but to prevent the people within it being attacked and destroyed by forces stronger than themselves breaking in. Selfishness, the desire for pleasure, the wish to be free of responsibility – these are all-powerful pressures that will destroy a family if they are allowed in.

Family life needs to be kept strong and healthy. Where it is, society too will be happier and healthier. Where family life is under pressure from divorce, adultery and abuse, society itself begins to break up. We need Jesus' boldness to come out and say so; it's not a popular claim to make today.

Of course, we must not condemn those families that are suffering from breakdown. As well as Jesus' boldness to state the facts, we need his compassion for those who are hurting. Salt isn't meant to make a wound worse! It's put into a wound to help heal it. As grains of salt, you and I are sent into lives that are hurting, in order to bring love, warmth, support and practical care. When people talk to us about their divorce, or about a breakdown in relationships in their family, there's no point in pretending that it's all OK really. The divorcee *knows* the divorce wasn't, in itself, a good thing. It's not the best that God had wanted for that family. But we can also assure people that God continues to want the best for them and will not abandon them – certainly not just when they are most aware of needing his guidance and care.

We preserve society from moral corruption and social disintegration when we proclaim that God's standards are eternal and certain. That message won't be welcome; it will sting like salt in a wound. And so we must go on to bring people the good news that God loves them and longs to bring back to himself those who have fallen from the standards he has set out for us – and that includes all of us. He longs to bring us back to a glorious wholeness of life in him.

Materialism

Materialism is the other big 'rot' in our society. In its broadest sense, it means a greed for things, status, power or influence, that overrides relationships and flattens values. It's the urge to 'get on' in the world at any price; to make a name for yourself. Suppose you've been offered a really good job three hundred miles away with a big pay increase and a leap in status, but your wife or husband doesn't want to move house. Some people would size it up, then ask, 'Well, do I really need this person anyway? If she's not prepared to see how important my career is, I'd be better off without her.'

Materialism lives for the things that can be seen, and for personal pleasure. The big problem with it is that it has lost all sense of duty. Again, to say that we have a 'duty' to do certain things – to love our wife or husband, to put their interests before our own, to be honest at work – is to say something sharp, painful and unpopular. It's like salt in the wound. But without that salt sprinkled into their lives, our work colleagues, friends and family members will make decisions that will gradually destroy them.

Taking steps
What practical steps can we take to stop the rot in our society?

— Talk about God's values. People won't know what they are unless we tell them. When moral subjects come up in conversation, take the opportunity to say what you believe and why. Emphasize that it is what God says, not just what you say – and that's why you think it's important to take notice of it.

— Model God's values. If people see God's values lived out in the lives of their friends, it helps them understand those values better. Try to provide a model, in the way you live, of God's values: in your marriage, in your friendships, at work, in your use of money, and so on.

— It is important to pick our own models carefully, too. For example, if you are married, whose marriage do you model your own on? We need to adopt attitudes and ways of behaving that are really God-honouring because our non-Christian friends will assume that the way we live is the 'Christian' way to live. Our words alone won't carry any weight unless they are backed up by our own lifestyle. As someone has said, 'I can't hear what you're saying, your actions are speaking too loudly!'

— Provide positive alternatives. Some Christians are so scared of doing anything wrong that they never do anything at all! Take

Hallowe'en: it's not very helpful to go around saying, 'Hallowe'en is bad; you shouldn't have anything to do with it – and make sure your children aren't allowed to make witches' hats at school!' Instead, plan an exciting, positive alternative. Perhaps you could have a 'Family Carnival' on that night. Focus on angels or famous Christians. (After all, it is the evening before All Saints' Day!) Have lots of games and fun planned, and invite your non-Christian friends – especially those with children who might otherwise be going to Hallowe'en parties. Don't let the Church be seen as something merely negative.

— Do you belong to a local residents' association that holds its meetings at the local pub? If everyone usually ends up smashed it can be pretty difficult to know whether you ought to go or not. So why not provide an alternative: offer to host it at your home instead and lay on a good meal for everyone.

— Alcohol is a real problem for many people. It's part and parcel of 'being sociable'. But non-alcoholic drinks can be just as varied. We have about ninety teenagers coming to a non-alcoholic cocktail bar at the church on a Saturday night. Instead of commanding the local young people not to go to the pub (so guaranteeing that they will!) we offer a positive alternative: 'Hey, have you heard about this place? Come and play pool and meet your mates and try our "Gulf War Cocktail" (brown and horrible!).' We have a wide range of non-alcoholic drinks and are always expanding and varying the selection. We'll also throw in things like a 'Cocktail of the month' and the odd, tropical 'special'.

Creativity and imagination will help people to be receptive to the salt we want to sprinkle in their lives!

Add some flavour

Jan, my wife, is not a very big salter of food. So, when we have company, people often ask for the salt and they pour it on their meal with great abandon because it doesn't have the flavour they're used to or want it to have.

Jesus calls us to be the flavour of the world, to influence everyday life in a way that makes it more palatable for others. Perhaps we could create a better working environment in the office. Are relationships sour? Then they need the saltiness of a peacemaker. Is the atmosphere very competitive, people doing each other down in order to get promoted in their place? Model a servant attitude to others instead. Does everyone rush off as fast as they can at the end of the day? Show what it is to care about a job being finished well. Do your workmates read porn magazines at lunch time? Take your Bible in to read instead, or a Christian book, and talk to them about it. This is what it means to 'flavour life'. Or, to put it another way, 'We are the deodorant on the body odour of life!'

Getting out of the salt cellar

There's one big problem to this flavour business. We have to get out there! We have to be shaken out of the salt cellar into the world.

I'm sure grains of salt are much more comfortable and happy when they're with lots of other grains of salt, sitting minding their own business in the salt cellar. As Christians we like to do the same. All around the country, grains of salt get together Sunday by Sunday. They look around at each other and think, 'Well, here we all are in the salt cellar again; isn't it wonderful!' Then we all go home again in our little family packets, like the blue ones Smiths used to put in crisp packets. And once home, we only mix with our Christian friends, being salty with one another. Then, come Sunday, we all pour ourselves back into the salt cellar again; one great salty mob. 'Food', however, doesn't get a look in!

Jesus said that we are to the world what sprinkled salt is to food. So we need to get out there! We can be so concerned for our own purity that, though we might take a peek at the world out there, we rush back in quickly, in case we get contaminated.

At Stopsley, we occasionally used to pour out onto the streets in 'Make Way' marches. Yet these were little more than quick trips out of the salt cellar to look at the food, and then to come rushing back in again to safety. We have to do something more.

It's contact that counts. Salt is useless unless it comes into contact with the food. Salt doesn't just shout at the food from a distance, it gets thoroughly involved in it! So how do we make contact?

Use their language

I was in Oxford one day. Walking round the street corner I bumped into someone with a big black Bible, and he was preaching his heart out – or had been until I walked slap into him. I walked into him because I couldn't hear him, the noise of the traffic and of the milling crowds was so great. He stopped preaching momentarily and said, 'Excuse me!' somewhat surprised. 'That's fine,' I said, 'feel free!' And his friend gave me a tract. As I wandered off I took a look at it. Now, we *do* need people who are ready to take the message of the gospel onto the streets; it's very important that we are open with our faith. But what the tract had inside as its basic message was, 'He is the propitiation for our sins.'

If I asked you now to stop reading and to write down what that means, how would you get on? Some of you would say, 'Propitiation. Oh, yes! that's no problem – there's a subtle difference between that and expiation, and actually it's quite interesting that ....'I guess most of us, though, would say, 'Propish .... what?' It makes me wonder what all those people in Oxford thought when they looked inside that tract.

That is not being salt in society. In fact, simply as an exercise in communication I would count it a failure. Of course, some people may have found Christ through that witness, and I would certainly not want to knock the commitment of the preacher and his helpers. But communication with other people has to be real. It has to be on their terms, in their language, with their dialect. The salt has to make contact with the food.

Go into their territory

Jesus was often found in places that 'religious' people didn't approve of. That's because he was looking for the people who needed God, and a bit of thought showed where he was likely to find them.

Similarly, if people are to talk with us at any depth we need to be prepared to go to the places where they will feel relaxed enough to be able to do so. Sometimes if a guy starts to share something with me but is obviously finding the church building or my office intimidating, I might say 'Look, let's talk about this over a drink,' and we'll go across to the pub for a while.

Are there lots of keen footballers in your church? Well, do you really need to start a church football team? Why not suggest they join a local team instead? Is there a group of people talking about setting up a church photography group? Why not join a local group instead or throw it open to the community as a whole and hold it on 'neutral' territory – the community hall or a local school?

We need to look for ways of making long-term contact with folk in our neighbourhood, if we are to have any effect on them as salt.

Restoring your saltiness

The mums you stand with as your children come out of school, the people you meet in the shops, office, classroom or staff room – how aware are they that there is something different about you? How much are you flavouring the society in which you find yourself? I wonder if you have lost your saltiness, your ability to reflect to others what God has done for you? If so, there are some steps you can take to put things right:

- Tell God about it, and about how you feel. Ask for his help.
- Tell one of the church leaders about it, or a mature Christian friend.

• Do whatever flows out of that discussion:

Perhaps there is a need for repentance. Perhaps a coldness and hardness has crept into your relationship with God. That needs to be broken through.

You might just be going through a 'low' time and are generally run down and have no enthusiasm for anything.

Perhaps you need to get back into serious Bible reading and to set aside time for prayer.

Perhaps the problem is that you don't have a 'role' in your local church. We are only being salty when we are *doing* something. It may be that you cannot actually see any opportunities open to you; your church leaders should be able to help there. They can tell you what needs to be done and can talk over with you how you might best be able to help.

On the other hand, it may be that you *are* actually being salty in your community, you just don't *feel* that you are. Remember that saltiness is what we *do*. When Jesus calls us to be salty, he calls us to action.

Dispel the darkness

Some friends of mine were on holiday in Devon, getting away from it all at a picturesque old farmhouse. In the middle of their first night there the wife had a coughing fit and wanted a glass of water. The husband dutifully found his way down the creaky, uneven stairs and into the kitchen. After a bit more fumbling he found the light switch and the place blazed into life – and the kitchen floor scattered in all directions as hundreds of cockroaches ran for cover! In mere seconds they had all melted away into the shadows. He didn't have the courage to tell his wife about this darker side of their holiday house until long after they'd left!

Light destroys darkness instantly, and sometimes shows up some pretty unpleasant things. When Jesus said, 'You are the light of the world', he might have had several things in mind.

Light and darkness cannot co-exist

I worry about people who seem to want to be 'secret' disciples. Basically, they are committed to being Christians: they come to church, probably go to a house group mid-week too, but in their place of work no one would suspect they were Christians. Their discipleship is a secret one. Now that is a fundamental contradiction. It's like saying 'I'll put the light on but I want it still to be dark.' Either our secrecy will destroy our faith, or our faith will destroy our secrecy. The two cannot live in tandem.

Yet many Christians try to live with this fight going on inside them. Some want the satisfaction and fulfilment of knowing Jesus, but they also want the comfort of not having to live up to his demands on them. If no one knows I am a Christian, perhaps I won't really have to change very much; the cockroaches can stay undisturbed in my life. But if I make too much of a song and dance about it, everyone will expect me to be some sort of angelic superman, always being kind, helpful and cheerful. And that's a bit much!

Jesus' words tell us clearly: 'You can't have both. You can't be filled with light *and* filled with darkness. You must choose to be either one or the other.' Nicodemus came to him by night, wanting to find out how to be a disciple but not prepared to be seen doing so! He found that to follow Jesus was going to make such radical changes in his life that he could not avoid being branded as 'one of them'. He had to make a clear choice.

Besides secret disciples, there are ignorant disciples! People who want to live a Christian life, but are secretive about it because they're slightly ashamed of what they believe. Others keep quiet because they aren't sure what they'd say if anyone asked them about it. That is basically a lack of knowledge. It can be cured easily enough by a long talk or two with other Christians who clearly *do* know what their faith is all about, or a visit to a Christian bookshop to find a book explaining Christian beliefs clearly. Don't let a lack of knowledge prevent your witness for Jesus being truly effective!

Light is visible!

D. L.Moody, the nineteenth-century American evangelist, said, 'We are told to let our light shine, and if it does we won't need to tell anybody it does. Lighthouses don't fire cannons to call attention to their shining. They just shine.'

We make our discipleship visible in two ways:

By living for God. Our honesty, quality of friendship, reliability and care for others will all be noticed. The sort of neighbour, worker or parent we are speaks volumes about the revolution that has happened in our lives because we met Jesus. A constant, steady witness to this in the way we live is the only thing that will convince people that what has happened is not just superficial or some passing fad, soon to be given up in despair like the low-fat diet. Rather, this encounter with Jesus has been so stunning that it has fundamentally affected every area of my life. My home, work, career, impact of the gospel of Jesus Christ. Only a gospel with effects that are radical will actually give the light that the world needs.

By speaking for God. The fact is, we can't *just* do our work and assume that people will realize we are Christians. It is very difficult to do some jobs 'Christianly'. How do you type like a Christian? You just type! It's a myth to say that if we only live the life people will start asking us questions. Some of us have been living the life for twenty years or more and no one has said two words to us about our faith other than something like 'Do you go to church?' And we've even found that hard to respond to! There must be both life and speech if our Christian witness – our light – is to be visible. We have to learn to speak about God and the effect that Jesus has had on our lives.

Light guides

We need the light on to see where we're going. Just as the Bible is a constant light to *our* path (Ps. 119:105), so we are called to hold it up as a light for the rest of society.

Help people find the right path

If you've ever had a holiday in the Mediterranean you may have had the experience of going out for the evening to the local village taverna, quite sure you know your way around such a small place. And later on you start back on the ten-minute walk to your villa, gazing up in wonder at the amazing assortment of stars sprinkled about in the sky. After you've been walking a while you begin to wonder why you aren't recognizing the path – but then, it is pitch black now, and everything does look different at night. But half an hour later you're still trying to figure out exactly where you are; all these houses with shutters and little low walls look just the same! If only there were a light *somewhere so* that you could get even a rough idea of just where you were in relation to the village! Eventually you figure out where you've gone wrong, and end up scrabbling through fences and melon fields to get back to the path you really should be on!

We are to shine God's word onto the paths of life that people are walking on. Sometimes they're on roads that are dead ends, but they don't realize it. Perhaps they think their good works will 'see them all right' in the end. But God's word has already shone a light onto that path to show us it will get us nowhere.

Other people have all sorts of ideas of what gives life meaning and purpose. Many think they have to 'make their mark' at something – working their way up their career, getting the next car up in the range, being seen with the 'right' people. An interview with Marlon Brando showed up the emptiness and futility of this path: Despite intimations of a comeback, Brando's life remains shapeless. He said recently:

> I don't like people; I don't love my neighbour. Every time I put any faith in love or friendship, I only came through with deep wounds. Today I am truly a person not open to relationships; this isn't a lie but a very true fact. I am deeply lonely, alone. I enjoy life, up to a point, but I no longer have dreams. Death and old age are events which I accept

and await with all feasible serenity. To a certain extent at times I make of them the purpose of living: I work toward the point at which I can accept them with equanimity.

Sunday Mirror Magazine, January 1989

There must be more point to life than this! How are people to know that they were created for fellowship with God, and for exciting, creative stewardship of the earth, unless we tell them and help them to find their way back onto that path?

Go with them on the way

If there's a power cut, we immediately search for the candles – and rack our brains to remember where we put them after the last power cut! It would be pretty useless to light a candle, stick it in a holder on the living room table, and expect it to give light all round the house. If we want to go into the kitchen or upstairs, we have to take the light with us.

In the same way, you and I are called to walk alongside people as guiding lights, helping them to see their way because of the way we are living, allowing them to copy the example we are giving. We lead the way by modelling it.

Bring the future into the present

We also lead the way in another sense. The God who has called us to serve him is the God who holds the future in his hands. As his servants, we are called to be 'makers of the future' with him. Gerald Coates calls it 'raiding the future for God'. With the insight God gives us, the power of prayer and with courage and determination, we are called to bring as much as we can of the kingdom of God and his future reign – into the present. Our brief is to change society in order to bring it into line with God's plans for it.

Light warns

Light is often used as a warning perhaps over a hole in the road to show us where it is, so that we don't fall in. We are called to be warning lights in a society that is full of holes people are always falling into. We are to be like lights warning people away from styles of life, habits and attitudes that will corrupt them and destroy others.

A captain of an aircraft carrier was sailing up the channel, his lights all ablaze. In the distance he saw another bright point of light so, as he drew nearer, he sent out a message: 'Move two degrees to starboard.' The message came back, '*You* move two degrees to starboard.' Annoyed, the captain responded, '*You* move two degrees to starboard; I am a captain!' And the reply came back, '*You* move two degrees to starboard; I am an able seaman!' Infuriated, the captain sent back the command, 'Move two degrees to starboard; I am the captain of an aircraft carrier!' And the reply came back, 'You had *better* move two degrees to starboard; I am an able seaman in a lighthouse!'

Lighthouses are found in dangerous and lonely places. They get battered by storms in the course of their work, yet if they didn't stick it out many ships would be wrecked. Part of our calling to be the light of the world is to act as lighthouses in our society. That means we can't always stay comfortably on the shore, but may be called to go out to the black spots of life, where danger, unhappiness, violence and despair are at their worst. Many Christians are helping to care for the residents of 'Cardboard City' at Waterloo, in London. Some work on the city streets among prostitutes and drug addicts, bringing them the love of God. Some have established drug rehabilitation centres, like Yeldall Manor, and give their lives to working with potentially manipulative and violent people.

As a last point, remember that the light we are to shine into our world is not our own. That would never be strong enough to challenge the world nor to withstand the advance of darkness. To show others the light, we have to keep walking in the company of the Light himself, allowing him to shine into the dark corners of our own lives, sending the cockroaches running.

4

Playing by the Rules

I've seen some tremendous cricketers play. Some of them are 'naturals': with very little practise and effort they are simply brilliant! Of course, they *do* practise, but their performances *look* effortless. Others practise for hours at the kinds of stroke they need and they do OK at the match. They do all the right things, keep the rules of the game and produce a very workmanlike job. But it feels a bit of a plod. They don't have the sparkle of the genius who seems to live on a plane above the rules, creating a game that is a work of art.

Their gift seems to transcend the letter of the rule book. They are playing according to its spirit, rather than its technicalities.

It's the same with music. I am capable of playing every song in *Songs of Fellowship,* and I'd be really happy to lead worship on Sunday morning at church. But you would need to give me a year's notice for each song so that I could practise it! Eventually I'd be able to play them – and it would be a workmanlike job. But it would have nothing of the freedom and vitality that our 'real' musicians could give them. They play with an ease that betrays a gift; they do not have a commitment just to getting the notes, timing and rhythm right, but they are gifted by God with the ability to make it live.

When Jesus was baptized, God announced: 'You are my Son, whom I love; with you I am well pleased' (Luke 3:22.) The appearance of the Spirit, like a dove above him at his baptism, confirmed that Jesus' life was totally, 100 percent, pleasing to God. He wasn't just a 'plodder' who took care to keep every last little detail of the Law. Rather, because of his anointing with the Spirit, he was supernaturally endowed by God to live out the implications of the Law. That marked him out as someone very different and put him in conflict with the Pharisees – the best 'Law keepers' of the day.

In Jesus' time 'the Law' sometimes meant just the Ten Commandments, sometimes the first five books of the Bible, sometimes all the Old Testament teaching and sometimes, and it's in this last way that the Pharisees and Scribes saw it, a vast collection of rules and regulations that had been written to explain exactly what the Ten Commandments meant.

For example, one of the ten commandments says, 'Remember the Sabbath day by keeping it holy ... on it you shall not do any work' (Exod. 20:8, 10). The Pharisees had become terribly nit-picking about that and had tried to define it. What does it mean to 'work'? Well, it means you mustn't carry a burden. Well, how heavy is a burden? There was a debate raging among the Pharisees at the time of Jesus about whether a tailor was working on the Sabbath if he inadvertently went out with a pin in his coat! Things had got to that level of legalism and stupidity.

When the Pharisees spoke of the Law, they meant the whole thing including all that they had added to it. When Jesus spoke of the Law he spoke of its heart – the Ten Commandments, and the meaning behind the words.

Jesus said:
'Do not think that I have come to abolish the Law or the Prophets; I have not come to abolish them but to fulfil them. I tell you the truth, until heaven and earth disappear, not the smallest letter, not the least stroke of a pen, will by any means disappear from the Law until everything is accomplished. Anyone who breaks one of the least of these commandments and teaches others to do the same will be called least in the kingdom of heaven, but whoever practises and teaches these commandments will be called great in the kingdom of heaven. For I tell you that unless

your righteousness surpasses that of the Pharisees and the teachers of the law, you will certainly not enter the kingdom of heaven' (Matt. 5:17-20).

In other words, Jesus was saying he had not come to make the ten commandments redundant, but to live out their teachings perfectly. He didn't do so in a legalistic way, saying to himself, 'I must obey this rule, and I must not do that.' Rather, his life was so filled with God that he obeyed the Law supernaturally. The Ten Commandments are a written expression of what God is like, what he values and what he hates. God was so present in Jesus that the commandments were fulfilled naturally, almost automatically, by him. He was gifted by God with the Holy Spirit, who enabled him to do so.

Two pits

Jesus' fulfilling of the Law has massive implications for us. The fact that he kept it underlines that it is permanent. He said as much: 'until heaven and earth disappear, not the smallest letter, not the least stroke of a pen, will by any means disappear from the Law until everything is accomplished.' This tells us two things:

We must ourselves, as Jesus' disciples, keep the Old Testament Law of God, the Ten Commandments.

But we do so not because we *must*, but because we are *empowered* to do so, by the same Holy Spirit who empowered Jesus. When we are filled with the Holy Spirit the Law really can work its truth out in our lives.

If either of these two things is separated from the other, we will end up with either legalism or licence.

Legalism

Many Christians are 'dry as dust' Christians. Perhaps they grew up in a traditional Christian home, they're nice people, they're clear about the need to obey God's Law – and they do so. But there's no life in it, no anointing of the Holy Spirit in their lives. We can

keep the Law thoroughly in every tiny detail – even be the sort of
Christians who won't use dried milk because the Bible says, 'Marvel
not'! Our lives can be bound up with rules and regulations –
mostly self-imposed ones like the Pharisees' – because we're afraid
of stepping out of line and doing the wrong thing. Sometimes
we can end up with a modern equivalent of the Pharisees' list of
commandments: 'You shall not do the washing on Sunday. You
shall not go to the pub. You shall not swear when you feel angry.
You shall not spend lots of money on a holiday ....' And if we
break one of these self-made rules, we feel as guilty as if we had
committed murder.

License
On the other hand, many people down through history, and some
in recent years too, have said that the Law is dead and finished
because we live in the age of the Spirit. They believe that because
we have God's Spirit in us, we no longer need to bother with
external law-keeping. Rules and regulations don't have any hold
on us any more, we're free. We can forget the Ten
Commandments.

But that is not the view of the New Testament. Yes, we *are*
free, and we can be filled with the Holy Spirit, but this is so that
we are *able* to fulfil the Law, not so that we can discard it. It is the
Holy Spirit who takes it up and applies it in our lives, just as the
gift of a musician enables her to use her technical skills to produce
a real work of art.

Some of us are filled with the Spirit and our lives are full of
vital signs of God at work. But is there also a moral maturity in
our lives? The things we say and do should reveal a character in
whom the fruit of the Spirit is at work. The standards and objective
teaching of the Old and New Testaments should be evident in
our lives.

Our salvation does not depend on our keeping the Law, but
our desire to do so will flow naturally from our desire to please
the God who has saved us. So we might not worry about doing

the washing on Sunday, but we will look for positive ways to make not just Sunday but every day 'holy' to God. We may have the freedom to enjoy a pint in the pub, but we will be aware that it is not always helpful to do so – alcoholism is a big problem today, even among some Christians. Our first desire will be to honour God in the way we live and the example we set for others, not to exercise our new freedom in Christ at any cost. It's the same with swearing and holidays. Freedom in Christ does not mean we can throw off all restraint. Rather, Jesus urges us to turn our minds to the positive, to look for the good things we can say and do that will build others up.

We cannot, then, sit loose to the great moral commands of the Old Testament. To do so would be to cut off Christianity from its roots. That would soon make our faith grow weak and wither. A rootless, subjective Christianity, based on a vague feeling of spirituality alone, is a useless Christianity. Our faith must have both an objective basis in the word of God, and the subjective anointing of the Holy Spirit.

The Ten Commandments are like channels down which the water of the Spirit flows. Without the Spirit they're just dry ruts. But our life in the Spirit will only be fulfilled when we are living in obedience to God as already defined by him in those commandments.

Steering clear of the pits
How do we make sure we don't fall into the pit of legalism or the pit of licence?

Ask for a change of will
Paul wrote, 'Where the Spirit of the Lord is, there is freedom' (2 Cor. 3 :17). Liberty, or freedom, is not the same as licence. We are not free to do as we please, but neither are we to allow ourselves to get locked into obedience from a sense of duty. Our freedom is the freedom to be filled with the Holy Spirit so that by his

power our will is changed. If we *want* to do the right thing, doing it is not so much hassle!

You might be very attracted to someone of the opposite sex who is not your wife or husband. It is virtually impossible *not* to want to take things further, unless that would mean throwing away something you want more badly. Perhaps you want more than anything else to cultivate a good relationship with your spouse. Or it might be that you want above all to honour Jesus in the way you live. And because those desires are greater than the desire to give in to temptation, you end up doing the right thing.

Duty and love are intermingled in our obedience to God. Our wills are *informed* by the Ten Commandments, but *motivated* by love for God.

It's the difference between doing something because the headmaster tells you to, and doing something because your father asks you to. A child will obey the headmaster out of fear of what might happen if he doesn't. But he'll obey his father out of love and trust, and because he wants to please him. Once we know we are forgiven and accepted by our heavenly Father, we no longer keep his laws out of fear of reprisals – we know he's not like that; we keep them out of love for him.

Or take marriage. If I say to Jan I'm going to be back by a certain time in the evening, I usually make sure I am; not because I'm afraid of what Jan might do if I'm late, but because I love her and don't want her to be worried.

Depend on God's grace

It is important to understand what we *cannot* achieve by keeping the Law. Jesus must have sent shock waves through the crowd when he said, 'Those leaders you've got – the Scribes and Pharisees– look at how righteous they are! They keep every minute detail of the law. But if you want to get into the kingdom of heaven, you will have to be even more spiritual and righteous than they are!'

Why did Jesus say that? Because keeping the Law will not save us. We do not earn salvation; we are given it as a free gift when we put our faith in the righteousness of Jesus.

Many people today believe they will be accepted by God on the basis of their works. Almost anyone who doesn't really know the heart of the gospel message will say to you and me, 'Well, I go to church; I try to be kind and neighbourly; I do my best – and you can't ask more than that, can you?' What they're saying is that obedience to some law, their own set of ideals and values, will make them acceptable to God. And that was the Pharisees in a nutshell. 'If we obey all the laws in the Old Testament, and throw in several thousand of our own too, then we'll be acceptable to God.'

But Jesus cuts a knife right through that way of thinking: 'You can obey every single law, and a thousand more you haven't even thought of yet, but you'll never get into the kingdom of God because that's not the way to get in. The only way is through faith in me.'

Many people are trying hard to 'win God over' to their side, by doing a lot of good things. Perhaps you are one of them. Although you became a Christian by faith, perhaps you now feel you need to live it by works. It's as if there's a list of things in heaven that we can get Brownie points for; a sort of house points system. If we're nice enough and good enough, often enough, God will bless us and our crown will be bigger!

Have you noticed, for example, that new Christians often catch a disease called 'Meetingitis'? We can feel we need to prove ourselves worthy of being saved, or we want to express our gratitude to God in a visible way – hence Meetingitis: an unfortunate compulsion to attend every house group, prayer meeting or Sunday service possible! It isn't necessary. We stay saved, just as we *got* saved, by God's grace, not by our good works. For new Christians with husbands and wives who do not yet share their faith, it can in fact be far more important to stay at home with them! Many non-Christian husbands feel they've lost their wives to 'God' when their wives become Christians. If such wives are not careful about the number of meetings they go to, their husbands can become very resentful of having lost them to 'the church' too.

An example
Jesus wanted to make sure the people really understood what he was saying about keeping God's rules, and about the need to go further than simply keeping the rules. So he went on to give them an example:

> 'You have heard that it was said to the people long ago, "Do not murder, and anyone who murders will be subject to judgment." But I tell you that anyone who is angry with his brother will be subject to judgment. Again, anyone who says to his brother, "Raca," is answerable to the Sanhedrin. But anyone who says, "You fool!" will be in danger of the fire of hell' (Matt. 5 : 21-22).

Murder dissected
If you dissect murder, taking it apart bit by bit, you will find particular attitudes, opinions and values at its heart. All of these desperately need to be dealt with long before they develop into actual murder.

It seems that Jesus had in mind three 'stages' in the development of murder:

Smouldering resentment
'Anyone who is angry with his brother will be subject to judgment,' said Jesus. The word Jesus uses for 'angry' means 'to go on being angry'. It's the sort of situation where you have been wronged and hurt. Perhaps someone at work has hurt you by what they've said or how they've treated you. Perhaps it's your husband, wife or parents. 'How could they say such a thing?' You ask yourself. 'I was doing my best; couldn't they see that?'

We can be wounded easily – and deeply – by our marriage partners. Sometimes the hurt and resentment can go on festering for years because we've never come to terms with it. We haven't forgiven them. Superficially your relationship may look great but deep inside resentment continues to smoulder.

The Lord wants us to be free from this because, if we allow it to carry on unchecked, it will eat away into our souls, as deadly and destructive as any physical cancer. It will poison our relationship with our partner, damage our relationship with God because we are not being totally honest with him, and make our worship and witness shallow.

Sooner or later, the smouldering volcano erupts. We may strike out at someone, or perhaps a family relationship is blown apart. Sometimes we're so good at containing the way we feel that the emotional pain surfaces in the form of physical illness.

This resentment, allowed to burn unchecked, says Jesus, lies at the heart of the act of murder. And the commandment, 'You shall not murder', given so long ago in the Old Testament, means first, 'You shall not allow resentment to smoulder away inside you. Deal with it!' We deal with it by taking it honestly to God, confessing it to him, and asking for his forgiveness. Forgiveness doesn't mean pretending something bad didn't happen after all, but it cleanses the wounds so that we can be healed of its effects. Forgiveness doesn't mean allowing things to go on as before, but it enables us to go on loving, and to repair relationships. God longs to give us his healing for those wounds, deep in our beings. By opening the door of forgiveness we open the door of our lives again to the person who has wronged us, and we open the door to Jesus too, so that he can come in to heal and restore.

Contemptuous dismissal

'Again, anyone who says to his brother, "Raca," is answerable to the Sanhedrin.' This is the next stage that Jesus points to. If you've read this passage before, I expect you've wondered what on earth 'Raca' means. Is it short for racoon?! What is a raca? Well, the reason why it has not been translated from the Aramaic is that it is impossible to convey its meaning in just one or two words. I suppose the nearest equivalent might be something like 'brainless idiot!'

The attitude betrayed by such a derogatory insult is one of contemptuous dismissal. The person doing the insulting denies the other person's ability to think or reason. It's exactly what happens if we allow our anger and resentment towards someone to go unchecked. We begin to be contemptuous of them and everything about them – their thinking, their gifts, abilities and the things they do. We are always criticizing and finding fault. We dismiss their ideas without a second thought. They could suggest something really good, or at least perfectly sensible, but because we've already shut ourselves off from them we instantly dismiss their suggestions. It's the smoke from that smouldering resentment, blinding our eyes to all that is good in them and clouding our judgment so that we are unable to make wise and godly decisions about them.

Jesus calls us to take a fresh look at ourselves. OK, so we might not have murdered, but is our attitude one that lies at the heart of murder? We might not have run someone down in our car, but are we running them down by what we say – belittling their mind, gifts and all that they do? What is it that we're holding against them, resenting about them? We must search our own hearts and dig out every last little bit of it.

Degrading the person

'Anyone who says, "You fool!" will be in danger of the fire of hell.' This is Jesus' description of the third stage on the road to murder.

It is not much easier to translate the word for 'fool' than it is to translate 'raca'! It doesn't mean just ignorant, unwise or unthinking; rather, it denotes a moral stupidity. It is a criticism of someone's total personhood. He's a total 'waste of space'; 'good for nothing'; of absolutely no value whatever. In biblical language, a 'fool' is someone who has no moral sense at all. He has become incapable of doing anything good.

If we think this about someone we are in severe danger of treating him as an 'it'. And that is the ultimate blasphemy – to look at someone for whom Christ died and to dismiss that person as worthless. Once we think of someone as less than human it is a short step to abusing them and even to feeling there is nothing wrong with their murder. Religious people are often the worst culprits here. Think of Saul of Tarsus. He was so contemptuous of the bunch of oddballs who said that a man, Jesus, was God, that he regarded them as less than human – a disgrace to good Jewish society – so not fit to live. And so he did all he could to destroy them (see Acts 7:54-8:3; 9:1-2; 26:4-11). Jesus, however, reminds us that because all people are made in the image of God, all people have unique dignity and value.

Coming into line with the rules

So we have to get rid of our resentment and bitterness in order for God's Spirit to be able to work effectively in us and help us live according to the Law of God. That's all very well, but how?

Be honest with God

If we allow ourselves to be controlled by our feelings we will find that our relationship with God is stunted, just as much as our relationships with other people are.

'Therefore, if you are offering your gift at the altar and there remember that your brother has something against you, leave your gift there in front of the altar. First go and be reconciled to your brother; then come and offer your gift. Settle matters quickly with your adversary who is taking you to court. Do it while you are still with him on the way, or he may hand you over to the judge, and the judge may hand you over to the officer and you may be thrown into

prison. I tell you the truth, you will not get out until you
have paid the last penny' (Matt. 5:23 - 26).

Bad relationships can hinder worship. Superficially, our
relationship with Jesus may seem all right, but deep inside we
struggle to be released into worship and praise. It's as if we've
covered our spirits with a veneer of resentment, and it prevents
God breaking through to us in the way he wants to. And often
we're hindered even from coming into the presence of God
because of our anger and frustration about other people.

Bad relationships hinder our corporate worship too. If a
congregation is divided and hurting from broken relationships
and bitterness towards one another, the body of Christ is
fragmented and cannot offer him true worship.

The whole purpose of Jesus' death on the cross was to reconcile
us to God, and ourselves to each other. When you get your bank
statement, you probably go through your cheque book stubs to
see what you think the balance of your account should be. And
then you check with the bank statement again and wonder why it
says something completely different! So you try to reconcile the
two, seeing if the bank has lost a cheque, or hasn't acted on a
request to cancel a standing order, or if something else has
happened. You try to bring the two accounts into line so that they
balance and match. Reconciliation is what we need to work for,
too, in our corporate life as God's people. It's not that we need
always to think the same or do the same things, but by becoming
reconciled to God we have entered into an agreement with him
to love and be reconciled to one another, too. If our *worship* of
God for what he has done for us is to have any meaning, we need
to be *acting* on what he has done for us – being reconciled to one
another.

As we allow God to deal with us in this way we will discover
new freedom and release in our worship, both individually and
corporately.

Be prepared to forgo your 'rights'

Jesus calls us to a maturity that is prepared to forgo our 'rights'. When I'm really hurt or angry about something that has been done or said unjustly about me, I find it helpful to remember that my suffering is nothing compared to the unjust hurt Jesus suffered on my behalf. Sometimes when we're criticized unjustly we can get all upset and stay in a crotchety, bad-tempered mood for months! If it weren't so sad, our overreactions would really be quite funny: it's strange that when we get *praise* which we don't deserve, we don't seem to mind that at all! Nor do we plunge into the same terrible moods!

Sometimes people say to me, 'I've got a right to be angry about this.' 'Yes,' I'll agree, 'you have. But it's still not right!' We need to learn to sit more loosely to our 'right' to be judged for who we really are. It's probably a good thing people don't actually know what we're really like! Jesus calls us to forgo our 'rights' and to exercise instead our privilege as members of the kingdom of God – the privilege to forgive, to know his healing from smouldering resentment, and from the contemptuous dismissal of others.

Change the way you behave

We cannot easily change how we feel about someone, but we can make up our mind to behave towards them in a loving, gracious and kind way, despite our feelings. If I've fallen out with my brother or sister in Christ I must do something to change that situation: I must 'go and be reconciled'. It's no use carrying on as usual, coming to worship, offering ourselves and our gifts to God, and hoping we might just feel different afterwards.

Resentment is expressed as a feeling, but it isn't just a feeling; it is an action. It works its way out in actions. If I resent someone, I'll go out of my way to snub him and do him down. The answer is not to wait until my feelings change, but to act now *as if I did not feel any resentment to him at all*. So, although I may still feel hurt by a particular person, I'll go out of my way to encourage him, vote for him, take him a birthday cake – whatever I can to promote his good and well-being. If we *do* what we know is right, we will soon *feel* like doing what is right. Feelings follow actions.

In his book, *Mere Christianity*, C. S. Lewis points out that we are to become in practice what we already are in theory – sons and daughters of God who live like Christ. He writes:

> 'When you are not feeling particularly friendly but know you ought to be, the best thing you can do, very often, is to put on a friendly manner and behave as if you were a nicer person than you actually are. And in a few minutes, as we have all noticed, you will be really feeling friendlier than you were. Very often the only way to get a quality in reality is to start behaving as if you had it already ....
> Now, the moment you realize, "Here I am, dressing up as Christ," it is extremely likely that you will see at once some way in which at that very moment the pretence could be made less of a pretence and more of a reality. You will find several things going on in your mind which would not be going on there if you were really a son of God. Well, stop them. Or you may realize that, instead of saying your prayers, you ought to be downstairs writing a letter, or helping your wife to wash up. Well, go and do it .... The real Son of God is at your side. He is beginning to turn you into the same kind of thing as himself.'
>
> C S Lewis, *Mere Christianity*. London: Fontana, 1970.

5

Pure in Heart

The *Daily Mirror* ran an article in its 29 May 1991 issue, titled, 'Adultery ... the sin that dreams are made of.' It went on to say:

> Women are catching up fast in the sex war – but can men cope with this kind of equality? There's worrying news for them in a revealing *Daily Mirror* poll which paints a startling picture of Britain in the Nineties.
>
> 'It seems it's just as acceptable these days for HER to enjoy steamy fantasies about the man next door or imagine herself in a torrid clinch with a screen hero as it is for HIM to drool over a pin-up.
>
> 'But here's worse news: she might actually pop next door to try the real thing. For one woman in four, according to our amazing survey, now thinks that adultery is OK.

Adultery and divorce have affected society for many years. But in a society like ours in which divorce is an increasingly more popular way of dealing with problems within marriage, and when the sexual side of our lives is more open and more freely discussed, Jesus' words to us hit home like sledgehammer blows. What he expects from his disciples in terms of sexual purity is in stark contrast to what we see around us today:

> You have heard that it was said, 'Do not commit adultery.' But I tell you that anyone who looks at a woman lustfully has already committed adultery with her in his heart. If your right eye causes you to sin, gouge it out and throw it

away. It is better for you to lose one part of your body than for your whole body to be thrown into hell. And if your right hand causes you to sin, cut it off and throw it away. It is better for you to lose one part of your body than for your whole body to go into hell (Matt. 5:27-30).

Keeping sexually pure

No Christian writes out of perfection when he writes on the area of sexual sin. In becoming Christians we don't lose our humanity, or our capacity to be tempted. What does Jesus tell us about this area of our lives?

Control your thought life

In the last chapter we saw that it is our thought life that produces anger and hatred, the root causes of murder. Murders don't just 'happen'. Here again, Jesus gets to the heart of the problem of adultery. He leaves no room for the snooty and arrogant to say, 'Well, of course, that's not my problem – that's something other people do.' Tragically, many Christians are involved in adultery and many have suffered divorce.

Jesus shows that adultery is not simply a matter of expressing sexuality outside the marriage bond. It's more a matter of the thought in your mind, dwelt on, entertained, encouraged – *even though no action occurs as a result!* That, Jesus says, is what is at the heart of adultery. The challenge to all of us, then, whether we're married or single, is to exercise holiness and purity about our thought life. God is concerned that our whole being should reflect his own holiness. King David put it this way, 'You desire truth in the inner parts' – in our thoughts and desires, not just in our actions; 'you teach me wisdom in the inmost place' (Ps. 51:6). It is that inner purity which we need to cultivate, with God's help.

What kind of pictures are we letting our minds feed on? They need to be rigorously monitored. If you watch a lot of television or see adverts in the press or on hoardings, you can't possibly be in any doubt that our sexual desires are being exploited for commercial purposes. In the advertising industry, sex is used to sell everything from cars to cat food! Quite unjustifiably and illegitimately, we are being conned into believing that sex and sexuality are the yardstick by which the value of everything in life can be measured.

As a result, hardly anyone can have failed to get the message: 'Have you noticed that all the best people are sexually attractive? You want to be one of the best people in your town? You buy this fantastic product and you'll be an instant hit! Just you see if you don't get all the admiration and respect you deserve! Be wise! Get on in the world! Buy X!' The pressure is on to *prove* that we're sexually attractive. What better proof than having an affair?

This invasion of our minds is persistent and subtle. We hardly notice that our attitudes and expectations have changed.

This doesn't happen just to non-Christians! Of the people I trained with for the Baptist ministry, six of them had left the ministry before they'd been in it seven years, because of adultery. In one eighteen month period a major denomination removed twelve ministers from office, because of their adultery. Of the first fifty people to die of AIDS in this country, two were Anglican clergymen. I am saddened to hear almost weekly of Christian leaders I have known and cared for personally, or known by reputation, whose marriages are in a mess. They are broken, hurt, defeated men and women, trying to put their lives back together again.

And those are just the leaders! We all seem to have swallowed the world's poisonous message that free sexual expression is a legitimate 'bit of fun' – in fact, it is our 'right', and crucial to our emotional and psychological well-being! It's not given a second thought. So now, even to most Christians, the church's traditional teaching of 'chastity outside marriage and faithfulness inside marriage' sounds embarrassingly old-fashioned. The word 'chaste' is seen as something dredged up from the dark ages of repression, and words like 'liberated', 'freedom', 'self-expression' and 'self-fulfilment' have become the new religious catchwords.

It is, in fact, something of a new religion. And in a society which follows that religion slavishly, Jesus calls his followers to be the heretics.

How do we measure up to his expectations of us? Which of us men has not seen an attractive woman on television, or walking down the street, or even in church, and not let our minds do things which they ought not to have done, and then dwelt on it and encouraged those thoughts? If you allow your thought life to wander, beware! I am convinced that the only reason there isn't more sin in this area among Christians is not that we're spiritual enough to resist it, but simply that we don't have the opportunity. If we did, many of us would find that our thoughts were quickly leading us on into action.

Be aware of your weak points

God is not calling us to be paranoid! Neither should our concern to be pure, sexually, lead us to see sex as something unclean. It sounds as easy as walking a tightrope blindfolded! Well, here are some of the problem areas we'll be hitting sooner or later, and some steps to take to overcome them.

The need for friendship and affirmation

We need friends to share life with; we often need affirmation. But how do we try to meet these needs? It's flattering to have someone of the opposite sex take an interest in you and want to spend time with you. But it's easy to take advantage of that friendship and use it simply to bolster your own ego. It's hard to be honest with ourselves about our motives, which is why it's doubly important to be transparently honest with God, bringing all our friendships, all our words, thoughts and actions into the powerful light of his gaze. Charles Finney said, 'Keep short accounts with God'. And John Donne strongly advised going over those accounts with God at the end of each day: 'Sleep with clean hands, either kept clean all day by integrity or washed clean at night by repentance.'

A marriage under pressure

All marriages go through rocky patches – perhaps the husband is under a lot of pressure at work so time together is short. And when they are together, he's so preoccupied with work that he's deadly boring! Perhaps finances are strained and the pleasure of going out somewhere together is spoiled because you're wondering what you're going to have to go without as a result. Perhaps the children are being a real pain and each partner ends up ratty and blaming the other for not controlling them better. The devil is always looking for chinks in marriages, especially Christian ones, that he can exploit, widening the divisions between husband and wife. Keep your eyes open to what's happening in your marriage – no one but the devil wins the battles between you and your spouse!

Gerald Griffin has said, 'Society creates the myth that marriage is the proper haven for all our longings and a cure for all our shortcomings. People are programmed to believe that marriage will automatically give them individuality, identity, security, and happiness, when as a matter of fact marriage gives them none of these things unless they possess them in the first place.' Trouble can start when either marriage partner realizes that the other simply cannot meet all their human and spiritual needs, so assumes that their partner is failing. That's the time when many people feel justified in looking to someone other than their husband or wife for the fulfilment they think they should be getting. Of course it's vital that we have close friends outside our marriages – but a substitute husband or wife is another matter altogether. It's important that we find our ultimate confidence in Jesus, not our marriage partner. It's Jesus who gives us dignity and respect. It's his honour and reputation we live for. And that will radically affect the way we relate to our marriage partner. It will mean that, even if they are short-changing us in some way, we'll be able to go on loving and caring for them, for Jesus' sake.

Opportunity

Perhaps you work closely with someone of the opposite sex. Perhaps people come to you to talk about their problems and you find yourself drawn very close to someone in particular. Perhaps you are just sociable and enjoy other people's company.

It is vital to give ourselves some basic 'ground rules' that we will always stick to in these situations. What those are will vary to some extent for each of us because we each have different areas of weakness. In his book, *Hedges*, Jerry Jenkins lists six 'hedges' or rules he's given himself in order to protect his marriage: First, if he needs to meet, travel or eat out with another woman, he'll always make it a threesome. He believes it's important that his actions could not be misinterpreted by anyone looking on. Second, he's careful how he touches people, and will embrace others only in public. Third, he's careful about how he compliments other women. Fourth, flirting is out, full stop. Fifth, he makes sure his wife knows his ground rules, and that he keeps to them! Sixth, he sets a curfew on work. He leaves it behind at a certain time, and refuses to let it encroach on time that belongs to his wife and family. (See *Hedges: Loving Your Marriage enough to Protect it,* Jerry Jenkins. Brentwood, USA: Wolgemuth & Hyatt.)

Discouragement

This can hit us at any time – and it usually seems to come when we're already down and depressed! Instead of looking for a quick 'fix' in the supportive friendship of someone else, channel your time and energies back into your family. Other projects we work on come and go. We can put a whole year's work into something only to find it all collapse. God has entrusted us with our families for the whole of our lifetimes, so it is never a waste of time or energy to give ourselves whole-heartedly to them.

A false sense of security

The people I fear for most are those who think they will never succumb to sexual sin. A healthy scepticism of our own ability to resist temptation is a surer safeguard. 'God have mercy on me, a sinner,' is a wiser attitude than, 'Look at me! I fast twice a week – aren't I good?' We're all fallible. Let's not forget that nor belittle the strength of the opposition. We're never strong enough to risk walking into temptation.

Many of these factors recur again and again. And so will the temptations that go with them. O A Battista has said, 'Temptations, unlike opportunities, will always give you a second chance.' The battle is one that has to be fought and won time and again as we struggle to fix our eyes on Jesus.

Divorce

> 'It has been said, "Anyone who divorces his wife must give her a certificate of divorce." But I tell you that anyone who divorces his wife, except for marital unfaithfulness, causes her to become an adulteress, and anyone who marries the divorced woman commits adultery' (Matt. 5:31-32).

Jesus again cuts to the heart of this issue and says that divorce isn't something you just do, one day; it's built up over a number of years. Bad attitudes that go unconfessed and unforgiven, resentments that build up and increasing hardness of heart are what eventually lead to divorce. Divorce doesn't come suddenly out of a loving relationship; it's built up over months and years of unresolved conflict, pain and tension. And sometimes one partner can be completely unaware that these things are building up in the other.

God's view

In Malachi, God states clearly, 'I hate divorce' (Mal. 2:16). He binds two people together as one flesh in marriage and when that's ripped apart he hates it. He hates the pain, the crying of the children feeling confused, guilty, frightened and bereft of a parent. He hates the desperate pain of the wronged partners who cry themselves to sleep at night unable to find relief from their hurt and powerlessness. That's why God hates it, because he sees his creation smashed beyond recognition; hurt, damaged and bent out of shape. God never thinks divorce is good, although sometimes it appears to be the better of two very bad options. Personally, I could never actively encourage anyone to get a divorce, although if they felt they had to, I as their pastor, along with the entire congregation, would want to pray for them, give them support and love, and not be judgmental.

The Old Testament could not have been clearer about God's view of marriage and divorce, but in Jesus' day Jewish men said that if you wanted to divorce your wife, you could. Just give her a certificate to confirm it! It was fairly easy, really – if she put too much salt in your food, or you saw someone who looked a bit better, you could just divorce her.

Of course, that was a gross travesty of what God had intended for marriage and Jesus reaffirmed that divorce is always wrong – except in the case of 'marital unfaithfulness'. Exactly what he meant by this is not as clear as it might seem. The Greek word used is *porneia,* from which we derive our word pornography and the associated idea of sexual abuse. The way the NIV translates it 'marital unfaithfulness', implies sexual unchastity, though Jesus might have meant unfaithfulness more broadly. Perhaps, for instance, the wife is undergoing persistent physical violence; her husband is thereby denying their marriage relationship and being unfaithful to it. Perhaps she is subjected to a different sort of 'marital unfaithfulness'.

Whatever it was Jesus had in mind, it was certainly something severe and destructive. He wasn't thinking of the trivial 'we just don't seem to love each other any more' reason for divorce. It's actually not until that point has been reached, when the *feeling* of love goes, that *real* love starts! Love is a commitment of the will. In my view, there are very few occasions which genuinely justify divorce, and those are mostly to do with the sexual immorality of one partner.

God longs to restore

If you have been divorced, know that Jesus doesn't write you off in any way, shape or form. He hates divorce, but he loves people who have been divorced, because he loves people. Divorce is not the ultimate sin. God can forgive you of all that led up to that, just as he can forgive you of any sinful thinking or behaviour. Perhaps you're living in the pain of a broken relationship, perhaps you're in the middle of divorce proceedings. Or perhaps the agony of a past divorce, maybe from many years ago, is still with you. Know that God, too, is with you in that. He feels the pain with you, and he longs to build you up again from it. He wants to bring you to a point of repentance and faith where the past can be put behind you and the sins and mistakes that led to that marriage breakdown are forgiven and resolved by his power.

God is not a God only of the past, he's a God who can take the mistakes of the past, help us face them square on, and bring blessings out of them for the future. Joel brings us God's promise: 'I will restore to you the years the locusts have eaten' (Joel 2:25). He wants us to have a renewed, guilt-free relationship with him. He can take and deal with all the years of pain and twistedness that we've lived through, and wants to assure us of his love. If you've been through divorce, you will know that much of the pain comes through being avoided by your neighbours, criticized by your friends, and having previously mutual friends take sides over who is to blame. God's love for us is constant. He sees all that is worst in us, and loves us anyway. He looks at all that is good in us, and encourages that to develop. He never avoids us, rejects us, or writes us off.

Divorce, a heart attitude

Yet again, Jesus is not content to say, 'So, you've never been divorced ... then this doesn't apply to you.' What about those of us who are married, and for whom divorce is something we've hardly considered – at least, not seriously? This week, we may have taken a step down that road without even realizing it. The moment we hold onto a dark resentment, refusing to bring it out into the light of the open, or are hurt by our partner and won't admit to it or talk it through, then we have pushed our partner a little further away. It only seems one step, hardly any distance at all, but it's the beginning of the movement away. Divorce is not a piece of paper that says, 'you two are now separated.' It's a heart attitude that keeps a partner at arm's length.

Such heart separation may never end in the divorce courts, in physical separation. But in heart and mind we have divorced our partner; we can already be distancing ourselves from them in a way that God never intended. Jesus' word to us is, 'Deal with that now. Make sure your marriage relationship is right today.'

As husbands and wives we need to speak openly with each other about the sexual temptations we face, and to pray together about them. Single people need friends with whom they can share their struggles – friends who will be sensitive to their needs, pray with them, help and comfort them.

A 10,000 mile service
Every marriage needs regular servicing if it is to keep running smoothly. How can we do this?

Several Christian organizations run 'marriage enrichment' weekends; it would be worth having a look at them and considering going on one.

Ask some good friends, preferably a couple who have been married longer, to talk with you about your marriage. What does it look like to them? Do they see how things could be improved? Do they recognize any danger points? We need people who are close enough to know when things are going wrong, objective enough to help us sort out what we should do to put things right, and laid-back enough not to be embarrassed about it!

From time to time, review what is happening in each of the four areas that cause most trouble in marriage: communication (lack of it), money, in-laws, and sex. As our circumstances change, so our relationship with each of these will too. Broadly, are things better in each area than they were, say, a year ago? Why? What has caused the changes for the better or the worse? How would you like things to be in this area of your marriage? What can you do to help work towards that?

6

A Transparent Life

When he was twenty-four years old, Abraham Lincoln served as the postmaster of New Salem, Illinois, for which he was paid an annual salary of $55.70. The New Salem post office was closed in 1836, but it was several years before the tax man arrived to settle accounts with ex-postmaster Lincoln, who was by then a lawyer, struggling to make a living and not doing too well. He was informed that $17 was due to the government. Lincoln crossed the room, opened an old trunk and took out a yellowed cotton rag bound with string. Untying it, he spread out the cloth and there was the $17. He had kept it untouched for all those years. 'I never use any man's money but my own,' he said. No wonder his nickname was 'Honest Abe'!

No hidden meanings

> Again, you have heard that it was said to the people long ago, 'Do not break your oath, but keep the oaths you have made to the Lord.' But I tell you, Do not swear at all: either by heaven, for it is God's throne; or by the earth, for it is his footstool; or by Jerusalem, for it is the city of the Great King. And do not swear by your head, for you cannot make even one hair white or black. Simply let your 'Yes' be 'Yes', and your 'No' 'No'; anything beyond this comes from the evil one' (Matt. 5:33-37).

Cross my heart and hope to die!
This passage is not really to do with our language, words that

your parents would tell you off for saying. It's more to do with telling the truth: 'Let your 'Yes' be 'Yes', and your 'No', 'No'. It was a custom in Jesus' day to swear by something in order to confirm a promise. You would swear by something enduring, or something whose continued existence was of major importance to you. So a devout Jew might swear by heaven, earth, Jerusalem, or even by his own bushy beard. What their swearing meant was, 'I promise you that my word will hold good for as long as the heavens/ earth/Jerusalem itself stays intact.' Or, 'If I don't fulfil this promise to you, I will shave off this bushy beard of which I am so proud.' Sometimes they would swear 'by my strong right arm' meaning, 'If I don't do as I say I will, may my right arm and all its power wither away.'

We don't swear to a promise in this way today, but I have heard people say, 'Oh, I didn't feel I had to keep my word; after all, I hadn't promised.' Does this mean we can say what we like and not be bound by it as long as we don't put 'I promise...' in front of it?

As children, we used to have a game. We'd cross our fingers and put our hands behind our backs and then whatever we said didn't count. So if Mum asked, 'Have you done your homework?' you could lie and say, 'Yes', provided you'd got your fingers crossed behind your back! I remember one occasion when I came unstuck with this. In our hallway was a huge mirror and I made the mistake of standing in front of it when Mum asked me about something. I lied, keeping my fingers crossed behind my back so that there wouldn't be any need to keep to what I'd said. But, of course, Mum saw exactly what I was doing. From then on, any important questions had to be answered with our hands held out in front of us! We could no longer worm our way out of doing something we didn't want to!

As adults, we go on playing children's games when it comes to transparent honesty. We'll sometimes do anything to get out of keeping an agreement, particularly if we've promised something rashly, in a hurry or under pressure. When we genuinely can't

keep a promise, we ought to be up front about it and say so. Go
to the person concerned and apologise. Instead, we often just
hide. Quietly we just don't do as we said we would. If we're
ruthlessly honest about it, we often let one another down, often
fail to deliver on something we promised we would: 'I'll let you
know on Monday.' 'Don't worry – I'll run that errand for you.'
Or the classic one, 'You can tell me; it won't go any further!' I've
heard children in the playground saying, 'I won't tell anyone!
Honest! Cross my heart and hope to die!' Well, that's our equivalent
of the sort of oath undertaken in Jesus' day and, if God took us
up on it, we'd all have been dead long since!

Say what you mean and mean what you say

Jesus points out that this sort of playing with words is an attempt
to hide ourselves and our true intentions. It is an attempt to foil
the other person. 'That's not the way you should carry on,' he says
to his disciples. 'Simply say what you mean, and mean what you
say.'

Much that happens in the church would be transformed by
this simple principle! Life would be so much easier if we knew
we could always rely on one another to do what we've said we
would – or not do what we said we wouldn't. As someone has
commented rather cynically, 'A secret is something you tell one
person at a time!'

No hidden resentments

Jesus' country was in the grip of an occupying power – the Romans.
Their soldiers were everywhere. And they took advantage of
their power. A Roman soldier, fed up with carrying his gear,
could say to anyone passing on their way to the shops, 'Oi! Carry
that stuff for me for the next mile.' And the unfortunate shopper
would have to forget his trip and concentrate on the soldier's
baggage. Someone commandeered in this way would feel resentful
and totally humiliated. So the next words in Jesus' sermon would

have jarred horribly on any Israelite ear – most of the situations here are probably descriptions of encounters with Roman soldiers:

> 'You have heard that it was said, "Eye for eye, and tooth for tooth." But I tell you, Do not resist an evil person. If someone strikes you on the right cheek, turn to him the other also. And if someone wants to sue you and take your tunic, let him have your cloak as well. If someone forces you to go one mile, go with him two miles. Give to the one who asks you and do not turn away from the one who wants to borrow from you' (Matt. 5:38-42).

Revenge is usually our first, instinctive thought when we have been wronged and humiliated. For the Israelites under Roman occupation it was doubly galling to be abused and have no way of redress.

They hated the Romans and wanted nothing to do with them. The thought of having to help one of them by carrying his bags (who knows what people he might be laying into when his hands were free?) was just sickening beyond words. You would feel like an accomplice, a forced traitor.

The 'strike' on the right cheek would have been a brutal blow from a soldier's right fist. In a way, it would have been a 'compassionate' bashing, as it meant he had decided not to go for you with his sword. But as he gripped his sword in his right hand, so he would knock you viciously out of his way with the butt of the sword or his right fist. A knock to the jaw like that could knock you out. It wasn't a gentle slap Jesus had seen – it was a fist in the face.

The quarrelsome person eager to sue another would demand the defendant's coat as surety against the claim. That would be humiliating enough, but Jesus tells his disciples to offer their cloaks too – their warm, outer garment – even though that was against the law on humanitarian grounds. Poor people used their cloaks as blankets at night (see Exod. 22:25-27).

The person who constantly wants to borrow things can be a real pain! It's often inconvenient to lend things; you don't know how they'll be treated or if you'll even get them back in one piece.

The principle Jesus lays down in each of these examples is: Always be ready to forgive. Don't hold resentments and grudges against people. Don't look for revenge or even a fair return – give freely. In Paul's words, 'Do not be overcome by evil; but overcome evil with good' (Rom. 12:21).

Jesus' command to the disciple who has just had his dentures knocked out by a Roman soldier is to forgive him. Instantly. So instantly, that he can turn the other cheek to him there and then. If someone hurts me a little, I can usually find it in me to forgive him. But when someone hurts me a great deal, it is very painful – not physically perhaps, but emotionally and mentally. What if they have done damage to my family? My career? My reputation? Jesus' teaching is clear and firm, 'Don't look for revenge.'

If someone offends us at work, makes us look stupid in front of the boss, or lies about us behind our back, we want to get back at them. As a child, if someone bullied me at school or got me into trouble with the teacher, I could always get some of my friends together, lie in wait for the culprit after school and duff him up on the way home. As adults we just duff them up in a more sophisticated fashion! We hope the person who's ruined our chances gets their own chances ruined. We hope their next bit of work is a failure. We exclude them from our conversations at coffee break and avoid them in the staff canteen. That's revenge – it just comes in a different guise.

If I'm resentful of things someone in the fellowship has said about me, it's very tempting to give a subtle 'slant' to my next sermon. That person will know exactly what I'm saying and why – and the feeling of getting my revenge would be sweet! But it is still revenge and I cannot hide it under the guise of 'relevant teaching'. Or I think, 'Perhaps I won't invite them round to our house after all.' But, according to Jesus, the principle I *should* be working on goes something like this: 'The nastier and ruder you are to me, the nicer I'll be to you and the more interesting things I'll invite you to!' In practice this means that if someone is derogatory about something I've written, I'll try to recommend something of his. If someone tears into something I've been trying to do, saying what a hopeless mess it is and what a stupid idea it all was in the first place anyway, I'll try to find some way of encouraging her in something she's doing.

Defensive action

When Saddam Hussein invaded Kuwait in August 1990, the western world was appalled and promptly set about counter attacking in order to get him out again. Does Jesus rule this out? What about self defence – should we simply let people pulverize us into the ground?

Many people have got their thinking tangled up here because they take Jesus' words to individual disciples and apply them to the national policies of world powers. Jesus wasn't addressing governments. Neither is he wiping out all differences between good and evil, justice and injustice. At both national and individual level it is right, wise and good to defend ourselves against those who attack us.

On a personal level, it is important to take defensive action against those who attack us, if at all possible, whether that attack is verbal or physical. Take steps to defend yourself emotionally. You may need to withdraw from fraught or harmful situations that you know will only get worse. Defuse your own anger by talking it out with your church leaders or friends you trust.

Plan an evening off. Criticism can really get to you after a while. It won't destroy you but it will 'terrorize' you if you allow it to dominate your perception of yourself and others. You begin to think, 'Well, I can understand Mrs Bloggs feeling that way, but what if *everyone is* thinking like her?' Take evasive action. The more up-tight you feel because of someone's insensitivity or hurtfulness, the harder it is to relax - and the more important it is to do so!

Listen to God's defence of you:

'You are precious and honoured in my sight, and ... I love you' (Isa. 43 :4).

No hidden motives

A noted Christian doctor has listed several emotions which produce disease in human beings. Heading the list is fear, followed by frustration, rage, resentment, hatred, jealousy, envy, self-centredness, and ambition. The one and only antidote that can save people from these, he says, is love. He would have approved of this prescription that Jesus gave his disciples:

You have heard that it was said, 'Love your neighbour and hate your enemy.' But I tell you, Love your enemies and pray for those who persecute you, that you may be sons of your Father in heaven. He causes his sun to rise on the evil and the good, and sends rain on the righteous and the unrighteous. If you love those who love you, what reward will you get? Are not even the tax collectors doing that? And if you greet only your brothers, what are you doing more than others? Do not even pagans do that? Be perfect, therefore, as your heavenly Father is perfect. (Matt. 5:43-48)

Let me tell you about some of the things I love. I love my wife, I love my children, I love my parents, friends and cream cakes. I love those chocolate eggs with the gooey bits in the middle. I love wine gums, old films (some new ones too), and I love sport.

But I don't love all those things in the same way! I don't love my wife in the same way that I love gooey chocolate eggs. The word has different meanings in different contexts. Sometimes we mean 'like' when we say 'love'. When Jesus said, 'love your enemies', he didn't mean, 'like your enemies'. He wasn't saying, 'when you meet that person who's been really rotten to your child at school and is always insulting your wife, you are to like him.'

That would be asking us to play emotional gymnastics in a way that would soon have the men in white coats coming for us. To try to twist our emotions and thoughts towards liking someone we honestly don't, would be harmful, false to the reality of the situation, and ultimately destructive.

Let's be honest: I can't stand my enemy. I hate his guts! The things he does are mean, cowardly and selfish, and I just don't want to know him. So how do I square that with what Jesus is saying in this passage?

Jesus says to us, 'I want you to come to me, recognising that on your own you cannot like or love this person. And I want to fill you with *my* love for him.' Anybody can love the people they like. Jesus' revolutionary principle is that we should love even the people we *don't* like – and who don't like us. If we want to become like Christ, 'perfect' children of our Father in heaven, this is the only option open to us.

To be perfect means to be completely fulfilled, doing the job we were meant to do. When we love our enemies we are being the sort of people God meant us to be. If I find that one of the shelves in our living room has a screw missing and is coming off the wall, I'll search around for the screwdriver. I've got to get the one with the end that's the right shape and precisely the right size. If it fits the screw just perfectly, and the screwdriver fits into my hand perfectly, if I can get it in under the shelf perfectly, and it screws in perfectly, then the Greek word *teleios* would be a perfect description of my screwdriver. *Teleios* means complete, or perfect. It's the word Jesus uses here: 'Be perfect as your heavenly Father is perfect.' The screwdriver is exactly right for the job, doing exactly what it is meant to do and in the way that it should. When we love our enemies we are doing precisely what God wants us to do in the way he wants us to do it. We are complete, perfect.

Jesus is again homing in on motives. 'There are no free lunches' is a fairly well-established principle in the business world. So when we see the managing director taking his rival out for a meal, painfully keeping up polite conversation and an ingratiating smile, you know there's a deal in the offing. He has a particular motive for loving his enemy. Jesus turns the 'no free lunches' principle on its head. My motive for loving my enemy should never be a pretence, in order to get something from him, nor should it be a subtle form of revenge – a way of making him feel awful about the way he's treated me. My motive must be simply that of obeying Jesus – I will love my enemy because I love Jesus.

So how do we do that? Love is not primarily what we feel, but what we do. The way to start to love our enemies is not to try to work up a nice feeling towards them, but to start treating them the way God wants us to. It means behaving towards them in a way which honours God. If you are a boss, this might mean that you start praying for the trade union official who's such a pain in the neck. (And vice versa!) You'll stop to say hello to him when you pass him on the stairs or in the lift. You'll remember the names of his children and ask how they are. And gradually your perception of him will change. Feelings follow the facts. Act as if you care about him, and you soon will.

Someone has put it well; 'It is not love when one simply draws a beautiful picture in one's soul and endows it with every perfection; rather this is love: to love people as we find them, and if they have weaknesses, to accept them with a heart filled with love' (Quoted by Lloyd Cory, *Quotable quotations*. Wheaton: Victor Books, 1985).

Insides that match the outsides

There's a parody of Longfellow's poem, *Hiawatha*, that leaves you totally confused about the guy's mittens: are they inside-out or outside-in?

> *A Modern Hiawatha*
> When he killed the Mudjokivis,
> Of the skin he made him mittens,
> Made them with the fur side inside,
> Made them with the skin side outside.

He, to get the warm side inside,
Put the inside skin side outside;
He, to get the cold side outside,
Put the outside warm side inside,
That's why he put the fur side inside,
Why he put the skin side outside,
Why he turned them inside outside.

(George A Strong)

Jesus was concerned that our lives should be so much of a piece that there is no difference between what we seem to be and what we really are. The image of ourselves that we project to others should genuinely reflect what we are like inside. Our constant prayer should be 'Lord, let my inside match my outside!'

Jesus said:
'Be careful not to do your "acts of righteousness" before men, to be seen by them. If you do, you will have no reward from your Father in heaven.
So when you give to the needy, do not announce it with trumpets, as the hypocrites do in the synagogues and on the streets, to be honoured by men. I tell you the truth, they have received their reward in full. But when you give to the needy, do not let your left hand know what your right hand is doing, so that your giving may be in secret. Then your Father, who sees what is done in secret, will reward you' (Matt. 6:1-4).

Inside giving

There are two quite different aspects to the Christian life. One is the external 'doing' or 'good works' aspect. The other is the inner relationship with God. In this bit of his sermon, Jesus shows how we can easily allow the two to drift apart, keeping up the show of a life lived in harmony with God and in obedience to him, yet in reality that being far from the truth.

It's clear from what Jesus says here that he expects his disciples to be giving to the needy, otherwise he'd have said, 'If you give ....' not 'When you give ....' People who live under the rule of God are going to be the sort of people who give to others, care about the oppressed and get bothered when they see people in need.

What does it mean to make our 'insides' match our 'outsides' in the area of giving?

It means being reflective *and* active. Evangelical Christianity is known for its emphases on the need to be born again, to keep up a committed prayer life and to read the Bible daily. All those things are good, but there is a danger that we can be so absorbed in this 'reflective' side of Christianity that Jesus' commands to care for the hurting go unheard. We neglect the more active aspect of Christianity. I find it very easy to be so preoccupied in reading, prayer or preaching that I forget the needs of those outside the kingdom. We can simply fail to notice that someone needs the loving hand of a Christian individual reaching out to meet his needs in a practical way. Jesus reminds us of our responsibility, as his representatives, towards those in need in our communities.

It means maintenance *and* mission. Tunnel vision can afflict whole churches as well as individual Christians. We can become inward-looking as churches. Sometimes we need to ask ourselves how many of our structures are designed with our own needs in mind and to make us feel good, and how much of our time, work, effort and vision we give as a church to those outside the kingdom. As we experience God, come to church regularly, continue in our faith year in year out, we can take for granted our relationship with Jesus Christ. We can become blasé and casual about all that the Lord has given us. Yet 'out there', not so far out there, either, are thousands in our community who are desperately searching for something that will give their lives meaning and purpose. They busy themselves with their families or bury themselves in work – or sometimes in drugs and alcohol – just to blot out the insistent questions that bother them in any moment of silence or aloneness: 'What's the purpose of all this? So you are earning more than last year, so your family is better off – but what's the point? Is it day after day of just the same, all the way until the children leave home and it's just the two of us again, and then there are grandchildren and then we die? Is that all there is?'

It is this kind of need Jesus expects his followers to do something about too; not just the practical, physical needs for enough to eat, somewhere to live, and work to do.

It means global *and* local. It's not too hard to be caught up in all the emotion of an international appeal for aid, and give generously to something like 'Live-aid'. There are lots of big, national crises that cry out for our money and gifts of clothing and medicines. And it is right that we should give as generously as we can to these 'outside' concerns. But we should take care that we are not at the same time ignoring needs closer to home, the 'inside' ones in our own community. We can be very concerned about the needs of those in Sudan, Romania or Iraq but neglect the needs of our own elderly parents or handicapped next-door neighbour.

It means meeting needs 'in secret'. If you went into the temple area at Jerusalem you would come into a courtyard. In the courtyard was a little room set aside called the Chamber of the Silent. No noise or chatter was allowed there. When you had a gift to bring for the needy, you would bring it into this room and leave it there. After you had gone, the priest would come and take the money to distribute it to those who were most in need. It was a gift given and received in secret – no one knew how much you were giving, the priest didn't know who had put what there, the giver didn't know who would receive it and the recipient didn't know who had given.

The Chamber of the Silent is a picture of how we are to give: in secret, not looking for any praise or reward, not making people feel 'beholden' to us.

Sometimes we like to get full value for money out of our giving. A big company gives a lot of money to a charity and there will be a photo of the hand-over in the local paper, with someone from the company holding up a huge replica cheque with the sum of x-thousand pounds clearly written on it for all to see. That company is hoping for some sort of commercial spin-off as the local community becomes more favourably disposed towards it.

It means giving for God's glory, not our own. There have been a number of times when I've given to someone, anonymously, because I felt that's where God wanted my money to go. And sometimes I hear second or third hand about how much that money was needed and that it had arrived just at the right time. These have been some of the most thrilling moments of my life! It's great to be able to provide the answer to someone's prayer, and so be the cause of their giving glory to God.

Inside praying

Our society values the public performance. Television, which absorbs so much of our time, is all about image. Politics is often about a public performance; preaching can also be no more than a public performance. But the image and the performance are not what really matters. What is crucial is what a man or woman is on the inside, on their knees before God:

> And when you pray, do not be like the hypocrites, for they love to pray standing in the synagogues and on the street corners to be seen by men. I tell you the truth, they have received their reward in full. But when you pray, go into your room, close the door and pray to your Father, who is unseen. Then your Father, who sees what is done in secret, will reward you. And when you pray, do not keep on babbling like pagans, for they think they will be heard because of their many words. Do not be like them, for your Father knows what you need before you ask him. (Matt. 6:5-8).

The reason why there is so much bankruptcy in the corporate prayer life of many churches, is that there is bankruptcy in our individual prayer lives. When we have the chance to pray together, whether in church meetings or in house groups, prayer is often very, very hard going! There is no power or authority in our prayers because the group is simply pooling its bankruptcy. We have nothing to bring. There is an emptiness inside because we have neglected the private place with God.

What factors have contributed to this, and how can we restore the heart of our Christian lives – our secret walk with God? We need to make choices each day on a number of issues:

To pray or just to think about it?

Prayer is something we continually have to decide to do. We cannot just decide one day to 'pray better' or 'every day for an hour' and then do it. We need to take that decision again each day. It is time for us to stir ourselves into serious praying, as individuals and as churches. God works in our lives, bringing us to maturity and carrying out his purposes in the world, only in response to our prayer and commitment.

Time for God or no time left?

We live in a world where the private, devotional life has never been harder, because the pace of our lives and world, particularly the western world, is so rapid. The place for prayer – private communion with God – is squeezed out.

At the end of the last century, a man called F W Norwood was living in London and went to see a huge mansion that he was thinking of buying. It was in the process of being renovated and redecorated by its current owner. The workmen were hard at it as he wandered through room after room – dining rooms, leisure rooms, bedrooms, and rooms for a whole range of other things. When he had worked his way to the centre of the house he found a very small room where the builders were at work. 'What's happened here?' he asked. 'Oh,' they replied, 'this used to be the chapel where the family met for prayers; the owners want it turned into a living room.'

Norwood couldn't help being struck, even all those years ago, that in an already massive house with a room for every purpose, even the smallest room once set aside for prayer was being turned into a living room. In the heart of modern man and modern woman, the room for God is rapidly being squeezed out by the busyness of the process of living. In the centre of our lives, where God wants to be, there is nothing but a continual rush and bustle of activity. In the heart where there should be peace and a centring down on God, there is the same frantic activity that there is at the periphery of our lives.

In the words of C S Lewis, we are breeding men and women with no chests, no heart, no inner reality. (See C S Lewis, *The Abolition of Man*. London: Fount Publications, 1984) We are all periphery, all edge, all activity. Sometimes we say that we can't get to the activity. Sometimes we say that we can't get to the bottom of someone, we can't fathom them. But modern men and women are like onions: you peel them away one layer after another - and find you have peeled them away entirely! There is simply nothing of substance at their core.

Many Christians live at that level. They go to church, they pray, they worship, they may even attempt evangelism, but in their hearts there is no true heart. The hidden reality, the inner room with God, the moment by moment truth of the Christian faith, is tragically absent. The oyster remains but the pearl is gone.

What is at the core of your life? If everything were stripped away from you, your husband or wife, your family, wealth, job, would God still be there, at the very centre of your being? Make sure you have that quiet, inner place set apart for God.

And what about our church fellowships? If we stripped away the excitement of Sunday worship, the preaching, teaching, the activities of the various organizations, the structures that give it all shape, would we find a heart that pulsates with God? Would we find anything there at all?

Professional distance or personal commitment?

Helmut Thielicke, a German theologian who died a few years ago, warned that preachers were often the most guilty of inner emptiness. He described them as building houses for their congregations to live in: houses with foundations of biblical study, walls of prayer, a roof of church attendance and windows of evangelism. It's a good description of the shape our Christian living should take. Yet, Thielicke said, the preachers weren't living in those houses themselves. He didn't hesitate to call this hypocrisy. It's the trap of 'professionalism', the belief that it's my job to know all about a subject, but I don't need to be personally committed to it. I can stand outside it and advise people about it without having to get 'personally involved'.

Everyone who leads, speaks or teaches in the church is in danger of making their role a 'professional' one only. Each time we encourage others to do something that we are not doing ourselves there is a conflict between our inner self and our outer self. The Baptist hymn book has a great hymn which says, 'Awake, O Lord, as in the time of old .... Make us to be what we profess to be; from unreality set us free.' We need to pray that God will set us free from any trace of unreality, and that what we are in public and what we are in our private devotions are identical.

Trusting or bargaining?

Again and again in the Gospels, Jesus reveals that God is the loving Father of all who accept Jesus as Lord. That fact of God's fatherhood determines how we relate to him. Trust is in, bargaining is out. 'So don't get the idea,' says Jesus, 'that prayer is some sort of arm-twisting ritual: "Look, God, I really want this and that, and I'll say so three hundred times just to prove it!" Don't think of God like that,' Jesus says, 'he is your loving Father: he heard you the first time! And he wants to give you everything that is good.'

Campbell Morgan used to say, 'Prayer is laying hold of God's willingness, not overcoming his reluctance.' Prayer isn't about manipulating God into giving us the answer we want. It's about bringing to him, with our mind and laying it out before him. As we grow in prayer in the secret place of our hearts and understand more about what he wants, we will see more and more how willing God is to respond.

Inside fasting

'When you fast, do not look sombre as the hypocrites do, for they disfigure their faces to show men they are fasting. I tell you the truth, they have received their reward in full. But when you fast, put oil on your head and wash your face, so that it will not be obvious to men that you are fasting, but only to your Father, who is unseen; and your Father, who sees what is done in secret, will reward you' (Matt. 6:16-18).

Here is another area where our insides should match our outsides – in more ways than one! The modern equivalent of 'disfiguring their faces to show men they are fasting' is to turn up to the midweek prayer meeting after a day of fasting, not having shaved, looking pretty dishevelled, wearing a hang-dog sort of look – just to make sure everyone knows you've been very spiritual today!

For us to fast for a day is almost nothing in comparison with what was common practice for many people in the past. We do it so badly, and so rarely, that we make an enormous deal of it. Even though we might not let other people know – perhaps we dress smartly and don't tell anyone at all that we're fasting – inside we might be on a spiritual 'high', saying to ourselves, 'Lord, you must be delighted with me! I've fasted all day today! You just can't believe your luck with a Christian like me, can you?'

Well, it's better not to fast at all than to have that attitude! We're not meant to fast for our own benefit, nor for a reward, but because our whole life is given over to God and committed to him. Fasting is symbolic of that and is a natural consequence of it.

Fasting has been part of committed Christian witness down through the ages. Generally speaking, this century has seen less of it than perhaps any other – certainly in western Europe – and only in the last twenty years or so has much been written and said about it by Protestant circles. Fasting should accompany our prayers, not to show how spiritual we are nor to get a warm spiritual glow, but as a way of saying that we are really serious about a particular issue. Just as we lose our appetite naturally when we are churned up inside about something, so the decision to fast should reflect a genuine 'churning up' inside about something in particular. It might be that you are desperately concerned to see the forces of evil bound, and their power over our social structures evaporate. Perhaps you really want to see your church move on in its praise and worship.

There are frequent occasions in the Old Testament when a fast was called. It was usually in response to a crisis – perhaps an army was invading (2 Chr.20:3-4), or because a daunting and difficult task was about to be undertaken and the people wanted to commit it to God (Ezra 8:21), or because the people had become aware of a particular sin in their lives and wanted to show their repentance from it (Jer. 36:1-10). Today, perhaps we do not fast more as churches, small groups and individuals, because we do not feel so strongly about the forces that threaten to disrupt God's church and ruin his world. On the outside we claim to be concerned, but is that claim matched by real concern on the inside?

Let us ask God to give us a glimpse of the world from his perspective, and to feel about it as he does. Then our prayers will take on a new life and integrity, and will be marked with a new urgency and effectiveness.

7

Handling the Pressure

Some days are better than others. Take the first day of your summer holiday for example: the day you've been looking forward to for the last three months. You wake up and what do you hear? Rain pattering on the windows. And perhaps a rumble of thunder. You discover that the kids have already been fighting for hours. When the sun eventually comes out and the car is packed up for the two weeks' holiday, can you get it started? Of course not. The hamster dies of fright as soon as you arrive with it at Mrs Jones', and you have to spend two hours explaining everything about heaven to a little cluster of tearful children. You vow you will never again try to spend a holiday anywhere other than at home!

There must have been a few days when the disciples wondered just what they were doing. 'Who is this Jesus? Have we really done the right thing, selling up and leaving home for the sake of this man?'

Jesus knew what they were thinking. He knew they were under a lot of pressure because of their decision to be with him. And he knew that this pressure would only increase for them after his death, resurrection and ascension. So he gave them a prayer that drew together all their main sources of worry and tension, allowing them to acknowledge the reality of their fears and then to lay them all at the feet of their Father in heaven:

> This, then, is how you should pray:
> 'Our Father in heaven,
> hallowed be your name,
> your kingdom come,

your will be done
on earth as it is in heaven.
Give us today our daily bread.
Forgive us our debts,
as we also have forgiven our debtors.
And lead us not into temptation,
but deliver us from the evil one'

(Matthew 6:9 - 13).

My Father, in control

There is a story about a Roman emperor, returning to Rome in victory after a long war. His wife and children were watching the triumphal procession from a raised dais. Suddenly one of his little boys rushed down through the crowd, pushing through people's legs, and ran out into the main parade. He was grabbed by a Roman soldier and yanked back. 'Where do you think you're going?' he demanded of the boy. 'That's the Emperor you were heading for!' The little boy replied, 'He may be your Emperor, but he's my father!'

That's the picture the Lord's Prayer gives us; it has all the weight and solemnity of addressing an emperor, but all the trust and intimacy of running up to a loving father. To those who belong to Christ, God is not a distant despot, the Dictator of the universe; he is a gentle, loving, approachable Father.

It's difficult for us to realize what a revelation this would have been to the disciples. They had been brought up, as all Jews would have, to believe that God's name was so holy you mustn't even say it. After all, God had not even told Moses his name. When Moses had asked what it was, God had simply replied, 'I AM WHO I AM' (Exod. 3:14).

Jesus puts things on a different footing. He doesn't focus on the distance between God and people, but on a relationship. God is our Father because we have been born into his family. The Lord's prayer becomes ours when we become Christians. Nowhere does the Bible say that God is the Father of every person in the world. He is the Father of those who have come to him in faith through Jesus.

What a lovely image! Those who have been badly treated by their human fathers have in God a Father who is totally good, kind and perfect. A young mum might be bringing up children on her own without the influence and support of their earthly father, perhaps because of divorce or bereavement. In God they have the perfect Father-figure. He can come into that painful situation and be the father those children never had and the supporting husband that the wife has lost.

Approachable, caring, loving – yet also fatherly in his discipline of his children. I wouldn't be much of a father if I didn't discipline my three children. One thing parents seem to disagree over more than almost anything else is about how much discipline is necessary. In our house the arguments go something like this:

'Don't shout at them – they couldn't help it!'
'Yes they could!'
'No they couldn't; you've got to make allowances for the fact that they're tired.'
'Why should I? That was still naughty ....'

As parents we worry about the discipline of our children. As our Father, God worries about our discipline, in the sense of being concerned, bothered. He's not a doddery old fool whom we can con; he's a Father with enormous discernment, who knows us completely, and who has absolute authority over us. His discipline of us is always right on target, exactly what we need; neither too little nor too much, and always at just the right time.

And this Father is also King. He is 'in heaven', on the throne of the whole world. What a relief that is! So often we can feel real anger and despair when we read the papers and see the TV news. The world is such a desperately evil place, there are times when we wish we were out of it. International terrorism, petty squabbles between super-powers that suddenly assume an awful

importance, more hostages taken, aeroplanes hijacked, another
tornado and an earthquake, thousands more deaths in Africa from
famine and AIDS. Tensions mount and the whole world looks
terminally sick. Jesus himself warned his disciples that things would
stay looking pretty bad: 'When you hear of wars and rumours of
wars ... Nation will rise against nation, and kingdom against
kingdom. There will be earthquakes in various places, and famines
... those will be days of distress unequalled from the beginning...'
(Mark 13:7-19). Yet in the light of all that, he could still teach his
disciples to say, 'Our Father, in heaven – in control.'

There is a limit to which Satan will be allowed to operate.
There is a limit to the level to which God will allow the world to
descend. Ultimately the destiny of our planet does not depend
on its political leaders. Ultimate power lies in the hands of the
living, loving God. That is a fact which we grasp by faith as we
come to know God as our Father, and gradually begin to perceive
how he is at work in the world.

Honour where honour's due

'Hallowed' is not a word we use very often! 'Honour' is the idea
behind it. God is to be honoured, taken seriously, respected.
There were many idols and images of gods around in the first
century, all of which were honoured to a greater or lesser degree.
But they were simply lumps of wood, stone or metal; they weren't
remotely worthy of being honoured.

But God is real, and his greatness should challenge our tendency
to be flippant about him. Much of today's popular humour is
flippant and destructive. It's hard to know where to draw the
line. I find much 'alternative humour' really funny, but it sometimes
pushes the boundaries back too far. Humour can push back
boundaries of acceptability that nothing else can budge. When
the satirists started poking fun at politics, none of us minded too
much. On the whole, we probably felt that the politicians got
what they deserved. Then they began poking fun at religion, but
it was usually stuffy old services and weird vicars who came in

for it, so again we didn't mind that either. Then they began to poke fun at God. And even that wasn't too bad because it was people's caricatures of God that were being demolished. We felt quite safe with that because we didn't actually believe those things about God. But when Jesus, his life, death and resurrection become the source of amusement and entertainment, and the very heart of all that we stand for is ridiculed and pooh-poohed, we suddenly find ourselves exposed, caught out.

Humour can be far more dangerous than antagonism or persecution. Those things produce martyrs; humour and ridicule simply make us look idiots. Yet we often take ourselves too seriously. It is our own reputations that we're usually concerned for, not God's.

And that spills over into our church life. The insidious influence of public satire, and our own pompous concern for our 'image', lead us almost to 'downgrade' God. Our attitude to corporate worship can become casual, even irreverent. When we gather together, we come to honour our special guest, the king of the universe, who has promised to be with us. Yet we find it hard not to be distracted. We have irrelevant chats with people about nothing at all, and can slide into thinking of Sunday worship as 'just another service' rather than an incredible opportunity to meet with our great king, the living God.

A little bit of heaven now

Life is a bit like a story in which the characters inside it are always trying to guess how it will end. But no one stuck inside a story that is happening can possibly say what the outcome will be. Neither can they tell what the point of it all is. We can only know that if someone from outside the story lets us in on the secret. The Bible tells us that this is precisely what has happened in our world. We have been 'let in on the secret' of what it's all about and how it will end. It's what we call 'revelation'.

What we're shown is that, at the end of the story, God's kingdom will be firmly established on this earth. Everything else in life may be uncertain, but this fact is absolutely beyond doubt.

Jesus told his disciples to pray that it would happen sooner rather than later: 'Your kingdom come, your will be done on earth as it is in heaven.' In other words 'pray that the reign and rule of God in heaven, a reign which is perfect and total, will begin to manifest itself on earth now, so that heaven will happen here more and more.' That's the whole point of the story: that Jesus Christ, the king of heaven in human form, will be given kingship and bring all people under his rule.

Praying for God's kingdom to come is what we do every time we intercede with God on behalf of others. We're inviting the Jesus who rules in heaven to bring about here on earth the same situation that already exists in heaven. When we ask for the forgiveness of sin, we're asking that it will be taken away as it's already been taken away in heaven. When we pray for healing we're asking that there will be wholeness of body, mind and spirit, as there is in heaven. We pray that heaven may touch earth and spread its power and influence throughout it.

The ministry of intercession is an exciting one! It's praying God's power out of heaven into earth, asking for the joy, peace, healing, forgiveness and wholeness of heaven to become more and more apparent here, both in our church family and in the whole world. What a great thing to pray for!

Daily renewal

The next bit of the Lord's prayer seems totally out of place. After that magnificent glimpse at the great sweep of world history, Jesus seems to be saying, 'And, God, if we could have lunch every day, that would be nice. Give us today our daily bread.'

The Greek word used for 'daily' only appears in the New Testament in the context of the Lord's prayer. It doesn't come anywhere else. It's an unusual word and, for years, scholars didn't know what to make of it. Then some archaeologists found an ancient shopping list, dating from the first century, written in Greek. This word 'daily' appeared beside a number of items on the shopping list. It could, perhaps, have meant 'large size' or 'on special offer', but the archaeologists decided it was more likely to mean, 'you've got to get this stuff each day.' Some of the items on the list could be bought and stored for a month or so, but other things, with this special word written alongside them, would go off quickly. They had to be bought fresh each day.

To the Jews, then, the request, 'Give us today our daily bread' was a very simple, practical prayer. But it packs a big punch! Behind its simplicity is a tremendous truth that many of us fail to grasp. People today and many Christians among them, are either living in the past or in the future! We thank God for what he gave us yesterday, for his blessing and for filling us with his Spirit, and we live our Christian lives in the strength of those past blessings. Or we live in hope for tomorrow. 'Maybe tomorrow will be better. Maybe I'll get those things done then. As soon as I've got into that new job I'll be able to spend time properly with my family.' We need instead to live in 'today', the place of daily blessing that God longs for us to know.

We might have had all sorts of great experiences of God in the past, but they were for then, not now. We might have been filled with God at one time, our lives radiating his love. When we went to church God's presence was real, we could almost feel him! Witnessing was no problem and life seemed to be one long, intimate conversation with the king. But, somehow, that has gone flat and stale on us, like a bottle of fizzy lemonade that has lost its fizz and taste. If we live on yesterday's spiritual bread our spiritual lives will go flat and not be very tasty.

We need God's blessing and provision each day. God longs to give us this daily renewal in his service; let's come to him each day to receive it.

Clearing out the cellars

God is in heaven. He is all-powerful and worthy of being worshipped. His kingdom will most certainly come. But if we want his will to be done on earth as it's being done in heaven, and if we want our daily bread, God's blessing for today, there is a big problem. Something stands in the way of that happening. That is why Jesus tells us to come to God and say:

> 'Forgive us our debts, as we also have forgiven our debtors...'
> For if you forgive men when they sin against you, your heavenly Father will also forgive you. But if you do not forgive men their sins, your Father will not forgive your sins. (Matt. 6:12, 14-15)

There is a stark principle here. If we don't grasp it and put it into practice, we'll be unable to receive the daily, fresh anointing that God wants to give us. The principle is simply that God calls on us to forgive those who have hurt, wronged or abused us, in whatever way.

Over the years an amazing quantity of hurts, fears and damage can accumulate in our lives. It builds up like toxic waste, but because it is usually too painful to live with we stuff it all down below in the cellars of our minds and hearts. And there it festers away, poisoning the way we respond to other people, damaging the way we view ourselves and crippling our spiritual development. But there is also some particularly poisonous stuff that we put there too, stacking it in neat, careful rows: unforgiveness and bitterness. Jesus is adamant that we need to clear out this bitterness; it's a spiritual and emotional health hazard. If we don't, we'll be the losers, for two reasons.

Firstly, bitterness eats away at our spirits like a cancer. When I was a student pastor I was placed in a church away from London. One of the church leaders there said something to me that I felt was quite unjustified. I was very hurt by it and angry with him. I didn't say anything at the time but I brooded on it. Over a matter of months I found myself getting angrier and angrier about this person's attitude to me. And then I began to catch myself wishing bad things on him. If he wasn't at church on a Sunday, I'd hope it wasn't just for some trivial reason but that he'd got his 'just desserts'.

That's a dreadful condition to be in. Unforgiveness destroys us and our relationships with others in the family of God. God calls us to a revolution in our ideas and practices of forgiveness.

Secondly, while we continue to be unforgiving, we allow the person who hurt us, and his or her action, to carry on having a hold over us. It's like being trapped emotionally while the resentment, grief and bitterness work away inside. In a book that looks at the stories of people who have been abused, the author describes one young woman who hated her father because of the way he had damaged her. The author comments:

'The strange paradox of the whole matter is that until she forgives her father, he (though now in prison) has the power to go on ruining her life. When she makes the choice to forgive him, his power over her life is destroyed.'

And she adds, 'The key of forgiveness is a heavy one, and it is a painful struggle to turn it in rusty locks.' (Maxine Hancock and Karen Burton Mains, *Child Sexual Abuse: A hope for healing.* Crowborough: Highland Books, 1990.)

It is a hard principle. Gandhi recognized this when he said, 'The weak can never forgive. Forgiveness in an attribute of the strong.' This strength can come only from a deep sense of security in God. When we know he is our Father, that we are infinitely precious to him and that nothing will shake his love for us, we can reach out to others with forgiveness, without fear of being diminished.

I wonder who it is in your life that you most need to forgive. Perhaps your wife who criticises and nags you? Perhaps your husband whose attitude towards you is demeaning and humiliating? If you are in this situation, seek counsel and help from your church leaders to enable your relationship to get back on an even keel.

As parents we need sometimes to ask the forgiveness of our children. As children we may need to ask the forgiveness of our parents. There are colleagues who need to ask forgiveness of one another; church leaders and church members who need to say sorry to God and one another. Forgiveness is the key to spiritual release and blessing.

Save me from the monsters

Satan can be a real pain, constantly looking for ways of tripping us up, appearing as an angel of light – and we can be so gullible! Even if he worked only part-time he'd probably still trip most of us up. We have to be so alert to the work of the evil one. His job is to bring division, gossip and condemnation into God's family; God's job is to bring brothers and sisters together again. Satan's job is to make us feel disgusted and depressed with our spiritual lives. God's job is to point out the sin and then to forgive and restore us. It's Satan's job to sow doubt, fear and tension; it's God's role to bring certainty, wholeness and a relaxation in his presence.

Satan is at work in our lives, our churches and our land. Before we know it, we've been caught in his trap and suddenly find ourselves dangling helplessly and miserably from the monster's jaws. We need to pray to be delivered from temptation and protected from evil.

Such prayers are prayed by realists, people who know themselves and have no illusions about their own strength. God does sometimes allow us to go through difficult times to test and strengthen our faith. But that doesn't mean we should ask for such testing. Peter Kreeft, an American theologian and philosopher, explains it like this:

'Compare the following two prayers ... (1) "Lord, I thank thee that I am not like other men. I can and will endure heroic sufferings for you. Please send them my way" and (2) "God be merciful to me, a sinner. I am weak. I can hardly endure even a little pain for you. Therefore, please do not send me great pain."

Self-delusion prays, "I am strong." Self-knowledge says, "I am weak." Self-knowledge says, "I am riddled with evils – physical, psychological, and spiritual, as with bullets or cancer. Therefore, I need deliverance. Deliver me from evil."' (Peter Kreeft, 'Tribulation within limits', *Christianity Today,* 16 May 1986. Carol Stream: Christianity Today Inc.)

The IRA has a motto: 'England's difficulty is our opportunity.' In February 1991 during the Gulf War, the IRA exploited the fact that the cabinet was totally preoccupied with the Gulf War, and launched a mortar bomb at Number 10, Downing Street. In the same way, Satan is an opportunist who exploits our weaknesses. We are either fools or fatally proud if we do not realize this and ask for God's protection.

Into new dimensions

What is your prayer life like? If your parents were Christians you were probably taught to pray as you grew up. My mother used to come into my bedroom at bed-time, kneel down by my bedside hold my hand, and say, 'Now, let's pray,' and we'd say, 'Jesus, tender shepherd, hear me, bless thy little lambs tonight.' For a while that was fine, but eventually I got bothered by these lambs; I couldn't work out where they were. Then our prayer would go on; 'God bless Grandma and Grandad, and the other Grandad and Grandma ...' (I never knew which was which, but it didn't seem to matter) '... and Mummy and Daddy and Sue.' And then we'd say a prayer at the end about something different each day.

Now that was right and good – I'm not knocking it at all. But I suspect that, years later, many of us simply put adult phrases on that same model and are carrying on praying in exactly the same way. We're still saying nothing much more than, 'God bless Grandma and Grandad; God look after this and God do that; God help me at work tomorrow and please give me a better day. And if you could arrange a rise in salary ....'

I believe God is calling us out of that immaturity into new levels and dimensions of prayer. The devil is more concerned about our praying than about any other aspect of our living. That's why the church prayer meeting is often the last thing to be revitalised. If we really want to see God's kingdom come and his will done on earth, as it is in heaven, we must understand that this will not happen simply through the vehicles of worship or evangelism. It is only the serious praying of the people of God that will bring it about.

8

Ultimate Commitment

Throughout the centuries, people have worried about what might happen should they suddenly fall on hard times. In the twentieth-century western world we expect life to give us more than ever before, and our concern for the future has a new complication: we believe that the ultimate aim in life is to be happy. So we take every step we can to make sure of our present and future happiness. We scrutinize the adverts of the banks and building societies to see which one will be able to give us the biggest nest-egg on our retirement. We don't want to get caught out by sudden redundancy or illness, so we save up for that 'rainy day'.

As Jesus' disciples and all the hangers-on sat or stood nearby to listen to him, he gave them some advice on sound investments against the ultimate 'rainy day'.

> Do not store up for yourselves treasures on earth, where moth and rust destroy, and where thieves break in and steal. But store up for yourselves treasures in heaven, where moth and rust do not destroy, and where thieves do not break in and steal. For where your treasure is, there your heart will be also. (Matt. 6:19-21).

As Jesus looked around at the crowd he would have seen fishermen, farmers, lawyers, probably Roman soldiers too. To each one he directed the same question: 'Where is your treasure?' He was talking about far more than money. 'What is it that really matters to you?' was his meaning. 'What are you living for? What's your aim, your goal in life? Where are you heading? What is it that you're prepared to sacrifice for? Because in that place where you've committed everything – time, money, effort, imagination, will – that's where your heart's going to be. What you devote your life to will ultimately define who you are as a person. So it's important to know what your goals and desires are. Fishermen, is your goal to catch more and bigger fish? Farmers, is it to have more crops and own more land? Religious lawyers, is it to know more of the Law by heart and stun people with your wisdom? Soldiers, is your aim to get promoted from the ranks to be centurions?'

This is a bit of Jesus' questioning we feel we can skip as Christians. After all, the answer is obvious, isn't it? 'My treasure is in heaven, of course! Why don't you ask non-Christians that question? They're the ones with their lives all wrapped up in these earthly things!'

Well, that may be true. But as Christians who have made a commitment to Jesus and known the touch of his hand on our lives, we are equally prone to keeping God on the edges of our lives. There are Christians who are so absorbed in the process of 'getting on' in their careers that they have failed to get on in the kingdom. Ambition is not wrong. It is good to want to be the best teacher, accountant or worker on the shop floor. But the reason for our ambition needs to be looked at carefully. Ambition is bad when our aim is to be seen, praised and admired for being such a wonderful person. Our aim then is not really to be 'the best teacher', or whatever, but 'to be well-known and admired'.

Many of us claim the Lordship of Christ over our lives, but in practical terms we are more committed to our careers, homes, or some other physical thing. How can we tell, honestly, what our aim is in life? Try the burglary test: what would you miss most if it were taken away from you? The TV or video? For many of us our leisure time is more dominated by these things than we would like to admit. What about our career? If that was taken from us would life still have meaning for us? What about our family? It could happen. What about our reputation in the local community? Are we prepared for that to suffer for the sake of Christ?

World at war

Perhaps we would see our daily life in clearer perspective if we reminded ourselves that we are in the middle of a war. Many Christians live a leisurely life in the kingdom as though it were peacetime. The recruits turn up occasionally for combat exercises with the commander-in-chief, and they go through various drill routines Sunday by Sunday. But basically, they do much as they like during the rest of the week.

The kingdom of God is a battleground, not a playground. That is why God's first concern is not for our happiness but for our wisdom and maturity. The call to Christian conversion is a call to engage in spiritual warfare with the kingdom of darkness. The fact that there is a 'kingdom of God' implies that there is an area outside it, opposed to it.

We are caught up in a war whether we like it or not. The only choice we have is which side we're going to be on! As members of God's kingdom we're involved in a fight against evil social structures, against Satan's activity in the world, against our own sinfulness, and against any number of problems in society that arise from people's sinfulness. What are we investing in this battle? Are we spending so much time and effort investing in things of this world that will soon be as insignificant as dust, that we leave no time to invest in things of eternal and lasting significance?

The *Queen Mary* is a large ship that has been used in peacetime and in times of war. It is now docked just off the Californian coast and is a major tourist attraction. When you board it to see round, you come across its huge dining room, divided down the middle by a massive partition. On one side of the partition the tables are laid out as they were in peacetime. The place settings are set a comfortable distance apart from each other, each with seven or eight plates and a myriad of cutlery. I wouldn't know where to begin with it! It's a bewildering display of opulence.

One corner of that room has been made up as a bedroom suite, just to show what it would have been like. There's a four-poster bed, and an amazingly luxurious range of other furnishings.

Then there's the partition. On its other side the tables are set out as for war-time. One metal tray marks each place. There's a hole in each tray for a cup, a little dent marking the place for the dessert, and a slightly bigger dent marking the place for the main course. Some of the places had a knife and a fork. The really lucky ones had a spoon too! In the corner of this room, there is no four-poster bed but a five-tier bunk.

In war-time the *Queen Mary* upped its complement from 3000 passengers to 15,000. Five times as many people, living in a completely different environment. One set of circumstances was appropriate for peace-time, a completely different set for war time. As Christians, I believe we are often living on the wrong side of the partition. We need to bring all our efforts to bear on things that matter and will last.

Pockets of resistance

It's a well-known fact that the last part of a man to be converted is his pocket. We resist yielding totally to the call of God to be committed to him. We are complicated people who can easily deceive ourselves about our motives and goals, and we can unearth pockets of resistance in the most surprising places.

As a preacher, I can kid myself that I don't have a problem with false goals; of course my treasure's in godly things. I'm constantly about the king's business! But am I? Aren't I in great danger of being so much in love with the work of the Lord that I forget the Lord of the work? Some of us so enjoy worship that we forget the God we're worshipping. We can so enjoy the fellowship and friendship of one another that the God who binds us together is somehow distanced. These are subtle temptations, but we are more prone to fall for them than we care to admit. 'My treasure in worldly things? Goodness, no! I've moved on from that; my treasure is now in *religious* things!'

Jesus says both of these are wrong. He wants our treasure to be *him*, because when he has pride of place in our lives as our most precious possession, all other things in life will fall into their rightful places. It's not that these other things are bad; they're mostly good and necessary, but if we seek the King and his kingdom first, 'all these things will be given to you as well.'

Jesus went on to warn his listeners about the dangers of thinking, 'I'm OK; I don't need to bother about all this treasure stuff just now. I'll sort it out some other time.' Don't be fobbed off by this sort of thinking!

> The eye is the lamp of the body. If your eyes are good, your whole body will be full of light. But if your eyes are bad, your whole body will be full of darkness. If then the light within you is darkness, how great is that darkness!
>
> (Matt. 6:22-23)

We need to see the real situation clearly. If we don't, how utterly blind we will be! If we can't see what the most important thing in life is, how on earth will we be able to see anything else clearly? We'll be condemned to wander around in this life like blind people, not sure what we are doing, where we are going or why we are going there.

A divided heart

> No one can serve two masters. Either he will hate the one and love the other, or he will be devoted to the one and despise the other. You cannot serve both God and Money.
>
> (Matt. 6:24)

If you've ever been in the situation of working for two bosses, you'll know how difficult life can be! One comes along and asks you to do something and says it's very urgent; then the other rushes up and says, 'Please could you do this, now! It's really important!'

Or they both give you horrible jobs and you don't want to do either of them. Or their conflicting demands mean that you don't get either job done properly so they both shout at you! Working for two masters is a real problem.

Even when we have committed ourselves whole-heartedly just to one master, Jesus Christ, we go on discovering pockets of resistance throughout our lives. It's as though we have to be converted bit by bit. When Richard the Lionheart came back from the Crusades, he found that Prince John had set up a series of rival kingdoms within the kingdom. Some people were loyal to him. He'd been telling them that Richard would certainly be killed in the Crusades, or at least be there for years – being such a religious fanatic. 'So follow me', he said, 'and I'll give you a nice little kingdom to rule over. How would Durham suit you?' So when Richard returned he found the kingdom divided into a number of different mini-kingdoms. With the assistance of his army he mopped up most of the south-coast resistance fairly quickly, but areas of rebellion remained, staunchly fortified with castles. The only way to defeat them was for Richard to lay siege to each one in turn, defeat the defenders and take it over.

There are many areas of our lives which we have not yet handed over to the King. We are perhaps not so up-front about it with God as Prince John was with Richard, but we have little private domains in our lives, little castles where we put our money or possessions, sexuality, time, job or something else, and try to keep them for ourselves. We don't want God to take control of that area of our lives. And because we're not fully God's, we aren't free to worship him in the way he deserves to be worshipped.

We can't be free to read the Bible, pray and grow as Christians. The internal struggle caused by those castles of rebellion brings tension, pain, emotional imbalance, stress and spiritual agony.

Taking back the areas of resistance

Set aside a chunk of time, perhaps an hour, and sit down with God to think over these questions:

What do I really want out of life?
What do I want to have achieved in ten years' time?
How do I want to be different in ten years' time from the
person I am now?
What do I use these things for most:
  my money?
  my time?
  my energy?
  my imagination?

As you answer these questions honestly, ask God to show you how you could invest more in his kingdom. Ask for a new awareness of the king, Jesus, calling you to be with him and to share in all that he does, as he goes out to battle.

It would be helpful to talk this over with a friend in your house-group or church, or with your church leaders. We need the encouragement of one another, and it helps us keep our commitment to Jesus fresh if we know someone else knows that we've made it!

God's commitment to us

We're in a battle, sure enough. But, says Jesus, 'Don't worry!' I've always thought that's a great deal easier to say than it is to do. But just as we have committed ourselves to God, so he has committed himself to us.

Therefore I tell you, do not worry about your life, what you will eat or drink; or about your body, what you will wear. Is not life more important than food, and the body more important than clothes? Look at the birds of the air; they do not sow or reap or store away in barns, and yet your heavenly Father feeds them. Are you not much more valuable than they? Who of you by worrying can add a single hour to his life?

And why do you worry about clothes? See how the lilies of the field grow. They do not labour or spin. Yet I tell you that not even Solomon in all his splendour was dressed like one of these. If that is how God clothes the grass of the field, which is here today and tomorrow is thrown into the fire, will he not much more clothe you, O you of little faith? (Matt. 6:25-30).

Worry can't change anything. How many of the things you've worried about have actually happened? Probably about one percent. How many circumstances have you managed to change by worrying about them? None. We'd all have to admit that Jesus' logic is impeccable – but still we keep on worrying! Jesus reaches out to you today and says, 'You worry so much! Don't you know that you've got a heavenly Father who knows your needs and who loves you?'

Jesus has good reason to tell us to stop worrying. He's not saying it just to gloss over our discomfort and fear, but because it's illogical, not sensible and won't achieve anything. And there's another good reason not to worry: of all people, we are most blessed. We have a Father who knows our needs and who cares for us. In a world where worry is endemic, we've got somewhere to run and hide, somewhere to go and be secure.

One afternoon we took Bethany to a little farm on the outskirts of Preston. She was about two at the time. The farmer's daughter took us to see a litter of week-old piglets. There were about twenty of them, and as we walked up to them they suddenly began to screech! Bethany had run on ahead but leapt back in fear, flung herself into my arms and almost throttled me. She wouldn't so much as look at them! So I said, 'Darling, the pigs can't get out, you're perfectly safe.' But by this time Bethany was making almost as much noise as the pigs! She was terrified.

You and I hear all the screeching and squealing of tomorrow, and we're terrified of what might happen – at work, with our health, in our job, with our family. And the devil turns up the volume so that we're even more afraid! But God is holding us securely in his arms, saying, 'Look, they can't get to you except through me. They can't hurt you; I'm your Father.'

Of course bad things do happen to God's people. Tensions, problems and difficulties do come our way. But we're given the gift of a Father who says, 'I care for the sparrows – and you can pick those up for 1p down the market! And I love them. I make the grass grow (and don't we know it!); I clothe it with its colours and its seeds, and yet I love you countless millions times more than the grass! Don't worry. I even hear it when a sparrow falls from the sky. So don't be anxious; you're surrounded with my love and compassion.'

> So do not worry, saying, 'What shall we eat?' or 'What shall we drink?' Or 'What shall we wear?' For the pagans run after all these things, and your heavenly Father knows that you need them. But seek first his kingdom and his righteousness, and all these things will be given to you as well. Therefore do not worry about tomorrow, for tomorrow will worry about itself. Each day has enough trouble of its own' (Matt. 6:31-34).

Have you ever met a great man or woman of faith, the sort who seem so sold out to God that their lives are totally absorbed in him and his kingdom? Yet somehow all the practical details of their lives seem to get sorted out, too. Their problems have a way of working themselves out, while you and I get four or five ulcers a week worrying about whether that is going to fall into place, or whether this is going to happen, and whether I remembered to do that. It's a struggle! But for those folk who seem to be committed to God's kingdom almost to the point of recklessness, the practicalities of their lives often seem incredibly well-ordered. I believe this is a promise which God honours literally, that when we put the kingdom first, other things will fall into place.

For some of us the answer to our worry and need is to change our focus. We should no longer look on the problems that cause us to worry, but look on Jesus and ask him to fill us with a vision of himself.

I vividly remember a time when I was a young child of about eight. I was out with my family late one evening walking through the countryside, and I had run on ahead of the others. Suddenly a huge dog came racing out of the darkness towards me and stopped abruptly in the middle of the path, barking and baring its teeth. I stood there paralysed with fear, not knowing whether to run, or if that would make it chase me, or whether to pray that I would die or that it would die! I didn't know what to do. And then my father, walking up behind and past me, stood by the dog. I have a mental picture of the dog suddenly shrinking in size, my father seemed so big in comparison. He went up to it and told it to clear off – or words to that effect! And the dog just ran away. My father seemed eighteen feet tall and the dog seemed like a midget! Some years later I told my father about that, and he confessed to having been terrified too! But the dog went.

As I focused on my father the dog seemed to grow smaller, because my dad was in control. Today, you and I are surrounded by the wolves and vicious dogs of problems that snarl and snap at us, making us fearful and preventing us from going any further. Jesus calls us to turn our focus away from those dogs on to the Father standing next to them, who is big enough and powerful enough to make all those things look insignificant. The God who closed the lions' mouth for Daniel is big enough to close the mouth of the yapping dog.

Where is your treasure? Let us put it in the hands of our loving, powerful Father who can silence all the yapping dogs of the world with his presence.

9

Sound Judgment

One of the criticisms commonly aimed at Christians – particularly evangelical ones – is that they are unthinking simpletons who have thrown out their brains in favour of a 'happy clappy' emotionalism. While this may be true of some people, the Bible emphasizes that the chief characteristics of a godly life include wisdom, discernment, integrity and sound judgment.

In today's secular world, these words carry a whole range of different meanings. We can damn people with faint praise, smudge someone's character or initiate a less than honest deal, all in the interests of 'sound judgment' and 'discernment'. It is hard to separate truth from falsehood, even when trying to be clear about our own motives? So is it better to throw out our brains after all and just rely on a sort of 'holy instinct' to judge what is right and wrong?

Jesus' sermon gives some clear guidelines on how to judge and discern properly. He starts by drawing a clear distinction between right and wrong types of judgment:

> Do not judge, or you too will be judged. For in the same way as you judge others, you will be judged, and with the measure you use, it will be measured to you. (Matt. 7:1-2)

Destructive criticism

We need to be clear first of all about what this passage is not saying. 'Judge' is used in two main ways in the New Testament. There are a number of Greek words for the idea of judging, but there are just two main groups of words. One of the groups uses it as in 'to condemn or criticize', and the other uses judge in the sense of 'to make a decision'.

At Wimbledon they have installed electronic judges, so that when the ball is going at 100 miles per hour and the umpire can't see exactly what it's doing, a little bleep will tell him whether it was on the line, just outside the line, or just inside – so that he can make an informed decision. That judgment is a decision on how to act, based on a variety of facts. This is not how Jesus uses the word here. He's not saying, 'don't be discerning', but 'don't be condemning and critical', the kind of person who, when she sees someone doing something she can't understand, appoints herself judge, council for the prosecution, and jury too! The force of his statement is, 'Don't go on habitually judging and criticizing. That kind of lifestyle is wrong. From time to time we need to take stock of ourselves and ask, 'Am I a judgmental sort of person? Am I a critical person? Is my first statement in any situation negative?'

An American psychiatrist has made a study of the case-histories of 10,000 people who were mentally or emotionally ill, or in some other kind of mental pain. As they asked for his help, he divided them into two categories. The first was made up of those suffering from mental and emotional disturbances; the second contained those who were largely free from such tensions. Gradually, one fact began to stand out. Those who were in the 'nervous and neurotic' group were habitual fault-finders, constantly critical of the people and things around them. Whereas those who were free from these tensions were the least fault-finding. His conclusion was that the habit of criticising others is related to mental imbalance.

Perhaps his conclusion is right, perhaps not. But if the art of continually criticising others does not indicate a state of mental imbalance, it would be fair to say it marks a state of spiritual imbalance.

When you think about it, the people you know who are good to be around are not those who are constantly critical. There is an ancient Greek legend about the god Monas. He had a reputation among the other gods for being a constant critic. One day the gods had a competition to see who could make something really special. One of them made a man – and Monas criticised it because it didn't have a window in the front so that he could see what the man was thinking. Another built a superb house – and Monas criticized it because it didn't have wheels so that it could be moved to another location. Another of the gods made a bull – and Monas criticized it too; he said the horns should be below the eyes so that it could see what it was goring. And at the end of the competition Monas got the boot out of heaven! He was banished to a domain of his own where he could criticize himself as much as he wanted to!

The order of the boot would be a good thing for some of us when we get into our 'moany' mood! How much easier it is to do a demolition job on someone's personality and character than it is to build them up. You've probably seen clips of film on TV which show a crowd of people standing at a safe distance from a tall building. Someone presses a button and there's a huge explosion. In a moment a block of flats twenty storeys high is reduced to a pile of rubble. It takes about ten seconds for the dust to clear – and then the building is gone. It took a great deal longer to put it up! You and I are guilty sometimes of being demolition experts on people's characters, personality and reputation, even in the life of the church. We are far more likely to point the finger of accusation than to reach out the hand of love; more likely to condemn than to congratulate.

What did Jesus mean by saying, 'in the same way as you judge others, you will be judged'? Probably without exception, each time we point a nagging, critical finger at someone else, we are condemning something we have done ourselves. Within days – even minutes – of accusing someone of a fault, we are doing exactly the same thing. We come under our own judgment. 'OK, you think that's wrong?' asks Jesus, 'Well, that condemns you, too, doesn't it?'

There are sometimes masquerade balls on television. A man comes in wearing a mask on both sides of his head – a frowning face on one side and a smiling face on the back, so you can't tell if he's coming or going, or whether you're talking to his face or his back! We are like that when we make ourselves judges of others. From the front we may look like the judge, wearing his wig and spectacles, but when people see us from the back they see the defendant in the dock.

In God's eyes, whenever we set ourselves up as judge, he sees us as the defendant.

Destructive criticism achieves nothing. It only destroys and hurts, and condemns the critic. Next time you feel like letting off steam about someone – perhaps a work colleague, a family member, a next-door neighbour or your house-group leader – stop to ask yourself these questions:

What will I achieve by saying those critical things?

How have I been guilty of doing exactly the same thing, though perhaps in a different situation?

What is there to praise about this person, even about the thing that I was going to criticize? What can I say or do to encourage this person?

If the thing I'm condemning is really important – if it's harming that person's ministry or destroying someone else – when am I going to make time to talk to that person about it face-to-face?

Deluded criticism

'Why do you look at the speck of sawdust in your brother's eye and pay no attention to the plank in your own eye? How can you say to your brother, "Let me take the speck out of your eye," when all the time there is a plank in your own eye? You hypocrite, first take the plank out of your own eye, and then you will see clearly to remove the speck from your brother's eye' (Matt. 7:3-5).

You know how painful and irritating it can be to get even the smallest speck of dust in your eye. You certainly know about it; it hurts! You want to get it out as soon as you can. But you can't, there isn't a mirror around and you need help. Then along comes a do-gooder who immediately spots your problem. He knows all about this sort of problem; he's dealt with it before. Lots of people suffer from it, but you're OK now because he will sort you out.

I can imagine all the self-made counsellors in Jesus' congregation sitting there nodding wisely. 'Yes, that's my particular gift – sorting people out, fixing their problems.' And then he shows them the rest of the picture. The counsellor heading for 'the person with the problem' has an enormous great plank sticking out of his eye! It's so big it covers both eyes. But he stumbles on toward the horrified victim, tweezers at the ready.

You must understand, says Jesus, how much you need forgiving and sorting out yourself; how much you need to put yourselves right with God before you dare presume to set yourself up as the person with all the answers.

Four things need to happen if we are to stop deluding ourselves about our own condition and that of others:

We need to get right with God. We can be living on such a 'low' spiritual level that almost all our judgments are suspect. We need to bring ourselves into God's searching gaze, asking for him to show us our faults and problems, and seek his forgiveness and help in putting things right.

We must find out the facts. Before so much as frowning, let alone expressing an opinion, we must find out the facts. As the pastor of a church, many people have come to me with a criticism of someone else in the church. It is right to share with our church leaders our concerns about others. But in all the cases I have been brought, not a single 'concerned critic' has known all the facts. People have pointed the finger of criticism at someone, not having a clue about the enormous pressures and hurt that person was suffering, and that were making him behave so unpredictably. We can only find out the facts by talking with the person concerned.

We must find out the feelings. Once we know the facts, we need to go further and try to feel how this person feels. What's eating away at him? Is he feeling depressed? Hopeless? Lonely? A failure? The French have a proverb: 'To know all is to forgive all' – perhaps not entirely true but it takes us a long way towards the truth. When we can stand in someone else's shoes and begin to imagine how his situation must feel, we will find that we are much less eager to judge and condemn.

This was what the incarnation meant for Jesus. God didn't stay up in heaven and bellow out his verdict on us. He came down to walk in our shoes, to live as we live, to experience all the pains and pressures of human life, with parents who didn't understand him and with friends who deserted him. That-same principle needs to be worked out in our lives before we get involved in criticising others.

We must act with compassion. 'Praying Hyde' was a missionary in India. One day he heard a bad report about a fellow evangelist, which incensed him. He immediately got down on his knees (which was his habit – hence his nickname), and said, 'Lord, I want to pray about this man because his faith is so ....' He was about to say '...cold', but before he could get the word out God spoke into his own heart like an arrow. 'Who are you accusing of being cold? Think about what that man has given up for me.' And as 'Praying Hyde' thought about it God reminded him of all that his fellow evangelist had given up to obey God's call: money, job, prestige, status, contacts. And he thought back to all the things God had done through the life and ministry of that man. Then he felt God saying to him, 'Now praise me for all those things.' So he began to pray, 'Lord, thank you for what you did in Calcutta .... I praise you for this man's life.'

When he had finished praying, Hyde travelled nearly 100 miles to the village where that man was holding a mission. To Hyde's astonishment, he came running to meet him and said, 'It's great to see you! I must tell you about the things God has been doing in my life this week. I've been feeling so cold recently in my spiritual life and I've found it really difficult to keep going. But this week God has been doing a fresh thing in my life; he's been real to me in such a powerful way!'

Our perception of a situation might be accurate, but there are two ways of responding to it. As Hyde focused on the positive things about the person of whom he was critical, so God worked supernaturally in that person's life to reinforce those good things and to cause the coldness to wither away. God acted with compassion, to change and improve the situation. So should we.

Discerning criticism

It is not always right to respond when asked for our opinion or judgment. I was once involved in a mission where we went into the local pubs to talk to people there, on their own home territory. On one occasion I was approached at the bar by someone with a slight stagger who demanded, 'Tell me about this Jesus, then.' And I said, 'No.' I simply refused to talk to him. But wasn't I on an evangelistic mission? Yes, but I didn't feel it right to talk to this particular, inebriated person about Jesus, when all I had heard from him throughout the rest of the evening was foul-mouthed obscenities and blasphemy. I was not prepared to put Jesus to further shame and mocking from someone who was not going to take the conversation seriously.

It is sometimes the case, of course, that when people mock and criticise our faith they are hiding a deep hurt inside and it would be right to share the gospel with them. But not always. We need to be discerning:

'Do not give dogs what is sacred; do not throw your pearls to pigs. If you do, they may trample them under their feet, and then turn and tear you to pieces' (Matt. 7:6)

How can we know it might be right or wrong to speak out, whether in constructive criticism or in sharing the gospel? Here are four things that will help us make wise decisions.

Get God's view. Most of us base our criticisms on things that have affected us personally. Perhaps we have been offended, hurt, or our values have been challenged. God asks us to look beyond all that and ask, 'What do you think about this, God?' Unlike us, God hasn't had his illusions about that particular person shattered; he didn't have any illusions about her in the first place but has always known the whole truth. His view of her is the only fair one, so we need his mind on the situation, not just our own limited perspective.

Be repentant. Each of us is guilty of being critical of others without a cause. We need to confess our guilt to God. That's not easy. Most of us are no better than our children when it comes to saying sorry.

'Say you're sorry.'
'Sorry ... grrrr.'
'Say it!'
'Sorry.'
'Now mean it .... !'

Unless we are humble enough to apologize to God, making no excuses for ourselves, we cannot move on from simply not criticising to being positive encouragements to one another. It is repentance – painful, and perhaps with tears – that breaks us of the desire to carry on doing what is wrong. Without this 'cleaning up' process there can be no healthy new life. It's like a visit to the dentist when you have toothache. As he reaches across for the dreaded drill you suddenly have a good idea: 'Tell you what, how about just filling the tooth – it would save all that drilling time!' 'Sorry' would be his response, 'no drilling, no filling.' God cannot build good things in our lives on rotten foundations. Without our repentance, how can God's blessing follow?

Go to the source, the person concerned. Most of us have shared our grievance with at least five people before we think about talking to the person who caused us all this bother in the first place! That's basically because we are cowards, or because we don't really want to confront the situation. Our concern isn't really to put things right, but to enjoy a good moan or a wallow in self-pity. If our first move is to talk to the person concerned, that will probably be the only move we need make.

Cultivate the positive. We must learn to be builders, not demolishers. God is at work in the lives of each of his children to build them up and display more of his kingdom glory in them. But if we are criticizing and tearing down those people, we are working against God, setting ourselves up in opposition to him. He calls us to give all that we have and are to him for his use – and that includes our tongues and our critical faculties. So let us use them to do his work.

10

Persistence

I am indebted to my young daughter for having given me a new perspective on what can easily become a routine: Sunday worship. One Sunday morning I was in the shower when Bethany came into the bathroom and yanked back the shower curtain – always a messy business. And as she stood there she asked, 'Daddy do you want to go to church this morning?' I thought about that for a moment and said, 'Yes! Yes, I really do want to go to church this morning!' And I became quite excited by the prospect and started singing in the shower about how good it is to be able to worship God and pray to him.

We don't always feel like that. But whether we feel glad to be worshipping God or feel it's a real drag, it's still right to do it. Someone once asked Spurgeon, 'When should I pray? Should I pray when I don't feel like it?' He answered, 'Pray when you feel like it, because God will bless you; pray when you don't feel like it, because that's when you most need it.'

Jesus laid a great deal of stress on the importance of 'keeping on', of persisting in our walk with God. In his sermon he outlines four major areas where we need to 'keep on keeping on' if we are to get anywhere worthwhile.

Persistent prayer

> Ask and it will be given to you; seek and you will find; knock and the door will be opened to you. For everyone who asks receives; he who seeks finds; and to him who knocks, the door will be opened (Matt. 7:7-8).

We are to keep on asking, seeking and knocking. If, at home, you say to your child, 'Pick up that pencil you've just dropped on the floor,' that's a 'one off' command. You don't mean 'keep on picking up that pencil and putting it back on the floor, then picking it up again.'

But if the child goes out of the room leaving the door wide open and you say, 'when you leave the room, please shut the door,' you mean that in a more general sense. In other words, 'every time you go out of the room or come in, please don't forget to close the door behind you.'

It's in the second sense that Jesus speaks of asking, seeking and knocking on God's door in prayer.

Prayer that keeps going

Much of my prayer life is very weak. One day I'll feel compelled to pray about an issue, but the next day I may have forgotten it.

In 1836 George Muller opened an orphanage for children in Bristol. He and his wife had no resources with which to run it, so each day he would pray for whatever they needed. He would pray very specifically: 'Lord, in the morning we will need three pints of milk and two loaves of bread.'

And, come the morning, there would be on the doorstep exactly three pints of milk and two loaves of bread. God answered those prayers in a remarkable way. Yet the same man was also praying for something else. Each day he would pray for the conversion of a particular friend of his and that friend's son. He prayed for that friend for over forty years! When Muller died, his friend still had not been converted. But God honoured his prayer and responded to it in his own timing: Muller's friend was converted while attending his funeral, and the friend's son a week later.

His prayers were effective because he was determined not to let anything knock him sideways in his prayer life or stop him being committed to something. What were you praying about last week? Last month? Last year? What were the matters burning in your mind? Have those prayers been answered? If not, perhaps you should still be persisting in bringing them to God.

Prayer that isn't a slave to 'fashion'

Part of the problem is that we are so fashion-conscious in our prayers. Ethiopia is 'in' for a month or two; then it goes out of fashion as Romania takes the stage. Then that's 'out' and the Middle East crisis is 'in'. But people are still dying in Ethiopia; orphanages in Romania are still desperately under-equipped; and the Middle East still needs all the prayer it can get.

Let me pull another name out of the pack: Rwanda. The plight of Rwandan refugees is still as awful as it was when they were hot news. But they are no longer 'media-worthy' so they drop out of our thinking. We need to be consistent as well as persistent in our praying. Keep a note book of topics and names of people that you feel you should pray for. Update it from time to time, and keep at it!

Persistent trust

> Which of you, if his son asks for bread, will give him a stone? Or if he asks for a fish, will give him a snake? If you, then, though you are evil, know how to give good gifts to your children, how much more will your Father in heaven give good gifts to those who ask him! (Matt. 7:911)

When God doesn't seem to be hearing or answering our prayers, our trust in his goodness or willingness to answer can waver. 'Don't let it,' Jesus says. God really is hearing and is concerned.

That was such a small thing, but our heavenly Father is interested in every little detail of our lives. He wants to listen to us, but sometimes we are so unready to ask. So what happens when our prayers don't seem to be answered? Is God sitting up there making fun of our puny requests? No, far from it. Jesus looked around at the crowds and asked which human father would do that to his child. If their child asked for a little round, flat loaf of bread, would any father give him a little round, flat stone instead? It would look just like the loaf of bread, and would shut the child up for a while. But it would be a cruel father who could watch his child bite into it and break his teeth.

God is nothing like that. He longs to give us good things. He loves it when we are happy. When we are thrilled with his gifts, he is delighted! I love giving treats to my daughters. Chocolate buttons used to be their favourite. I'd line up the buttons on the armchair at home and the girls would stand there, poised, looking up at me. Then I'd ask, 'What do you say?' 'Please!' came the reply. 'OK'. And if I didn't stop them they'd go down the line of buttons as fast as they could, cramming them into their mouths.

What I really enjoyed was seeing their faces light up just as they were about to launch into the chocolate. They were so good to be nice to, because they would get so excited about it! If I said to them, 'Do you want some buttons?' they would dance on the spot with joy! By comparison, people can do the greatest favours for us – and we're 'flat' and unresponsive.

Our heavenly Father longs to give us good gifts. Sometimes when I'm praying I hear an accusing voice in my head saying, 'God's not going to answer that prayer; you don't need that, you just want it!' Well, great! God sometimes does give us things we don't need but simply want, because he is a God of bounty and excess. He is the God who fed 5000 people and had enough left to set someone up in their own catering business. He didn't skimp on it, saying, 'There's just enough here for the picnic, folks; can you go easy on it, please.'

'Ask, and you will receive,' he says. 'I long to pour out my blessings on you.' Let's take him at his word and not doubt his love, his good intentions for us, or his generosity.

Persistent selflessness

> In everything, do to others what you would have them do
> to you, for this sums up the Law and the Prophets. (Matt.
> 7:12)

This saying of Jesus has become world famous as 'the golden rule'. The surprising thing is that before Jesus did so, no one had put that thought in the positive. The Jews knew the principle, it was stated in their Law, but it was put negatively: 'Don't do to others what you wouldn't like them to do to you.' Jesus cast that command in a totally new light by restating it positively.

There's a story of two famous rabbis who lived in New Testament times not long after Jesus. One was a mean old grouch and the other was a really approachable sort of guy. A Gentile came up to the mean old grouch and said, 'If the Jewish faith is so significant, tell me what it's all about, quickly. If you can sum it up in just a few minutes – while I'm standing on one leg – I'll believe you.' And the rabbi said, grouchily, 'Go away. I can't possibly do that.'

Then the Gentile went to the other rabbi. 'Tell me all about the Jewish faith,' he asked. 'And tell me while I'm standing on one leg.' And, quick as anything, the rabbi responded, 'Do to others what you would have them do to you. Everything else is commentary. Bye.'

This second rabbi had got to the heart of the Jewish law. And Jesus brought out that teaching clearly. Yet we Christians seem to have forgotten the practice of this 'golden rule'. How much of what I've said privately in the past week would have been said if my life had been governed by this rule? How many people have I let down in the past month because I didn't do something I said I would – and it was something important to them?

The reason why we have probably lost sight of this rule is that it sounds so 'unspiritual'. For one thing it's a 'rule', and we're into grace, not law. For another, it sounds as if we're trying to earn

God's approval by being do-gooders. For a third, shouldn't we be more concerned about preaching the gospel to people than being nice to them? These are all false distinctions. True spirituality will show itself in the way we love, care for and respect other people. The way to ensure that we're doing that to the best of our Spirit-filled ability is to try to put this rule into practice.

Persistent discipleship

> Enter through the narrow gate. For wide is the gate and broad is the road that leads to destruction, and many enter through it. But small is the gate and narrow the road that leads to life, and only a few find it. (Matt. 7:13-14).

This is the crunch point of Jesus' sermon; it's make-your-mind-up time. Jesus is looking for one hundred per cent commitment. There can be no half measures. We are either in the kingdom of God or in the kingdom of Satan. In wartime you can't be on both sides at once.

Disciples whose commitment is total
Jesus sums up the whole of his sermon in this stark either-or statement. There is a narrow way – do you want to choose it? That's the way of the beatitudes, being single-minded in our longing for God, putting into practise all that teaching about the Law, living a life of transparent integrity, clearing out the grime and dirt from the cellars of our lives, living by that clear, unbending 'golden rule'. There is also a broad way – it's much easier, you just do what comes naturally.

The broad way seems sensible and obvious. That's why so many people are on it. At work or with our friends the question will arise time and again in our minds, 'Why shouldn't I do it? Everyone else is.' 'Why shouldn't I take that from the store cupboard at work? Everyone else does. Why shouldn't I use language like that? All my mates do. Why shouldn't I cheat on my wife? Everyone does that sort of thing.'

Actually, there are some people living differently. Jesus invites you to join them – a group of people who, down through history, have either been persecuted or labelled 'oddballs' because of it. 'You need to choose,' says Jesus. 'I invite you to join me, to choose a life that is tough and demanding, that will take your total commitment, but that will also be deeply satisfying and have eternal value.'

Many of us have made that decision. We have taken Jesus up on his challenge and have committed ourselves to him for life. And yet there are still those pockets of resistance in our lives, areas where we have not allowed him to take control.

During the American Civil War, Abraham Lincoln met with the generals of the Southern armies on a number of occasions as the war progressed, to seek a peaceful end to it. The Southerners wanted to keep on these meetings because they were getting fairly profoundly bashed up. After one year of war they came to Lincoln and said, 'OK, we'll give in. Just let us have Texas, New Mexico, the southern bit of California and one or two other States. You can have everything else.' And Lincoln refused. Another year went by and the Southerners became more desperate. 'How about letting us have just Texas and New Mexico? The North can keep everything else.' Abraham Lincoln reached over the table, put his hand on the map of the whole of America and said, 'Gentlemen, this Government wants it all.' Then he left the negotiating table and refused to meet with his opponents again until they came back in unconditional surrender.

While we carry on trying to keep some sovereign States in our lives apart from God, he is unable to give us all that he longs to. He cannot fill us with himself or direct us fully, because there is civil war going on inside us. God is putting his hand on the map of our lives and saying, 'My Government wants it all. Not just the bits you feel you can spare; not some bits and not others; I want all of your life.'

Disciples who are mature

> Watch out for false prophets. They come to you in sheep's clothing, but inwardly they are ferocious wolves. By their fruit you will recognize them. Do people pick grapes from thornbushes, or figs from thistles? Likewise every good tree bears good fruit, but a bad tree bears bad fruit. A good tree cannot bear bad fruit, and a bad tree cannot bear good fruit. Every tree that does not bear good fruit is cut down and thrown into the fire. Thus, by their fruit you will recognize them. (Matt. 7:15-20)

As Jesus comes to the end of his sermon, he sees how the crowd has swelled in size. There are disciples, half-disciples, the vaguely interested, and their friends, families, cousins, aunties and uncles. They are fascinated by his revolutionary teaching. He acknowledges the interest and attentiveness with which they hear him and he gives them a glimpse of the future. Yes, he says, his teaching is good and true, and many in those crowds will become his disciples. But there will come a time when those who recognize the power of his teaching will want the power without the teaching. They will want for themselves the devotion Jesus' disciples are to give to him alone. They will be false prophets and teachers, wolves in sheep's clothing – the exact opposite of what they purport to be.

His words have proved to be true. Down through history, from the time of the first apostles, false teachers have done all they can to distort the truth and the minds of God's people, so that our walk with God is not an easy one. We are constantly presented with new ideas, more 'intellectually acceptable' ideas about the resurrection of Jesus, for instance; highways and byways to go wandering into, attractive-looking cul-de-sacs down which to walk.

Individual church fellowships are particularly prone to drifting into heresy, especially when they have a strong leader with no one seriously disputing what he decrees. A group known as the Children of God grew out of the Jesus movement of the 1960s and 1970s. They were a great bunch of people, sharing their faith warmly and openly on the streets and attracting many people to Christ. But where are they now? Under a strong leader, who calls himself Moses David, they have become a cult which is into 'prostitution', fund-raising, subversive high-pressure activity and gross distortion of the gospel message – all within just a few years.

Today in America, those who teach a 'prosperity gospel' are also, I believe, heading towards cultism. They teach that God loves us – yes, and that he wants the best for us – yes; so we should ask him for what we want: 'name it and claim it' is their slogan. If you want a Mercedes, ask God for it! If you've got enough faith, God will give it to you. Of course, if you don't get one, that shows there's something wrong in your life or with your prayers or faith. Well, if they're right, I obviously don't have a very good prayer life!

Satan is cunning in the way he entices us to swallow lies like this. He doesn't come straight out with rubbish or heresy; he latches on to a particular biblical truth, and then pushes it beyond the limits it was meant to go. He takes a single truth and blows it out of proportion or corrupts it in some other way. It sounds so logical and right, to begin with. And then you get involved with a closely-knit group of people and give its leader your loyalty. And then it is very hard to disentangle yourself. Any hint of dissent is condemned as being unspiritual and rebellious. You just can't win in that sort of setup. The wolves have got you fairly cornered.

It is crucial to know our Bibles and be able to test against its teaching the teaching of groups and sects we come across. But another test to apply is the fruit test: what are these people's lives like? Do they display the fruit of the Spirit? Do they uphold the great biblical moral values – chastity outside marriage, faithfulness within it, honesty and integrity in every aspect of life? Does their theology lead them to live Christ-like lives?

Jesus doesn't leave things here. It is easy enough to apply these tests to other people and denounce those we find to be at fault. But he suddenly makes things very personal.

Disciples who love their Lord

'Not everyone who says to me, "Lord, Lord," will enter the kingdom of heaven, but only he who does the will of my Father who is in heaven. Many will say to me on that day, "Lord, Lord, did we not prophesy in your name, and in your name drive out demons and perform many miracles?" Then I will tell them plainly, "I never knew you. Away from me, you evildoers!"' (Matt. 7:21-23).

I don't know about you, but I would be delighted to be able to stand in God's presence and say, 'Lord, I've cast out lots of demons, I've worked hundreds of miracles, and I simply couldn't stop prophesying!' To you and me, people who could truly stand up and say that would seem like spiritual giants, capable of anything in the realm of spiritual battle. Yet Jesus is going to say he never knew them. I find that amazing. What is he wanting us to learn from it? This: that it is obedience he has in store for his people, not simply the miraculous.

It is right that we look for the exorcism of demons, where that is appropriate, for miracles and for prophecy. But the ability to do those things is not the ultimate test of a person's walk with God. There is a great danger in judging either our own spiritual standing or that of others on the evidence of what we can see, rather than on what is unseen. The wolves in sheep's clothing look very much like the real thing on the outside, but inside they are very different. We might look very spiritual on the outside, but God knows whether our heart is right with him.

Many of us think, 'I know I've been saved by grace but, my word, God is going to be really grateful to me when I get to heaven because I've done quite a few good things!' When I get to the pearly gates, God isn't going to bring out a great check-list of things and tick off all those things I've accomplished in my life. The test is going to be, did I love Jesus and follow him? And whatever was apparent to people on the outside who looked on, was there a deep, God-given integrity about my life? Or did I urge people to spend time in prayer and reading the word of God, while neglecting to do so myself? Did I encourage people to share their faith, while having none to share myself?

Performance, skill, gifts, abilities – without inner integrity all these things are ultimately of no use to us. What counts for eternity is a heart that is right with King Jesus.

11

Building on solid ground

Some years ago I read the book *Spy Catcher*, by Peter Wright. In it he reveals an astounding level of lack of trust, lying, deceit and intrigue within the Secret Services and the world of politics. He portrays a world where you simply do not know who you can trust, who your friends are, or what you can say to whom. He shows a world where everyone is constantly watching their backs, constantly living 'on edge'.

In a smaller, less potent way, all our lives can be like that – looking over our shoulders, wondering who we can trust with a problem, which of our friends are genuine and which are simply fair-weather friends. We're always searching for a foundational security that will not waver or fail. Where can we find that?

> 'Therefore everyone who hears these words of mine and puts them into practise is like a wise man who built his house on the rock. The rain came down, the streams rose, and the winds blew and beat against that house; yet it did not fall, because it had its foundation on the rock. But everyone who hears these words of mine and does not put them into practise is like a foolish man who built his house on sand. The rain came down, the streams rose, and the winds blew and beat against that house, and it fell with a great crash.'
>
> When Jesus had finished saying these things, the crowds were amazed at his teaching, because he taught as one who had authority, and not as their teachers of the law. (Matt. 7:24-29)

Jesus asks some hard questions! Behind his words here are the questions, 'What do you want to build your life on? What really matters to you? What are you going to give your life for and to?' If we're building on something insubstantial, the whole edifice of our lives is likely to come crumbling down around us. On the other hand, if our life is built on values that hold good through all eternity, then what we build on them will last too.

What will you find when you get to the top of your particular ladder? That it was leaning against the wrong wall all those years? All the money you earned, all the status and success you achieved –was it all worth while? What a tragedy to get to the end of life only to discover that it was just one big waste of time.

Jesus offers us a rock-like foundation on which to build; something that will give strength to all that we build on it and stay firm through the bad times as well as the good. He says, 'These words of mine, these are the foundational facts on which you need to build your life. Everything else is useless and insubstantial. If you build on anything else, you're wasting your time.'

How do we go about building on Jesus' words? There are two things we must do.

Hear God's word
Speaking in this passage, Jesus was referring primarily to his sermon, but we need to go on hearing God's word if we are to build our lives on what he says. God wants to speak to us in our reading of the Bible, in our prayer life, as we talk with other Christians and listen to his word being proclaimed from the pulpit. So we need to make the time to hear him in all these ways.

We can easily fall into the habit of tuning God out, developing a screening system that prevents us listening to anything we might find challenging or uncomfortable. Perhaps I've decided that my house group leader isn't able to tell me anything I don't already know, so I turn up at house group with my ears firmly closed to anything God might want to say through him. We can be prejudiced about other Christians, through whom God might want to speak to us. They're 'too young in the faith' to be able to teach me anything, or they're really a bit thick. And God certainly wouldn't teach me anything through a woman, would he?'

Years ago when my wife asked Cara, our youngest daughter, to put away the toys Cara did not take a blind bit of notice. She had perfected the art of tuning out whatever she did not want to hear. She actually turned her head away when asked to tidy up, as if to prove that her ears did not exist! Jan sometimes had to get hold of her by the chin and turn her round to face her, saying, 'Look at me when I'm talking to you!' She demanded that Cara came out of her little world and listen.

We've muddled along in our Christian lives for long enough. God longs for our attention so that he can say something to us. He wants to take hold of our chins and turn us to look at him and listen to him, so that he can change us and give us the power to be different.

Obey God's word

I was marrying a couple in church and had got to the point where you look the groom straight in the eye and say, 'Will you take this woman to be your lawful wedded wife?' And you expect the quick response 'I will.' Now this particular couple both affirmed that boldly, but if the groom had hesitated I'd probably have said the words again, in case he'd not heard. And if he'd whispered back, 'I'm thinking about it', I'd have got pretty worried! He'd planned for this marriage for ages: asked the bride, asked the bride's parents, got all the arrangements done, and arrived at the front of the church with all their relatives looking on. All that he needed to make the marriage happen was to say the words, 'I will.' All of his previous promises to his fiancée would have been seen as so much twaddle if he hadn't carried it through to its legal conclusion.

Many of us have made all sorts of promises to God. We tell him that we want to do this and that for him, serve him and obey him, but when it comes to the crunch we are very bad at carrying through on those promises. There is a cost to building on solid, secure, reliable foundations. And that cost is obedience to God's word.

What is your life being built on? At the end, when you stand on the threshold of eternity, will you look back on it and see a wonderful edifice crumble to nothing before your eyes as the sand beneath it shifts and blows away? Or will you be able to look back and see something of lasting worth and value, built through obedience on the rock-hard foundation of God's word?

Growing your
Gifts

2 Timothy: Ministry in Today's World

Contents

Introduction...229

1 Discovering your gifts...................................231

2 Secrets of successful service........................239

3 A life investment..250

4 Growing Christian character 264

5 Strength for tough times.............................276

6 The art of friendship...................................290

7 Growing the gift of preaching.....................298

8 Held by God...312

Gift identification questionnaire...................315

Notes..320

Introduction

If terrorism is even more of a problem in two hundred years time than it is now, archaeologists in Texas will be in trouble. While I was working with a church in Lubbock, Texas, I spent some time in the church's library. Around the top of the room were air vents, which blew hot air into the room, and I was fascinated by a sign that hung above one of them. It said, 'Please do not adjust these vents, they are set to blow up'!

Knowing that America and Britain do not use the English language in the same way, and being aware of what sort of building I was in, I think I worked out what that notice meant! But if the church falls into disrepair and, two hundred years from now, somebody excavating it comes into the library and sees the sign, he may think he's discovered the headquarters of a guerilla organization and that the vents are booby-trapped!

Reading the New Testament presents the same sort of difficulties. We are trying to make sense of letters and other documents that were written not just two hundred but two thousand years ago – in another culture and another language.

So, why bother?

Paul's letter to Timothy, the young pastor of a growing church, is vital reading for anyone who wants to learn more about using his or her gifts to serve God. His message is for every Christian as he or she goes about daily life.

As we draw out the main themes within the letter we will discover that the questions Timothy had about the Christian life and how to use his gifts effectively were no different from those we face today.

Build on the principles Paul gives here, and you will be well on the way to a life of fruitful service.

1

Discovering your Gifts

It's the end of a busy day. There is a knock at my study door and my last 'visitor' has come, a young woman interested in finding out more about leadership. After talking for a while I discover that's not why she's come at all. Years ago her father sexually abused her and the emotional and spiritual scars have not healed.

Three lads in their late teens phone up in the middle of the night, obviously the worse for drink: 'We thought you could tell us about God.'

A letter arrives on my desk: 'The Lord has shown me that he's not going to bless your ministry. And he's told me why . . .'

A man who thinks he might have AIDS phones up. 'Can I come to church? . . . Is it all right if I bring my boyfriend?'

As I think about the problems that crop up in my role as pastor, preacher and teacher, I'm relieved to know that I didn't take on the task simply because I felt like it! Rather, I'm doing it because God gave me the basic gifts and called me to use and develop them in this way.

Gifted?

From time to time people come to me and say, 'What can I do in the church? I don't know if I've got any real gifts but I feel I'd like to help somehow.' Many people doubt whether they really do have any gifts that can be of use to God, but the New Testament tells us that God has given each of us gifts to use and develop in his service: 'Each one should use whatever gift he has received to serve others, faithfully administering God's grace in its various forms' (1 Peter 4:10). These gifts may develop in us as our spiritual life develops, or they may be given to us as a result of prayer or the laying on of hands.

The New Testament spells out an amazing variety of gifts. You will find them in, for example, Romans 12:6-8; 1 Corinthians 12:4-11, 27-31; and Ephesians 4:11-13. The sort of gifts mentioned divide into three main types.

- There are gifts of 'caring': encouraging others; showing kindness; giving pastoral care; serving others.
- There are gifts of 'thinking and talking': prophecy; bringing messages of wisdom; bringing messages of knowledge; the ability to distinguish between those messages that come from God and those that do not; speaking in tongues – spiritual languages; the ability to explain what is being said in those languages; teaching; evangelism.
- There are also gifts of 'doing': leadership; faith; the power to heal; the power to work miracles; administration; helping others practically; sharing resources with others in need.

Perhaps you are gifted in caring for others – you are good at encouraging others or at making people new to the church feel at home. Perhaps you have gifts of thinking and talking: you can get your mind round ideas and help other people understand them; you are able to give good advice when asked for it. Perhaps you have gifts of 'doing': if someone needs something mended, organized or fixed, they come to you knowing that you will make it happen!

If you are not sure what gifts you have, take a look at the gift identification questionnaire at the back of this book. This will help you to pinpoint the sort of areas where God might want to use you in the life of the church and the community.

Growing

Sometimes we look at how other Christians are able to serve the church and their community, and we think, 'I could never do that! I've not got much in the way of gifts.' It is true that God has given each of us particular gifts but at the moment they might just be gift 'seeds', waiting for us to water and feed from them so that they can grow into something powerful and useful.

These seeds will begin to grow as we dedicate all that we are to God and as we step out in faith to use the little bits of gift we know we have. As we grow more like Christ in our character, so he can use those gifts more fully. And as we use them more fully, so the seedling gifts grow into strong, mature, effective gifts to use in his service.

Finding your niche

Once we have discovered our main area of gifting, we will want to know how God wants us to use those gifts. It is important to know that we are using them in the way that will be most effective.

Paul's opening line in his letter to Timothy shows that he was sure he was using his gifts for speaking and teaching in the way God wanted him to:

Paul, an apostle of Christ Jesus by the will of God, according to the promise of life that is in Jesus Christ.

Paul was convinced that he was to use those gifts to tell others about Jesus. He calls himself an apostle, literally a 'sent one', and says that it was 'the will of God' that he should take on this task.

How could Paul be so sure? We tend to spend hours agonizing about what is 'the right' thing to do when we are faced with a change of job, a house move or which school to send the children to. How can we tell what is the right course of action for putting our gifts to good use?

One way is to think what particular 'ministry' you could take on because of the gifts you have. The gifts are what we have; the ministry is the way we use them and this can be either within or outside the fellowship. Although every Christian has gifts to use for the good of the church fellowship, most of us spend most of our time in a secular job or at home and in our local community, and our gifts can be of use there too. In fact, it may be that our ministry will mostly be to colleagues and our families. If, as a teacher, businessman, assembly-line worker, accountant or homemaker you are using the gifts God has given you in a way that shows people something of him, you are God's 'minister' in that place.

If you have teaching gifts, it may be that you should be developing a teaching ministry in the church – but perhaps your school teaching job should be your main ministry.

You may not be called to use your gifts of caring in full-time pastoral ministry but those gifts could be well used in visiting the elderly or in opening up the church on weekdays as a drop-in centre for those who are lonely, or by offering support and encouragement to colleagues at work.

Do you play a musical instrument? Perhaps you could develop that gift in helping to lead worship in the church or in a house group. Or it may be that you could give something more valuable as a Christian if you invested your time and talents with a local non-Christian music group.

Do you get heated and angry about social issues– the state of our prisons, the effects of the poll tax, the number of abortions carried out each year? It may be that God is calling you to use your gifts to minister outside the fellowship, prison visiting, campaigning, or forming support groups for expectant mums.

Or perhaps your ministry will be as a union representative in your office or factory.

As we think about the gifts we have, it is good to talk over with our church leaders and with friends who know us well, exactly how we can begin to develop them or use them more fully. Usually, the right decision here will be confirmed to us by a deep sense of peace and security.

This doesn't mean we always feel peaceful when we are serving God in the place to which he has called us – often quite the reverse! We will probably experience pressure, problems and even persecution from Satan. Let's face it, *he* certainly doesn't want us to be using our gifts effectively and, when we are, he'll do his level best to stop us enjoying it!

You may need to try a number of areas before you feel you have found your main sphere of ministry. You may, of course, have gifts in several different areas. In this case, church leaders and friends may be able to point to the tasks most in need of being done, whether in the community, at work or in the fellowship, and help you to plan where and how to put those gifts to use.

Right Reasons

Before his conversion, Paul had been a 'religious studies' teacher in Jerusalem. He had been educated by Gamaliel, a highly respected Rabbi, and had gone to the best universities of his day. He had been born into a city famous for its great intellectuals, Tarsus. But he didn't for one moment think that his academic qualifications gave him the right to teach others about Christ. Two other things did that.

Knowing Jesus

The first was his personal meeting with Christ on the road to Damascus. Paul was temporarily blinded in that dramatic event but when he was able to see again it was not just physically. For the very first time, despite all his years of studying the Old Testament law, he could see spiritually.

We can know all there is to know *about* Jesus but if we don't know him personally we will not be able to introduce others to him. In Christian service it's *who* you know, not *what* you know, that matters most. I can think of dozens of people who have proved this.

There's the young wife who was full of enthusiasm for the Lord after her conversion. She had no theological training at all but she knew Jesus and nothing would stop her telling others about him. She had a gift for spotting and doing practical things to help her friends and neighbours. While she helped out or made them coffee she would talk about Jesus.

There's the insurance salesman who gets to the end of his patter then adds, 'Actually, I'm a Christian and I think the greatest form of insurance you can have is to know Jesus', and gives his client a book explaining the Christian faith.

There's the elderly person whose special ministry is prayer. She spends so much time with Jesus that he seems to radiate from her. Being with her is a real encouragement and inspiration.

Being called

Secondly, even though Paul had all the right skills, they were not enough to make him an apostle. His ministry was something to which he had to be called. Being smart at sums, clever with kids or a genius with groups doesn't automatically mean you should volunteer to be church accountant, help in the Sunday School or lead a house group! It is likely that God will use those natural gifts that you have – but the call must come from him.

God's help guaranteed

God guarantees to give us his help in using, day by day, the gifts he has given us. This present of help comes wrapped up in three parcels labelled 'grace', 'mercy' and 'peace'. As Paul began to write to Timothy he wanted to remind him of all that God had ready to give him. He also wanted to be sure Timothy knew that it is only because God has already give us grace, mercy and peace that ministry of any kind is possible:

> To Timothy, my dear son:
> Grace, mercy and peace from God the Father and Christ Jesus our Lord.

In other words, 'remember how it all started,' says Paul. 'God took you from being outside his kingdom and gave you new life in Christ: that's grace! What's more, Jesus didn't *have* to die for you but, because he loves you so much, he would have done so even if you were the only sinner in the world: that's mercy! And he wants you to be sure of these things and of his constant care: that's peace!' As we prepare for ministry in the fellowship, home or our work places, we can depend on these three things to act both as first aid kit and as tool kit.

A hymn that was often sung in the church in which I grew up began, 'There is a balm in Gilead.' As a teenager, I couldn't for the life of me figure out what it meant! It was, in fact, a quote from Jeremiah 8:22; the 'balm' was a kind of ointment or eye salve that came from Gilead, an area of Israel famous for its spices and medicinal herbs. It was just the thing for soothing eyes that were irritated by the dust and grit of a hot, dry country. What Jeremiah was getting at was that the promises of God to his struggling and suffering people were the spiritual equivalent of that soothing, healing balm of Gilead. They were to remember those promises and be encouraged and renewed by them.

When we feel unsure of ourselves, uncertain that God really has called us to serve him, afraid of what it might involve, we need to 'apply' these gifts of grace, mercy and peace to ourselves. We need to absorb them until we can *feel* God's love for us and are assured of his power for the task.

There may be times in your ministry when you are depressed by criticism, overwhelmed by work and floored by the complexity of the people for whom you are caring. There are times when life at home is chaotic and demanding. Whatever problems and tensions you face, God wants to give you his grace to cope with them, the certainty of his constant love in the midst of them, and the peace that comes from trusting him to resolve them in his own time and way.

Getting started

It can take a lot of courage to launch out into using our gifts in a particular form of ministry, whether it is accepting speaking engagements, taking the initiative to visit elderly folk who cannot get out very much, offering Christian counsel to people when they tell you about their problems, or getting involved with running the local mother and toddler group. We need the help of others! Ask a few friends to support you in the following ways:

• Before you take the plunge: in helping you think about what it will involve – in time, in skills, for your family – and to help you prepare.

• During your first attempts: to pray for you and to cheer you on.

• After your first attempts: to encourage you, help you to assess which things went well and which were not quite so good, and to help come up with ways to do even better next time.

2

Secrets of Successful Service

It seems that all the churches Timothy established turned out to
be strong and permanent. Paul's letter to him gives us four clues
as to why Timothy was able to use his gift for preaching so
successfully:

> I thank God, whom I serve, as my forefathers did, with a
> clear conscience, as night and day I constantly remember
> you in my prayers. Recalling your tears, I long to see you,
> so that I may be filled with joy. I have been reminded of
> your sincere faith, which first lived in your grandmother
> Lois and in your mother Eunice and, I am persuaded,
> now lives in you also. For this reason I remind you to fan
> into flame the gift of God, which is in you through the
> laying on of my hands. For God did not give us a spirit of
> timidity, but a spirit of power, of love and of self-discipline.
>
> *2 Timothy 1:3-7*

1. Prayer

Firstly, Timothy was surrounded by prayer. Paul wanted him to
know how deeply committed he was to his well-being and that
he was always praying for him. Paul could encourage him to get
on and do his bit for the kingdom only because he was backing
Timothy up with his own hard work of prayer.

Timothy's ministry was undergirded by the prayers of many
others too, without doubt including those of Mum and Grandma!
The secret of an effective ministry is the prayer of the people of

God. In the long run, our ministry will only be as powerful as the prayers of those who pray for us. In the same way, a preacher or teacher can influence others by his or her skills of communication but the ability to build up a church is given by God. Even the most gifted speaker simply doesn't have the skill to do this without God's help.

When I was in the States I watched, with interest and amazement, some American television. For a start, the home in which I was staying had a television with eighty-three channels! I heard a variety of people preach and teach, some of them riveting, brilliant communicators who hold massive audiences in the palm of their hand. I also heard a number of other superb communicators; crowds had flocked to hear them off screen and they had seemed all set for a successful television ministry. But today they are nowhere to be seen, largely because they depended only on the skills of oratory and good communication. Their audiences were interested simply in the fireworks of a dramatic performance. The prayers of God's people were not under-girding those ministries, helping to transform them into something that would have eternal effectiveness.

If you have already found your ministry 'niche' in the church fellowship or are still thinking about it, ask a couple of friends to be your prayer partners, praying with you and for you. Keep them up to date with what you are planning or doing and what you want to see happen as a result. Then pray it into reality!

The same goes for your work and witness at home or in your secular job. If you feel you have reached a dead end in terms of being effective for God there, perhaps the answer is to enlist the support of others to pray with you about it. It is also very helpful to have a prayer partner who will pray with you about persistent problems at work or home. When you have to decide how to react to fraud or sexual harassment at work, or are expected to cover up for the mistakes of colleagues by lying and deceit, how do you cope? Who helps you think it through? A prayer partner whom you can trust with these problems is invaluable.

In addition, why not determine now to pray regularly for those who are using their gifts in some of the 'front-line' ways – in evangelism, youth work or teaching, for instance? Really pray! Your prayers could be the key to their success. There is no such thing as 'one-man ministry'; without the active, prayerful support of all God's people, there can be no ministry at all. When we finally meet God, will he have to explain that our churches have been so weak because the people of God never really prayed?

We need to commit ourselves to praying that each other's ministries of 'caring', 'taking and thinking' and 'doing' will be powerful and effective in our communities.

2. Role Models

Timothy's ministry was successful because he had good role models. He grew up in a home where Jesus was known as Lord and, later, he was able to work with Paul, watching and learning from him.

Role models in the home

Many Christian families suffer because Mum or Dad is so 'committed' to the work of the church or so 'conscientious' about his or her day-to-day work that the children don't see much of them. Timothy, by contrast, seems to have grown up with adults in whom he could see the power of the living God at work. 'Lois', the name of Timothy's grandmother, means 'desirable' and 'Eunice', the name of his mother, means 'good victory'. He saw the gospel lived out at home in a way that was both attractive and powerful.

Children naturally copy the behaviour and attitudes of adults. I remember the stage of fatherhood where my wife often had to tell me off. Apparently, I was teaching our small daughters to do things their mother didn't think they should! I didn't teach them deliberately – most of the time – but there were little things I would say, gestures I would make and things I did that called forth the comment, 'Now we don't want Bethany and Cara doing *that*, do we?!' I couldn't very well say to my children, 'Don't do that!' if, two minutes later, *I* was doing it!

As we observe children and see their family life, we can often predict how they are going to grow up. Already at seven, eight and nine, they are mirroring the bad habits and attitudes of their parents. Their attitudes to Christian things are becoming sour and twisted because they are growing up in a home where, although the family members go to church, the risen Christ is not known in a loving, gentle and attractive way.

Today we can get almost anything instantly, from coffee to credit. But we can't conjure up instant Christian character in our children. It is tempting to leave that to the church fellowship. We take our children along as though we were putting scrambled egg in the microwave. Two minutes teaching in Sunday School then 'ping!' out they come as strong, spiritual, mature Christians ready to give a lead to the next generation. Or so we hope!

Lois and Eunice put time and patience into nourishing Timothy's young life. We cannot over-estimate the impact on a person's future ministry of a godly Christian home.

Role models in the church

Paul comes across as amazingly arrogant at times! 'Timothy,' he says, 'you know all about me. You have seen my life, my purpose for living, my faith. You have seen how patient I am! How loving I am! How enduring I am! You have seen me suffer persecution ... Now model your life on mine':

> You, however, know all about my teaching, my way of
> life, my purpose, faith, patience, love, endurance,
> persecutions, sufferings – what kinds of things happened
> to me in Antioch, Iconium and Lystra, the persecutions I
> endured ...But as for you, continue in what you have learned
> and have become convinced of, because you know those
> from whom you learned it.   *2 Timothy 3:10-14*

Paul was not claiming to be perfect but he was right to encourage
Timothy to follow his example. We know we should follow the
example of Jesus but sometimes we need a model and guide
who is easier to 'see'. Who can we look to for this sort of model?

• The historical 'greats': people like Martin Luther, John Wesley,
George Muller or Lord Shaftesbury. Get hold of their biographies
and find out what it was that made them great.

• The contemporary 'greats': people like Billy Graham, Eva
Burrows, Desmond Tutu – people whose ministries have made
them nationally and internationally famous. What motivates them?
How do they cope with difficulties? What are the secrets of their
success?

• The mature Christians you will find in your own church
fellowship: people who are emotionally secure and spiritually wise.
Some will be particularly good listeners; what makes them so?
Some always seem to have the right thing so say to someone who
needs guidance; why's that? Some have the knack of making you
feel welcome and at home; how do they do it? We can learn
much simply by observing how others have put their gifts to use.

As well as looking for role models on which to pattern our
own ministries, we need to be aware that in the church family and
in the wider community too, people are looking to us to
demonstrate the truth of what we say. My wife once told me,
'You're a model husband.' I felt rather pleased about that! As I

basked in the warm glow it gave me I looked up 'model' in the dictionary. This is what it said: 'Model: small imitation of the real thing'! That can be the problem with us; we often do not show what real Christianity is all about. Unless our lives model what we say, our words will carry no weight.

Perhaps your children have grown up or maybe you do not have children; even so we all have some contact with young people, especially those in our church fellowships. Although we may not be their parents, they see us as 'The Church'. They draw conclusions about Christianity from what they see in us. If they want to know whether a particular kind of behaviour is acceptable, they look at us to find out.

If we are going to help our young people towards effective future ministries, we must set them the kind of example that Paul set Timothy.

3. Continuing Renewal

At some time, Paul had laid hands on Timothy, recognising his gifts and sending him out to use them for God's glory. Now that Timothy was hitting problems Paul was concerned that his enthusiasm might begin to tail off, just as a roaring fire slowly dies down when the flames bite into wet wood. So he reminds Timothy of that very special event when he was commissioned for his task and specially equipped to do it. He probably guessed that the memory of it would rekindle Timothy's determination and commitment:

> ...fan into flame the gift of God, which is in you through the laying on of my hands. For God did not give us a spirit of timidity, but a spirit of power, of love and of self-discipline.   *2 Timothy 1:6-7*

Camp fires have a habit of going out while you are not watching them – especially if they took hours of hard labour to light! There's nothing else for it but to get down on all fours and puff some life into them until the dying embers flicker into flame again. In the same way, in Christian ministry it's easy to get so bogged down by the wet wood of routine, tedious tasks, the everyday and the hum-drum that we run out of spiritual power to cope with them.

We know what this means in practise. Doing the washing up suddenly seems so much more exciting than planning tomorrow night's house group meeting! Or you suggest that it would be a good idea to hold the deacon's meeting at your house so that you could carry on painting the skirting boards while you talk. Or you 'forget' to visit old Mr Smith because there's that film on TV you really want to see. Our creativity easily dries up and we realize we are doing those tasks, for which we are gifted, out of habit rather than heartfelt commitment.

Sometimes it is simply the busyness of our daily lives – the pressure of circumstances, trouble, tensions or stress of a variety of kinds – that leads us into a mediocre spiritual life. That flame of spiritual vitality we once had has died down. That touch from the Holy Spirit when someone laid hands on us seems far away. The conversion experience in which we felt so close to God, or the time when God moved into our life in a new way, now hardly seems real. If we are simply going through the motions of spiritual life, we need to make the time to fan it back into reality. There must be a freshness and vitality about our own walk with the Lord if our ministry to others is to be effective.

The good news is that flagging ministries can be fanned back into flame. The bad news is that it takes a major act of will, strengthened and encouraged by the Holy Spirit. If you know this is what you need to do, share it with one or two trusted friends and pray with them. It may be that you are simply too busy and drained of all energy and enthusiasm, not just enthusiasm for using your gifts for the Lord. Your friends may not be able to help you reorder your priorities or see that you take a break. Perhaps you need to be reassured that you *are* gifted in the ways you think you are, and are using those gifts in the place God wants you to. Sometimes other people can see that more clearly than we can ourselves. Ask your friends to be honest with you; encourage them not to let you off the hook until your ministry is revived – and don't give up!

4. The Holy Spirit

Very often when I suggest to particular people that they consider training for house group leadership, they respond with something like, 'Oh, I couldn't do that; I haven't got my own act together yet!' Or, 'I'm not spiritual enough.' Those may be very true self-observations, but they should not stop a person from taking on that leadership role! I encourage them instead to trust the judgment of those who have spotted the gift in them, and to trust God to work through them, despite any inadequacies they feel. The attitude, 'I'm not good enough,' is actually an important one to maintain; it is only when we realize our own limitations that we are prepared to let God take the reins and work through us.

Timothy was young and probably not at all sure of his own abilities. When he took a cold, hard look at the responsibilities of his ministry he got frightened. But God had promised to give him power, love and self-discipline – vital gifts if his ministry was to be effective. The Lord wants to give those same three things to us, too, for the areas of service to which he has called us. The Spirit within us is *powerful*; when he is directing operations the work will be done quickly and expertly. His Spirit will give us *love,* so that the power is under control; and *self-discipline*, so that our weaknesses are kept in check and do not undermine our ministry.

Power

Before a new building can be put up, the old building on the site must be smashed to the ground and the rubbish cleared. In the same way, the Spirit of Christ has to do some demolition work in us before he can build something solid in us and with us. God hates all the sin in our lives and he wants to destroy it. Like the prophet Jeremiah, we are called 'to uproot and tear down, to destroy and overthrow' and only then 'to build and to plant' (Jeremiah 1:10). Selfishness, pride, fear, even feelings of insecurity need to be swept away if God is to help us grow in the use of our gifts.

The same can be true of a church fellowship as a whole. To begin with, most of our churches need a demolition contractor in to deal with their outdated organizations. It is easy to cling on to 'what we have always done' simply because we feel secure with the predictable. But might some of our many meetings actually be hindering God's work rather than achieving it? At Stopsley we decided to close down a midweek ladies' meeting because it no longer seemed to be meeting a need. We also wound up, with sadness, the Girls' Brigade. After a time each was replaced with more appropriate alternatives.

There may be destructive attitudes in a church that need to be rooted out before the ministry of the fellowship, as a whole, can be effective. In large churches where it is easy to form hasty opinions of others, gossip, back-biting and sniping may need to be smashed down and broken. Smaller churches, on the other hand, often suffer from a false sense of ownership on the part of their elders or deacons: 'It's my church!' is sometimes their real feeling.

If we allow the demolition contractor in, we are forced to let go of our own secure holds and reach out instead towards the marvellous future God has in mind for us, whatever that may be.

As we clear the site of all its clutter we will be able to gauge more clearly the ministry goals that *Christ* has for us and for *his* church.

Love

When the demolition work is complete the ground needs to be levelled out so that new work can begin. Demolition is costly and painful but God works to change us gently and lovingly, at a pace we can handle. Demolition work will need to be done in us throughout our lives but, as God does it, he smoothes out all the brokenness and pain we feel and gives us the security from which to launch out into new areas of service. He also develops this same love in us so that we can use it in our ministries to bring healing and encouragement to others.

Self-discipline

Thirdly, we need self-discipline if we are to mature as Christians and use our gifts to build up the body of Christ.

Western culture today looks on self-discipline as something deviant. We are bombarded by a hundred voices urging us to take up the latest fads and fashions. 'The good life is yours for the asking! Just buy this aftershave, that car, this box of chocolates and the world will be at your feet! It all looks and sounds so easy! But building a mature Christian faith that will stand up under pressure takes hard work and self-discipline.

Some of us can get stuck into a project that will take a month or two, but commitment to Christian living demands our attention week after week, year after year, until we die! Most of us find that our enthusiasm tails off very easily. Many of us, for instance, are bad at making time to read the Bible and to pray regularly – though we are very good at talking about it! We need the self-discipline of a devotional life which is feeding on God's word; a tongue under control – free from gossip, lies and negative cynicism;

an emotional life under God's authority and of a commitment to other people which goes beyond our feelings. Self-discipline enables us to do something because it is right, not because we necessarily feel like doing it.

A building worth having is not built over night, nor haphazardly and in a hurry – the bricks thrown together crookedly, the roof at five different angles, the windows all askew! It demands careful, painstaking work or we will soon see the cracks appear. God's work in us will take the whole of our life but will last for all eternity. In the same way, those who are called to build in the lives of others, in Christ's name, need to be determined and patient builders. If things have not 'happened' in one or two years, or even in six months or six weeks, we can begin to wonder if there was any point in it. Then it is a short step to giving up and going back to what is safe and predictable.

If we want to see God's glory descend into our churches so that the miraculous happens and individuals become filled with the Spirit of Christ, we must keep on looking to God to do his work in us and through us.

3

A Life Investment

After much prayer and enthusiastic cajoling, Carole has at last persuaded her friend, Sandra, to go with her to an evangelistic service at church. There is an 'appeal' at the end and, to Carole's delight, Sandra decides to become a Christian. Carole goes off rejoicing, glad to have been able to add another sheep to the fold. But Sandra, now left to fend for herself as a new Christian, stands as much chance of survival as an ice cube in the Sahara! As struggles with sceptical friends, old habits and pressures of time hot up, that initial sense of commitment begins to melt away. Why isn't it lasting? What's going wrong?

In his book, *Discipleship*[1], David Watson puts his finger on the problem: 'Christians in the West have largely neglected what it means to be a *disciple of Christ*.' Tremendous efforts are made to bring people to Christ but, having accepted him, they are given no idea as to what he expects of them from then on.

The Navigators, a Christian organization which works mainly among students, has taken 2 Timothy 2: 2 as its basic text for ministry. From this it has developed an excellent way of 'making disciples':

> And the things you have heard me say in the presence of many witnesses entrust to reliable men who will also be qualified to teach others.

Navigators 'invest' their lives in others. Their goal is to spend quality time with a new Christian – perhaps for as long as five years – helping him or her to learn about the faith and encouraging them to practise living it out.

Invest in People

Using the gifts that God has given us will mean investing time, energy, prayer and love in the lives of people. That is how the church grows! Jesus invested three years of his life in a small group of twelve disciples. He showed them how to grow the gifts he had, teaching them how to pray and how to do the miracles he did; teaching them about God and how to live together as his followers. It was a practical, day-by-day apprenticeship – learning on the job.

Timothy's gifts were in teaching and preaching so Paul encouraged him to pass on the tools of the trade to other potential teachers and preachers. At root, this meant passing on to them the things Paul had taught him so that they in turn would be able to teach them to others. This happened in a dramatic way in the early life of the church: the twelve disciples became the one hundred and twenty; those in turn were joined by three thousand on the day of Pentecost, and so on down the generations until the church became worldwide.

As parents, teachers, work friends and neighbours we are called to invest our lives in others, perhaps moving them on a little nearer to faith or helping consolidate the faith which they already have.

We spend a great amount of our time investing in things that are simply not going to last. They are trivial in comparison to investment in the things of the kingdom of God. It helps to remember that all our prized possessions will be dust in a hundred years time and our best achievements will have long since been forgotten! In the words of the old verse:

Only one life, 'twill soon be past

Only what's done for Christ will last

252   *Growing your Gifts*

Invest in yourself

We can also make a direct investment in our own lives. In fact, it is vital that we do it if we are to last any longer than Sandra did, because keeping up the Christian life is hard work. There are so many obstacles!

For one thing, the Bible is a difficult book to understand. It was first written in three languages, Hebrew, Aramaic and Greek, each of which is hard for the average twenty-first century reader to learn. But it is a book with which we are going to have to grapple. Sometimes people come to me and say, 'I'm having difficulty with reading the Bible.' I occasionally reach out and shake their hand. 'So am I!' The Bible won't reveal its treasures to the casual observer. It won't strengthen us at the deepest level if we simply flick through its pages, looking at the odd verse and hoping that something relevant will leap off the page at us. Sometimes God *does* speak to us in that way but the Bible yields its deepest treasure only to hard work, study and prayer.

Secondly, the church is hard work. To be honest, we don't always find it easy to maintain good relationships with others in our church:

> To fellowship above with saints we love,
> Oh! That will be glory!
> To fellowship below with saints we know,
> Well – that's a different story!

The church is hard work because it is made up of people like you and me! God has put us in a church family where we rub shoulders with real people, from different backgrounds to ourselves, with different upbringings, educational achievements, priorities and family circumstances. On top of these there are the simply 'prickly' who get offended at the drop of a hymn book!

Sometimes we turn the pages of the Old and New Testaments and think, 'Look at these characters! If only we could be like them! If only we could be like Daniel or David!' As if they were absolutely perfect and didn't have family problems, corns and dandruff, as well as all the pressures of a world that didn't want anything to do with their faith! The reality is that wherever God's people are trying to live out their commitment to him, some hard work is called for. Paul wanted Timothy to be clear about that:

> Endure hardship with us like a good soldier of Christ Jesus. No-one serving as a soldier gets involved in civilian affairs – he wants to please his commanding officer. Similarly, if anyone competes as an athlete, he does not receive the victor's crown unless he competes according to the rules. The hardworking farmer should be the first to receive a share of the crops.   *2 Timothy 2:3-6*

Clear out the clutter!

When we moved house, my wife took it as an opportunity to throw out a lot of things we no longer needed – and a lot of things I thought we still did! The first I knew of this was when a friend came to see me one day, and was wearing my jacket! It happened to be the day after a sale at church where there had been a 'good as new' stall!

House moves really are good times to get rid of all the clutter we've been tripping over for the last few years. Jam jars, paper bags, bits of old car tyres, boxes of rusty staples – all go to the local dump or recycling centre. We feel that we want to clear out the rubbish from the old house, the old life, and make a new start in a new house. As the deadline approaches, panic sets in and some of the stuff we probably could use goes out too! Better to throw it out, we think, than not be ready when the removal people come!

If we are to live an effective Christian life, everything else must take second place to that goal. Anything that hinders us must be thrown out ruthlessly. The imagery Paul uses is that of the soldier, utterly dedicated to his job, his single goal being to carry out well the orders given by his superiors. If we are determined to make a success of our Christian lives, it may be that some unhelpful friendships and interests will have to go. There are many lonely and marginalized people who need our care and support instead. Some attitudes will need to be rethought as we struggle to allow the mind of Christ to develop in us. Some time may have to be reordered – perhaps we should cut down the amount of time we spend in front of 'the box' and invest it instead in doing things with the family.

John Stott writes, 'Every Christian is in some degree a soldier of Christ, even if he is as timid as Timothy. For, whatever our temperament, we cannot avoid the Christian conflict. And if we are to be good soldiers of Jesus Christ, we must be dedicated to the battle, committing ourselves to a life of discipline and suffering, and avoiding whatever may 'entangle' us and so distract us from it.'[2]

Keep in shape!

Today's Olympic runners won't be awarded a gold medal – or even a bronze one – unless they compete according to the rules. Many have recently found that out to their cost. In the Olympics of the first century AD there were similar rules about training and preparation for the games. Before he was permitted to enter the games, each athlete had to stand before a statue of Jupiter and swear, with one hand on his heart, that he had been in hard training for six months. If he could not swear that, he was automatically disqualified from taking part. The judges didn't want to waste their time watching a motley crowd of no-hopers!

Paul was impressed by the athletes' dedication. But even he was afraid that after having coached people for the Olympic struggles of the Christian life he would himself be found out of shape, unfit to qualify for entry to the race.

It is vital that, as we use our gifts to help others live Christianly, we keep ourselves in shape spiritually. We need to develop a daily fitness programme that includes the press-ups of prayer, the body-building of Bible reading, and the weights of witnessing (not to mention the squat-thrusts of systematic attendance at Sunday services)! Fighting the flab takes time, effort and a commitment of the will.

Stick at it!
Paul thinks of another analogy: the hard-working farmer. Even in these days of tractor cabs with built-in stereos and wall-to-wall carpeting, a farmer's work still demands daily perseverance. The cows have to be milked at five o'clock each morning, whether dawn breaks warm and clear or the sleet is hammering down on the window panes! The fields have to be ploughed and the crops sown and weeded if the arable farmer is to reap anything worth selling at the end of the season.

We need to be aware that Christianity is not a soft option. 'You don't need to tell *me* that!' may be your response! But sometimes we do present Christianity as the answer to every problem without understanding that the message of Timothy, as of the whole Bible, is that it involves commitment to a lifetime of hard work.

Many an elderly Christian will vouch that living out their faith doesn't get easier as time goes on. One member of our church, now in his seventies, has had to cope with enormous changes in church life alone! New people, new songs, new forms of worship – and that on top of coping with the gradual loss of physical freedom and the grief of outliving longstanding friends. But his verdict on all this? 'It's good to see God at work!'

That is good news! God *is* at work. We will be sustained and strengthened by him throughout our lives. It is his Holy Spirit working through us who ensures that what we do will be effective and fruitful. We need to hold these two facts in tension: prayer as if the success of the ministries he has given us is all up to God, while working as if it is all up to us! Otherwise, we will find ourselves in one of two situations:

- Being too 'God-confident'. Some people over-emphasize the sovereignty of God in an almost fatalistic way and get bogged down in a porridge-like holy laziness. 'If God wants that to be done', they think, 'he will see that it is!' Then they hand back all the responsibility to God and convince themselves that the truly spiritual thing to do is – nothing. This way of thinking provides one of the worst excuses for lazy Christianity I have ever heard!

- Being too self-confident. At the other end of the scale are Christians who are so self-confident that they don't take God's Spirit into account at all. They work hard at things but nothing of eternal significance happens because God is left out of the equation.

It is only when the two facts of God's sovereignty and human responsibility are brought together that God's work gets done in God's way.

Relax! And trust God

The last letter John Wesley wrote before his death in 1791 was to William Wilberforce. Wilberforce had many gifts. He was deeply caring and was incensed at the way wealthy westerners were keeping the slave trade going. He was a thinking person and knew that slave trading was wrong. But he also had gifts of 'doing' and

God called him to combine all three areas of gifting to launch a campaign against the slave trade. This was his ministry. Thinking about Wilberforce's campaign, John Wesley wrote:

> Unless God has raised you up for this very thing, you will be worn out by the opposition of men and devils. But if God be for you, who can be against you? Are all of them stronger than God? Oh be not weary of well-doing. Go on, in the name of God and in the power of his might, till even American slavery, the vilest thing that ever saw the sun, shall vanish away before it.

Paul, like Wilberforce, knew what it was like to work so hard for years but feel he was getting nowhere. He knew the depths of despair and felt keenly the limitations of his humanity. But he had also found the key that unlocked the door of that cell:

> Remember Jesus Christ, raised from the dead, descended from David. This is my gospel, for which I am suffering even to the point of being chained like a criminal. But God's word is not chained. Therefore I endure everything for the sake of the elect, that they too may obtain the salvation that is in Christ Jesus, with eternal glory.
>
> *2 Timothy 2:8-10*

When the going gets tough, he says, 'Remember Jesus Christ, raised from the dead, descended from David.' This statement flatly contradicted a heresy of the day which denied that Jesus was both God and man. In being 'raised from the dead' Jesus was proved to be God's Son; the phrase speaks of his divine nature. 'Descended from David' speaks of his human nature.

There are two things we need to grasp if we are to escape being paralysed emotionally by problems that hit us in our ministries. The first is that Jesus understands us! He knows just how we feel – he, too, had the onerous task of serving God as a mere human being. But, secondly, because Jesus is also God, he has the power to *do* something about our pain and suffering.

I think the three most devastating causes of self-doubt and despair that hit us as we try to use our God-given gifts are these.

• Criticism. There is the one-off, insensitive or spiteful remark: a young woman who has practised hard and struggled with nervousness in order to sing a solo at the evening service is greeted at the door afterwards with, 'You didn't sing very well tonight; what went wrong?' It takes immense courage and a mature assessment of one's abilities to be able to weather that and sing again.

Living with a constant undercurrent of criticism is perhaps even harder to cope with. The feeling that people are not approving of what you are doing can make you wary and unsure of yourself. A creeping 'paralysis' can take over as you double-check all your plans, so making you less effective in your ministry.

• Facing limitations. Secondly, sooner or later you make the discovery that you are not omni-competent! It is hard to admit to having limitations. Physical energy, time, gifts, can all be exhausted; there is a certain point beyond which you cannot go. It is sometimes painful to have to admit that someone else will have to do that particular job you always wanted to – and it can be stressful, too, if you think you could do it better!

• Lack of job satisfaction. Thirdly, particularly for those whose gifts are in caring for others, there is the lack of tangible job satisfaction. With any 'people-centred' work it is difficult to assess how you are doing. You can't be encouraged by the sales figure, take pride in the fact that the books balance, admire the finished car or wave goodbye to a satisfied client! The carer is always in a vulnerable position as far as job satisfaction is concerned.

All three debilitating factors can hit us particularly hard as we try to balance the demands of work, home and church. Criticism can come from all sides when one or another feels they are not getting a big enough slice of our time. We become painfully aware of our lack of ability to be in three places at once, and we're never quite sure we have done *any* of the jobs well!

When they join forces these three giants prove formidable foes – strong enough, it would seem, to put anyone's God-given ministry firmly under lock and key. If that is how you feel, Paul would sympathize. Writing to Timothy, he comments that his preaching of the gospel had led directly to his 'being chained like a criminal'. But he doesn't write himself into a depression; rather, he adds triumphantly, 'But God's word is not chained!'

Martin Luther, the sixteenth-century German reformer, was once taken into hiding, for his own safety, to an old, disused fortress. He was there for over a year. At the beginning of that time, away from all the action of reform happening in his home town, he became very anxious and depressed. Writing to a friend he poured out his frustration but the friend's reply helped restore Luther's sense of perspective: 'Look, God's work is going on, Martin! You're not the only one doing it, you know!'

When the truth of this had sunk in, Luther wrote in his journal: 'While I sit here sipping my beer, the gospel runs its course.' He had got to the point of saying, 'Lord, I'm still asking you to get me out of this place but I praise you that, even while I'm stuck here, your work is getting done.'

From time to time we all need to be released from the pressure to be *achieving* something for God. We all go through periods of illness, hospitalization or family pressure when we are simply unable to be what we want to be. We are unable to witness or share

Christ with others as we would want to. It is then that we need to hear the Lord's assurance: 'I love you and I know about the situation you are in, and I want to tell you that even while you feel unable to do anything, I'm still getting my work done. Relax!'

While Jan and I were on a sabbatical visit to Texas, Jan took ill and I drove her to the emergency department of the hospital for treatment. When we returned she went straight to bed feeling worse than before! She remained ill for the rest of our time there and by the time we had to leave she was feeling very frustrated. 'While I lay there,' she said, 'I kept thinking, what a waste of a sabbatical this is! I'm supposed to be doing things that are useful here!' She added, 'Even when I tried to pray for you and for all that was happening I just couldn't concentrate.'

But what kind of God do we serve? Was he standing there at Jan's bedside saying, 'you know, this is really pathetic! I mean, you have started this sentence three times now!' No, God isn't like that. He understood the situation. Jan's little bits of heartfelt groaning to God were just as acceptable to him as any well thought out, carefully constructed prayer. The *last* thing Jan needed was a heavy-handed pastoral visit: 'Have you had your devotions this morning? Why not? Where is the Bible? Pray, woman!'

There will be times when you are simply unable to use your gifts. God wants you to know that he loves you very much and that his word is not chained even when you are. God is big enough to cope with your situation and will handle his world and his business himself for the time being!

Invest in Christ

Here is a trustworthy saying:
If we died with him,
We will also live with him;
If we endure, we will also reign with him.

If we disown him, he will also disown us;
If we are faithless, he will remain faithful,
For he cannot disown himself.

2 Timothy 2:11-13

Many people think these verses are part of a song that the early Christians sang. It could have been one of the first songs written for a 'Make Way' march or, at any rate, for an evangelistic presentation. Perhaps we should imagine Timothy at the head of a 'Make Way' procession, with his lyre or lute, leading the local Christians through the streets of their town declaring the good news of Jesus and singing the song, 'If we die with him we will also live with him.'

It was a challenge to the folk who heard it: 'You think you are living life now, but it is only when you have died to yourself that you will really live.' It speaks of the principle of giving all that we have and are into the hands of Jesus. The next phrase carries the same idea, 'If we endure, we will also reign with him.' It is an appeal to people, 'Come and die to yourself and live instead for Christ. And if you keep that commitment to him, you will find yourself reigning with him for ever.' What a great evangelistic message! 'Come and experience all the glory of the real kingdom!'

These verses are exceptionally difficult to understand though. The many commentaries on this passage all say different things. When we get to heaven we can ask Paul what he really meant! The difficulty lies with the phrase, 'If we disown him, he will disown us', because it seems, at first sight, to be a direct contradiction of what follows, 'If we are faithless, he will remain faithful, for he cannot disown himself.'

What Paul may be getting at is this. 'If we disown him' refers to something that has happened in the past. It was a one-off thing, a single event. If we, at one point, disowned him, 'he will also disown us'. Paul is probably remembering Jesus' words, 'Whoever acknowledges me before men, I will also acknowledge him before my Father in heaven. But whoever disowns me before men, I will disown him before my Father in heaven' (Matthew 10:32-33). If someone hears the message of Jesus and then says, 'I don't want anything to do with that, it's not for me,' God, in his infinite mercy and love, says, 'Fine, if you don't want me, I can't have you.' In that moment that person disowns Christ and is disowned by God. There can be no other outcome. God has given us the gift of free will and it is only as we exercise that free will that he can offer us his gift of salvation. If we say we do not want anything to do with his way, he will disown us. He is bound to.

This is a reminder we urgently need today. Many people seem to think that 'everyone will get there in the end'. It doesn't matter what you believe or don't believe, or what you commit yourself to or do not; God loves us so much, they say, that he will see we're all right in the end. But that is an outright denial of human liberty! If we disown God, he will take our decision *seriously* and will not overrule it. He will not make us *less* than human. Paul goes on to hammer the nail into the coffin. 'If we are faithless, he will remain faithful, for he cannot disown himself.'

'If we are faithless' indicates *going on* being. It is not referring to a single event in the past. If we continue to be faithless, we not only disown Christ once but reject the gospel message time and again. If we keep on refusing to have anything to do with him, 'he will remain faithful'. What does that mean? It does not mean that he will eventually say, 'All right, I know that you keep on rejecting me, but I've run out of patience and I'm going to accept you now despite your rejection.' It means, rather, that God is faithful to his original work, which was, 'he will also disown us.' So, if we continue to be faithless God will be faithful to himself and, being faithful to himself, will continue to disown us. That is why these verses have such a powerful evangelistic thrust.

We can be equally sure, however, that if we come to God, in faith, God will instantly cancel all our past rejection of him and say, 'Thank goodness for that! I own you. I love you. I want you and I will keep you for ever in my grasp.'

So, while these verses look forbidding in one sense, they contain a message of hope. They show that God is just, righteous and reliable and does not change his mind about things halfway through. We would never know where we stood with him if he did.

All this means that we are thoroughly wise to invest our lives, gifts and all our energies in serving Jesus. No fears here of a 'Black Monday' crash and of losing all our assets! Investment in serving Christ is costly and demanding but gilt-edged security is guaranteed. Christians intent on growing their gifts should invest in nothing but the best!

4

Growing Christian Character

'Building character' sounds a bit old-fashioned, straight-backed and army-like today, but it is still a crucial part of the Christian life. God is vitally concerned about who we *become* in the course of our lives – just as much as he is about what we *do* in life. This is because, in a real sense, 'character is destiny'. Who we are, in terms of character, will affect what we accomplish. We can have every gift going, but if our characters are not becoming increasingly Christ-like we will not be able to use those gifts effectively for him.

In practical terms, Paul pinpoints three aspects of character that should be apparent in our lives: integrity in handling the Bible, holy living, and a servant attitude. He weaves together teaching on all three in his letter to Timothy, showing how each is vital to the other two and how each undergirds and makes possible the others.

Integrity in handling the Bible

Do your best to present yourself to God as one approved, a workman who does not need to be ashamed and who correctly handles the word of truth.   *2 Timothy 2:15*

... from infancy you have known the holy Scriptures, which are able to make you wise for salvation through faith in Christ Jesus. All Scripture is God-breathed and is useful for teaching, rebuking, correcting and training in

righteousness, so that the man of God may be thoroughly
equipped for every good work.   *2 Timothy 3:15-17*

It is very easy to twist – ever so slightly – what someone has said,
so that it puts us in a better light. We 'reinterpret' a statement until
we are happy with what we have made it say: 'Well, I know double
yellow lines mean "No parking", but I'm not really *parking* here –
just stopping for a couple of minutes to get to the bank!' The
ticket on your windscreen when you get back will suggest that
you and the traffic warden differ over your definitions of 'parking'!

    Though we admit to being a bit free with our interpretation
of the comments and rules we come across each day, we need to
treat the Bible with respect. When we offer advice and teaching
to others, we must be sure that we are really passing on the mind
of God, not simply giving the thoughts that we or our hearers
find most acceptable. So we need to understand what the Bible is
teaching and we need to bring our own lives into line with what it
says.

Understanding the Bible

The Bible is no mere human invention; it is not just the product
of forty clever minds writing sixty-six books over a span of nearly
two thousand years, but the product of the mind of God. In
that case, how can we be expected to understand it?

    Firstly, God used ordinary people to write the Bible – it is
presented in normal, human languages and in concepts that can
be grasped by anyone familiar with those languages. We are not
all accomplished readers of Greek, Hebrew and Aramaic,
however! So, secondly, we have translations and books of
explanation written by those who are. There are also countless
commentaries on individual books of the Bible. Many of these
are designed to help the ordinary Christian learn how to handle

the Bible and apply its teaching with integrity. If you are in a position of church leadership, perhaps as an elder or house group leader, you should be building up a library of such books to help you as you teach others.[3]

Handling the Bible with integrity means taking all of it seriously – Old Testament as well as New. We tend to make a big distinction between the two, thinking that the New Testament is 'interesting' and 'all about good things', whereas the Old Testament is 'difficult' and 'some day I'll get round to looking at it!' Gordon MacDonald, the author of *Ordering your private world* and *Restoring your spiritual passion*, suggests that we think of the Old Testament as 'the older Testament', to help us see it in its true light. It is not like an old vacuum cleaner that we throw out once we've got a new one; it's more like the first volume of a two-book novel. We won't understand what's really happening in the second one until we know what happened earlier.

The picture of God that we have from the Old Testament is always in the background of what we read of him in the New. The Old Testament gives us clues about the nature of God and how he related to people in large groups, particularly nations. It shows his concern for their laws and general principles of social justice. It is also the canvas on which the New Testament picture of Jesus is painted; without the canvas, there is no picture. The New Testament unfolds the reasons why God became man in Jesus and shows how we can have access not just to a fuller understanding of God but can come right into his presence.

'Doing' the Bible

As Christians we recognize that God's word has authority over us: we will let it step into our lives and change the way we live. God's word comes to us most clearly in the Bible, and we can have every confidence in the Bible's truth. It describes itself as

'God-breathed'. That is, it comes straight from the heart of God and when you read it you recognize the Spirit that breathed it. *Mein Kampf* breathes the spirit of its author, Adolf Hitler. It simply reeks of his megalomania. You cannot read the book without knowing something about the man, even though he is not writing directly about himself. You cannot read *Das Kapital* without understanding something of the sort of person that Karl Marx was; it breathes out his personality. Neither can you read the Bible honestly without knowing that it breathes out a unique personality beyond those of its human authors – Peter, Paul, Isaiah, Jeremiah and others. It is because the Bible is God-breathed that it is authoritative.

We will not find God in his fullness nor know how to use our gifts fully in his service until his word is authoritative in our lives. We are far more comfortable when we sit in judgment over the Bible, trying to keep some measure of control over it: 'Well, I quite like that bit but not that,' and 'I don't think that bit applies to me but maybe this does.' Others would not claim to sit 'above' the Bible but think it is important to sit 'around' it, like nothing more than a discussion group, talking about it with other folk, seeing who can convince whom of their particular viewpoint. The only way we will find out what it is that God wants us to be and do is to sit 'under' the Bible's authority, accepting and obeying its teaching.

Many new Christians, and people thinking about becoming Christians, are sceptical about the Bible. They feel they need to give it time to 'prove' itself. I'm an intelligent person and I'm not going to believe a word of this Bible until I can see some reason to. Why should I take any notice of what uneducated, superstitious people thought in the first century?'

One Saturday morning you are walking along the street when you come across two people in their front drives, each with a car

Repair Manual, a broken-down car, and no idea how to mend it. One of them picks up the Manual and says, 'I'm not stupid. I'm just as intelligent as the person who wrote this Manual. How do I know if he's got it right? I think I'll check every single one of his instructions. In fact, at different points, I think I'll do things differently to the way he suggests because he may not have got it right at all.' For each instruction in the book, this person asks, 'How do I know *that* instruction is right?' Or says, 'That doesn't make much sense to me; I'll miss out that step.'

The other person takes the Manual, props it up against the garage wall and reads, '*Step one:* open Manual (you must already have done this.)' '*Step two*: the thing with four wheels is a car.' '*Step three*: open the front bit.' And so on. He just follows the instructions, one after the other. He has no idea whether the person who wrote the Manual is right or not but neither does he know how to mend a car! So he simply follows the instructions and gets his car back on the road long before the other guy!

Some people are very cynical about the Bible. They are bright and wonderfully sophisticated people but their lives go on rusting by the side of the road because they will not allow the 'Repair Manual' to sort them out. They would rather let the car stay off the road than trust themselves to what someone else says.

It is important not to ignore the questions that arise in our minds about the Bible, but it is important to put aside our cynicism. If the Bible *is* true, what it says will work and will make a difference to our lives. But we will discover whether or not it is true only if we take the risk of following its instructions.

Paul doesn't leave us simply with the assurance that the Bible is authoritative and totally trustworthy. He goes on to explain exactly how it is that the Bible helps us live Christianly.

Firstly, it 'rebukes' us. As we read it and open ourselves to the prompting of the Holy Spirit, we become aware of where we are falling short of God's standards. We invite the Holy Spirit to step in and point out where and how we need to change.

Secondly, it 'corrects' us: it brings us back onto the right track. The tense of the verb, 'correcting', is present continuous; the Bible keeps on correcting our way. Many young people today are subjected to orthodontic work, having a brace fitted to crooked teeth to pull them back into line. It's usually a long process. The orthodontist doesn't fit the brace one afternoon and say, 'There, take that off in the morning and you'll be all straightened out!' The brace works on the principle that it keeps on working. Over a period of time it pulls the teeth back into line. Our behaviour is not corrected simply by hearing once what God has to say about it. Rather, as we continually hear him, his Spirit continually helps us adjust.

Thirdly, Paul emphasizes that if we understand the Bible and do what it says we will be 'fully equipped for every good work' of Christian ministry.

When I first witnessed American football and saw all the gear they wear, I was fascinated. They are swathed in protective gear including helmets and huge shoulder pads. It makes you wonder whether the nine-foot high giants who come out onto the pitch are actually only three-foot-six midgets underneath all their padding! Imagine these modern-day knights in all their armour being joined on the field by an Englishman thinking he was going to play rugby, and had dressed accordingly. We are talking painful!

You and I need to be equipped for the battles of ministering in Christ's name, armoured and suited up. The only way we are going to be ready to face the hassles and aggro, pressure, and pain, is to be equipped by the Bible. Those who neglect it, both in its preaching and teaching and in its private reading, are going to be defenceless when exposed to the problems of the world. Spiritual injury is the inevitable result.

Holy living

The goal of the Christian life is righteous, holy living. Vance Havner, an American preacher, once said, 'If you want to be popular, preach happiness. If you want to be unpopular, preach holiness.'

Of course, happiness and holiness are not necessarily mutually exclusive! We sometimes have odd views, though, of what holiness is. We expect a holy person to radiate a sort of luminosity and always wear a serene, Mona Lisa smile. But real holiness is something very earthy and practical. It will affect the things we say and do, but above all it will affect the way we relate to other people.

In writing to Timothy, Paul speaks of a gentle and humble spirit as one of the main characteristics of a holy life:

> Keep reminding them of these things. Warn them before God against quarrelling about words; it is of no value, and only ruins those who listen...Avoid godless chatter because those who indulge in it will become more and more ungodly. Their teaching will spread like gangrene. Among them are Hymenaeus and Philetus, who have wandered away from the truth. They say that the resurrection has already taken place, and they destroy the faith of some...
>
> Don't have anything to do with foolish and stupid arguments, because you know they produce quarrels. And the Lord's servant must not quarrel; instead, he must be kind to everyone, able to teach, not resentful. Those who oppose him he must gently instruct, in the hope that God will grant them repentance leading them to a knowledge of the truth, and that they will come to their senses and escape from the trap of the devil, who has taken them captive to do his will.   *2 Timothy 2:14-26*

Sometimes we come across Christians who simply cannot discuss a point of conflict with humility, gentleness and love.

There was once a preacher, a Baptist and a staunch Baptist at that. No other denomination was really *Christian*, in his view. If you weren't a Baptist – well, you were just the pits! He went to preach at a church that was preparing to take part in a week of prayer for Christian unity. At the end of the meeting he asked, 'How many people in this church are Baptist?'

It was a Baptist church and, knowing his reputation, almost all the local non-Baptists had stayed away. So nearly everyone in the congregation put up their hands – all except one little old lady.

The preacher decided to embarrass her. He told the others to put their hands down and he said to her,

'What denomination are you?'

'I'm a Methodist', she replied.

'A *what?*'

'A Methodist,' she said.

'And *why* are you a Methodist?' he asked.

'Well,' she said, 'my father was a Methodist and my grandfather was a Methodist, so I'm a Methodist.'

The preacher decided that he would really make his point here, so he said,

'That's simply ridiculous! Suppose your father was a moron and your grandfather was a moron, what would *that* make you?'

The little old lady thought for a moment, then replied, 'I guess that would make me a Baptist!'

Sometimes there is an unhealthy arrogance about us. It is right to be confident about what the Bible teaches but we can become very conceited about our own interpretations of it. This shows itself particularly in personal conversation with other Christians. I have heard people from different churches getting together in a corner after joint events and arguing hammer and tongs about

which of them is right. Each says, 'But it says *this* in the Bible!'
And the 'discussion' ends up as a heated slagging match: 'You feel
free *not* to believe the Bible then!'

This is not warm, open discussion. Nor is it helpful to anyone.
God calls us to a new humility and gentleness in our personal
relationships. The bold proclamation of God's word is essential
and the strongest authoritative teaching is crucial. But when people
are hungry for the truth, or searching or disagreeing, the time for
arguing is over. In private, personal relationships with other
believers and with non-Christians, we need the spirit Timothy had
– one of confidence in the Bible but also of humility and a lack
of arrogance.

Holiness is a bit like measles: it's catching. But so is unholiness.
When we are away from strong Christian fellowship, our fellowship
with God grows weak. It is easy for our language to become
displeasing to him. It is also easier to hang loose to the truth of
the gospel and so undermine the faith of others.

Paul warned Timothy about two types of people. The first
are characterized by Hymenaeus and Philetus. Their talking had
affected their thinking and then their teaching, so that they had
ended up destroying the faith of some believers. People like this
know in their hearts that Jesus is Saviour, but are wilfully and
deliberately sinning. Those folk will not be brought back to the
kingdom of God by Bible-bashing, anger or rebuke, but only by
love.

The other group of people Paul describes are those who have
never found Jesus for themselves as Saviour and Lord. They, too,
are going to be won to him only by the quiet, gentle and humble
spirit of men and women of God who are so certain of their
ground that they don't need to shout or be abrasive or angry, but
can present the gospel lovingly and clearly. In our own day, many
have found this true of Billy Graham's preaching. The simplicity

of the gospel message he presents, combined with his certainty, gentleness and lack of pressurized 'hype', breaks down many barriers to faith.

A servant attitude

> In a large house there are articles not only of gold and silver, but also of wood and clay; some are for noble purposes and some for ignoble. If a man cleanses himself from the latter, he will be an instrument for noble purposes, made holy, useful to the Master and prepared to do any good work.   *2 Timothy 2:20-21*

Not everything that glitters in the church is necessarily gold – and that goes for the people too! Characters like Hymenaeus and Philetus seem to be really useful to begin with but their true colours soon show. Paul describes these people as 'ignoble', that is, unfit for use in God's work. We cannot always spot people like this, but God can! He won't use, for any of his 'noble' purposes, people who deliberately deviate from his word. We need to work hard to keep close to God, living in obedience to him. When we do this our gifts can be used by God with all the honour reserved for the best china – which is the marvellous alternative to being treated like a polystyrene cup!

The reward for holiness in our lives is service and not status. Being spiritually clean will make us *'useful* to the Master and prepared *to do any good work*'! William Barclay, commenting on these verses, challenges our motives and calls us to selfless ministry:

> A really good man does not regard his goodness as entitling him to special honour ... His glory will not be in exemption from service; it will be in still more demanding service.

No Christian should ever think of fitting himself for honour but always as fitting himself for service.'[4]

In practise, there are some steps we can take to help develop this attitude.

- Firstly, remember that it is not ability but availability that matters. Just because God chooses us to be his ministers in a certain place it doesn't mean that we are anything very special. After all, he has spoken through a donkey before now (Numbers 22:21-34)! The Sovereign of the universe chooses us for *his* reasons, not for who we are. God does not use us because we are specially able but because we make ourselves totally available to him.

- Secondly, remember that *our* accomplishments count for nothing; only those things done by God's Spirit will have enduring worth. The prophet Zechariah reminded King Zerubbabel of this at the same time as he encouraged him in his work of rebuilding the temple: 'Not by might nor by power, but by my Spirit, says the Lord Almighty' (Zechariah 4:6).

- Thirdly, remember that true Christian service springs from love. If we serve God from any motive other than love we will only be harming ourselves and those around us. If we are honest, we have to admit that much of our Christian service is done because we feel we have to. It may be that we think it is expected of us and that we won't be thought to be 'pulling our weight' in the church if we don't. Or we may not be secure enough in God's love. Deep down we feel that he won't *really* accept us unless we are running a weekly house group, transporting old ladies to and from the Women's Fellowship, preaching at least once a month, teaching Sunday School, witnessing to our neighbours *and* going to six services every Sunday.

But God doesn't need his arm twisted in order to love us. He demonstrated his unfathomable love for us long before we were in existence, let alone doing anything for him. All he wants from us in return is our love. True service will grow out of that.

5

Strength for Tough Times

If you have spent much time in Christian book shops, you will know that there are almost as many theories about the second coming as there are Christians! There are pre-millennialists, post-millennialists and a-millennialists.[5] There are those who believe the church will go through a time of intense tribulation before Jesus comes back and those who think Christians will be taken to be with Christ in the middle of those tribulations or a little later on, or at the end. It's all very confusing. I'm a 'pan-millennialist': I believe it will all pan out in the end!

While the Bible does not set out to give us a timetable, it is very clear about two things: firstly, 'the last days' are here. Secondly, they will, in places, be 'terrible'. They are 'the tough times' and Paul warns Timothy to be ready for them:

> There will be terrible times in the last days. People will be lovers of themselves, lovers of money, boastful, proud, abusive, disobedient to their parents, ungrateful,unholy, without love,unforgiving, slanderous, without self-control, brutal, not lovers of the good, treacherous, rash, conceited, lovers of pleasure rather than lovers of God – having a form of godliness but denying its power. Have nothing to do with them.
>
> They are the kind who worm their way into homes and gain control over weak-willed women, who are loaded down with sins and are swayed by all kinds of evil desires, always learning but never able to acknowledge the truth.

Just as Jannes and Jambres opposed Moses, so also these men oppose the truth – men of depraved minds, who, as far as the faith is concerned, are rejected. But they will not get very far because, as in the case of those men, their folly will be clear to everyone.   *2 Timothy 3:1-9*

The Jews of Paul's day divided history into two parts, current time and 'the last days'. The New Testament writers use the phrase, 'the last days', to mean the entire period after the death and resurrection of Jesus, up until his second coming. In the New Testament, the crucial words linked with the second coming are 'soon!' and 'be ready!' Whenever the apostles were asked about the second coming they said, 'The Lord is coming soon', emphasizing the need to be ready. The importance of that was stressed by Jesus himself. He warned his disciples to keep awake and alert, just as they would be at three o'clock in the morning if they'd had a tip-off about being burgled! (See Luke 12:35-40.)

But why should this time be particularly difficult for Christians? Paul mentions two pressures that we will feel and gives some hints on how to cope with them.

Pressure from society
The first pressure has two aspects. Society at large is going to be hostile towards the Christian faith; being different is going to be a real struggle. But at the same time God is wanting to change our characters so that we become more Christlike. As he does that, we will find ourselves swimming more obviously against the tide. Let's look at some of the characteristics of society which Paul highlights as hostile to Christian faith.

Personal qualities
'*People will be . . . boastful, proud . . .*' There is some difference

between the two. One evening some years ago I played football at Luton Town Football Club. As I ran out onto the artificial pitch the crowds cheered. All the old magic returned. The crowds gasped at the ability of this centre-forward, thinking, 'Why isn't he playing full-time – a man with this kind of skill?' Then, at the end, three laps of honour and back to the dressing room.

Now, there is only one element in that account which is true: I did play football at Luton Town Football Club but the rest is pure embroidery to make a good story. I actually felt sick after the first two minutes! Most of us are experts at dressing up a simple incident – something we did or that happened to us – in order to impress other people. You know the sort of thing: 'I had lunch with so-and-so today, the *very famous person* (along with – ahem – three thousand other people).' We try to make ourselves look good in other people's eyes – that is what 'boastful' means.

Pride is something more sinister because it is an inner attitude. Most of the time other people can tell what we are really like – they know when we are boasting! Pride is much harder to detect. It sometimes comes across as cynicism. We may not brag or boast about anything but inside we consider ourselves 'superior' to other people. We look down our noses at them, firmly believing that we are better than they are because of our intellect or because we are more spiritual or understand the Bible better.

Pride is a deadly disease in the church. It comes across in the way we can almost casually dismiss someone else. It can only be fought with constant vigilance, by regularly examining our attitudes or by giving a very honest friend permission to pull us up when he or she can see us slipping.

'People will be . . . abusive, disobedient to their parents, ungrateful.' Ungratefulness is a hallmark of our society. 'Demand your rights,' is the slogan of the day. We have a terrible inability to say 'thank

you' and to be gracious in thanking others for what they do for us. That applies in our church life too: we find it hard to praise, thank and worship God for all that he has done for us. If we organise a time to intercede for someone, many people may turn up and pray with passion. That's good! But if we hold a prayer time just to say 'thank you' to God and to praise him for what he has done, it could easily be the flattest and most difficult prayer time ever! Let's pray for the gift of gratitude.

'People will be ... unholy, without love, unforgiving, slanderous' – and when they are they will be thought of as witty, especially if they're writing in a satirical magazine! This sort of attitude is institutionalised in segments of our society, perhaps most obviously in the popular press where sales depend on sensationalism and 'shock reports'.

The word translated 'slanderous' is more often translated 'devilish'. The powers of the tongue and pen are devilish when they tear down others. It is so easy to criticise others, so hard to build them up. Building people up seems to be of no advantage to ourselves, whereas taking them down a peg shows us off, we think, in a comparatively better light. Yet when we withhold praise, and destroy a person's character instead, we are letting our tongues be instruments of Satan and not of God. A simple 'thank you', a telephone call offering help or expressing appreciation, even remembering someone's name – all these are positive up-building uses of our tongue.

'If you drop that glove once more, I'll throw you down those stairs!' That was how one young mother communicated with her shivering two-year-old at the top flight of concrete steps leading out of a London underground station.

'People will be ... without self-control, brutal.'
Even our humour gets more crude and brutal. You can learn a
great deal about a society by observing its humour, just as you
know more about someone from what they laugh at than from
almost anything else. Many of the things ordinary people in Britain
hold dear are now the targets of cynical and manipulative TV
comedians. As Christians we need to be careful that we do not
allow these attitudes to others to take hold of us.

*'People will be ... not lovers of the good, treacherous, rash, conceited,
lovers of pleasure rather than lovers of God – having a form of godliness but
denying its power.'* The word translated 'form' is an interesting one.
It means a 'model' and implies that a person can 'make a model'
of godliness.

Madam Tussaud's in London is always worth a visit. Have
you ever tried sitting very still on one of the seats they provide
round the sides of the rooms? You know what happens: people
wander past you and then they step back and take another look!
A friend of mine tried this once. He sat very still in a thoughtful
pose for quite some time, until an older lady came along with a
friend. She looked at him for a while. Then she turned to her
friend and said, 'This one's not very good.' She was startled and
rather embarrassed when 'it' moved!

All the actors, presidents and politicians at Madam Tussaud's
are only 'forms' of someone. Some of them are exceptionally
lifelike but they do not live. They could fool you in the half-light
or at a distance but they're not real.

The culture of Victorian England had a 'form of godliness'
but lacked its life and power. People went to church because
their bosses did or because it was what made them culturally
acceptable – but there was no life in their religious experience.
Today in America, particularly in the Southern States, being a

Christian can have the same air about it. Many people who go to church on a Sunday morning seem to do so with no real faith but because it is part of their culture.

It can happen to us, too. We can become 'Madame Tussaud Christians', sitting in church, saying all the right things, being part of the church family and even being heavily involved in its life – but being totally ineffective. We can perform the functions without allowing the Spirit of God to transform what we do into a reality that lasts. God wants us to have a real and satisfying faith. He is not interested in 'appearances'.

Public witness

Swimming against the tide of our culture doesn't stop with our private lives. Following Christ and using our gifts in his name is a very public business.

Some time ago I was talking with a BBC television commentator about Christian influence in the media. He said to me, 'While you were away in America, we heard a Chief of Police here talking about homosexuality and the AIDS issue, and saw him pilloried by every newspaper in the country, by TV, radio and by lots of very learned bishops and clergy. They were all outraged by any suggestions that AIDS might have anything to do with judgment and were saying, "We need to be very careful before we condemn homosexual practices." 'I looked in vain,' he said, 'for a Christian leader who was prepared to stand up on national television or say on the radio or in the press, "God has his standards and they will not be flouted."' There is a time to use our gifts for 'thinking and talking' in the public arena.

On 22 November 1963, two great men died. One of them was assassinated in Dallas, Texas; the other died peacefully at home in Oxford, England. John Kennedy and C S Lewis both had a massive influence on our world but in quite different ways. Take

C S Lewis, the author-theologian. In the academic environment of Oxford University, he said that the Bible was the word of God and that full-blooded Christianity was true. And they laughed at him. In the 1940s, 1950s and 1960s you were not popular in academic institutions if you had a committed faith in God. Lewis stood alone in an environment that thought his beliefs had gone out with the ark.

You also may have to stand alone as a Christian in your place of work, or perhaps you are the only Christian in your family. It may be that your actions or what you say will mark you out as being different. Through prayer and the support of other Christians, God wants to give you special grace for that situation. He loves you and does not want you to be afraid or to shy away from the cost involved in taking that stand for him.

There are times when even the strongest Christian feels shaken, unsure of himself and of God. At times like this it is good to remember three things:

• Your conversion. Think back to the time when Jesus Christ came into your life or first became real to you. He has promised that, once we are his, no-one and nothing can pluck us out of his hand: 'My sheep listen to my voice; I know them, and they follow me. I give them eternal life, and they shall never perish; no-one can snatch them out of my hand' (John 10:27-28). You can be sure that he has not let go of you, and will never do so! Relax in the security of this.

• Your call. Your call to use your gifts to serve God in a particular way came with an inner sense that you were doing the right thing. And this was confirmed by others in the church, either 'officially' at a commissioning ceremony, or simply by their comments that you had a gift in that particular area. Now that you have pushed out the boat and begun to exercise that ministry, don't let the descending fog fool you into thinking it was all a mistake. Once you have set your course, you will need courage and determination to keep going in it, especially when you can't see any land ahead!

- Your commitment. In a world which lives for the good times and goes for immediate rewards, our ministries can soon end up in the cupboard along with the skate board and the Rubick cube. But things of significance are only achieved with time and commitment.

Paul appeals to Timothy to swim against the tide of his culture. 'But as for you, continue in what you have learned' (3:14). It is vital that, if our ministries are to be effective, we determine to follow and serve God as closely as we can, regardless of what anyone else is doing. Joshua threw down the same challenge to the people of Israel in the Old Testament: 'Choose for yourselves this day whom you will serve . . . but as for me and my household, we will serve the Lord.' (Joshua 24:15).

Outright opposition

The prevailing attitude of our culture, along with the painful changes God wants to make to our characters, will make 'the last days' tough. But there will also be outright, open opposition.

Preachers are often tempted to be dishonest in their proclamation of the gospel. 'Come to know Jesus,' they say, 'and life will be great! Wonderful! Marvellous! It's the best thing that can happen to you!' All of that is true, but we do not often give prospective converts the other side of the picture: 'Everyone who wants to live a godly life in Christ Jesus will be persecuted' (3:12).

Who by? Well, Satan to start with. He is pretty mad when someone becomes a Christian. Though you may not even know of his existence beforehand, when you become a Christian you soon find out about it! He works to prevent God's people from being effective, by getting at them through two routes: other Christians and the hostility of people outside the church.

Opposition from fellow Christians

The history of the church is full of examples of Christians disagreeing with each other to the point of withdrawing them from fellowship. This is how most of our denominations have come into existence! It can be devastating to find that, on top of this, one's name is being tarred and feathered by those with whom one disagrees. It seems inevitable that any ministry will be damaged by this. Yet it does not always follow. John Wesley, the great eighteenth-century preacher who began Methodism, was always concerned to stay within the Anglican church, reforming from within. But many ministers barred him from their pulpits so he was forced to preach out of doors. Because of this, many thousands of people who would never have set foot inside a church heard the gospel and responded to it eagerly.

Paul warned Timothy to expect opposition to his ministry from within the church. It comes in many different forms. Sometimes there is stubborn opposition to the things of God. More often, opposition comes unwittingly from those who have forgotten Jesus' model of self-giving service and have taken on the models of the business world instead. Gifts can become fossilized until all that a person is doing is holding on to a position of power and prestige. Deacons can become dominated by traditionalism; youth workers start empire-building; house group leaders become motivated by pride, not by love; council members make decisions about the church's future ministry on financial considerations alone and not on the basis of Spirit-directed insight.

In his imprisonment, suffering because of the gospel he had preached, Paul soon discovered who was genuine in their concern to serve God and who wasn't:

You know that everyone in the province of Asia has deserted me, including Phygelus and Hermogenes. May the Lord show mercy to the household of Onesiphorus, because he often refreshed me and was not ashamed of my chains. On the contrary, when he was in Rome, he searched hard for me until he found me. May the Lord grant that he will find mercy from the Lord on that day! You know very well in how many ways he helped me in Ephesus. You then, my son, be strong in the grace that is in Christ Jesus.

2 Timothy 1:15-2:1

It seemed that Paul had called Phygelus and Hermogenes to work alongside him as trainees. Things appear to have started off well but very quickly they spotted that there was an angle of the gospel that could be exploited. Being in on the healings and miracles and seeing the way people were listening to the new teachings gave them a sense of power. What they needed in order to acquire that power for themselves was a slightly different version of the gospel, so they began to twist the message a little. When Paul tried to bring them back into line, he was not able to.

They distanced themselves more and more from Paul until they heard that he was in prison. Being connected with him then was anything but good for their image! They were ashamed to be associated with him. Although he had been their mentor, 'setting them up in business' and teaching them all he knew, they decided to have nothing more to do with him, his ministry or his name. But they went on manipulating and abusing the gospel for their own ends. Jesus denounced the Pharisees in strong terms for doing just this:

You clean the outside of the cup and dish, but inside they are full of greed and self-indulgence . . . You are like white-washed tombs, which look beautiful on the outside but on the inside are full of dead men's bones.

Matthew 23:25, 27

As we take on different sorts of ministry within the church fellowship we will discover that some people are supporting us only for their own ends and will be ready to dump us at the slightest hint of trouble. There were plenty of people who said to Paul, 'Thank you *so much* for your great sermon! What a *terrific* crusade you led when you came to Smyrna! What a *wonderful* preacher! We will *never* forget your ministry; thank you for all you gave us!' Six months later Paul is alone, rotting in a Roman jail. 'There you are,' says Paul. 'What kind of friends were they, really?'

Loss of support from fellow Christians can take a heavy emotional toll. The biggest knocks, however, may come from outside the church.

Opposition from outside the church

I sometimes wonder if I have really understood what 'being a Christian' is all about. I wonder how much opposition you and I face because of our service to Christ. It's not that we don't suffer at all – we all have toothache and family problems and our water pipes burst when it snows – the sort of suffering everyone else has. But what about suffering for Christ's sake?

I do not believe we should *look* for opposition, but it seems that Paul saw that Christian service was so revolutionary that it would involve a particular kind of suffering and pressure:

So do not be ashamed to testify about our Lord, or ashamed of me his prisoner. But join with me in suffering for the gospel, by the power of God, who has saved us and called us to a holy life – not because of anything we have done but because of his own purpose and grace. This grace was given us in Christ Jesus before the beginning of time, but it has now been revealed through the appearing of our Saviour, Christ Jesus, who has destroyed death and has brought life and immortality to light through the gospel. And of this gospel I was appointed a herald and an apostle and a teacher. That is why I am suffering as I am. Yet I am not ashamed, because I know whom I have believed, and am convinced that he is able to guard what I have entrusted to him for that day.   *2 Timothy 1:8-12*

For Paul, opposition came as a direct result of his preaching ministry and he ended up in chains in a Roman jail. How did he cope with that, and how should we cope with the opposition that comes our way?

• Remember the eternal time-scale. Paul had no doubts that all his suffering was worthwhile. He measured its worth on a longer time-scale than those around him: 'I . . . am convinced that he is able to guard what I have entrusted to him for that day.'

The word Paul used for 'entrust' was a banking term meaning 'to place on deposit'. He was convinced that nothing could rob him of the benefits of his faith. Life here and now was being made pretty unpleasant for Paul and many people must have wondered what on earth he was getting out of his faith. To the pagan in the street it must have looked as though Paul was losing out in every way – and should be ashamed of his losses. But Paul lived by the principle that 'you get what you pay for'. A person who buys a Rembrandt print from a High Street department store won't get more than a few pence for it at a jumble sale in a year or two's time. But a collector who spends all he has on the original work will find his sacrifice repaid many times over at a future international auction!

In his first letter to the Christians at Corinth Paul freely admitted that if he was looking for a return for his faith in this life he was backing a loser: 'If only for this life we have hope in Christ, we are to be pitied more than all men' (1 Corinthians 15:19). But, he said, faith in Christ didn't work like that. It was as though he had placed his faith on deposit in God's bank vault where it was not just being kept safe but compounding interest. Though the benefits of it might not be seen straight away, on the day of Christ's return his deposit would be given back to him with interest which is out of this world! Ministry in his name is never wasted.

• Trust God. God promises that we can trust our future to him. If we have given our lives to Jesus Christ nothing can take away our security. No problem in our lives, no disaster, failure or world catastrophe will be able to rob us of the eternal benefits of our faith. God will guard what we have committed to him and no bank robber can get past him! We need to be honest about where our security lies. Is it really with God and with his people? If we find that we are actually more concerned about losing favour and prestige in the world we need to re-establish a solid centre of security that will last into eternity.

• Go on the attack! Don't be forced onto the defensive! There is no need to be a doormat or to give a milk-and-water impression of Christianity to your work colleagues. I have often been challenged to explain why there is suffering in the world – and given about two minutes to do so! I sometimes turn the question back on the questioners: 'First I give *you* two minutes to explain why there is suffering in the world!' Needless to say, they usually cannot. We don't know all the answers to the problems people face day by day, but those who reject Christian faith do not usually have better ideas of their own!

• Gather support. When you are aware of opposition building up, share your concerns with friends and with others involved in the same sort of ministry as yourself. Ask them to pray with you and pledge yourself to supporting them, too.

So Paul encourages Timothy to be reckless for the sake of the gospel – to stick his neck out to the extent of suffering for it. He was to regard opposition to Christian service as something normal and to be expected. The good news for the Christian is that we can stand firm in the face of set-backs and say, 'Thank you, Lord, that in the middle of this swirling storm of problems, there is rock-hard certainty: I have trusted all my life to you and I know that you will not let me down. Ultimately, I will find that you have kept me and have completed through me the work that you asked me to do.'

The Art of Friendship

There are times when everything seems to conspire against you. Grandma had come to stay with us for a few days but no sooner had she arrived than our oldest daughter went down with a stomach bug. The next day my wife, Jan, went down with it too – not a very cheery welcome for Grandma. But someone in the church found out what happened. Next day, she was round at our house sorting everything out: organizing the children, looking after Jan, chatting with Grandma, getting the tea ready, even cooking an evening meal for those who were able to eat!

True Friendship

Tenacious, practical, loyal support is one of the most valuable gifts that one Christian can give another. As we assess our gifts and move out into new areas of ministry we need the honest and loving support of friends. We need to know that there are people we can always count on. True friendship shows itself in practical ways, in faithful prayer support and in public backing.

Paul was certainly not so spiritual that he didn't feel the cold or become dejected and suffer loneliness when no friends were around. His letters show a real mixture of the deeply spiritual and the very practical:

> Do your best to come to me quickly, for Demas, because he loved this world, has deserted me... Only Luke is with me. Get Mark and bring him with you, because he is helpful to me in my ministry... When you come, bring the cloak

that I left with Carpus at Troas, and my scrolls, especially the parchments.

Alexander the metalworker did me a great deal of harm... You too should be on your guard against him, because he strongly opposed our message.

At my first defence, no one came to my support, but everyone deserted me. May it not be held against them. But the Lord stood at my side and gave me strength, so that through me the message might be fully proclaimed and all the Gentiles might hear it...

Greet Priscilla and Aquila and the household of Onesiphorus... Do your best to get here before winter.

2 Timothy 4:9-21

Phygelus and Hermogenes had deserted Paul when he most needed them. Onesiphorus was a complete contrast. His name meant 'profit-bearing' and he was obviously profitable to Paul! He was not ashamed of Paul when he was in prison; on the contrary, he was prepared to risk his own reputation by visiting and helping him.

Practical friendship
True friendship is very practical. 'It's pretty cold here!' says Paul. 'So come before winter and bring my winter cloak; don't miss the boat or I'll freeze! I need your support, brother! Others have deserted me so it's bad enough spiritually, but it's worse feeling cold!'

When we say, 'Yes, I'll pray for you,' we need to be prepared to add, 'And what can I give you to help?' Good ministry always remembers the whole person. People are not just 'souls with ears' but have physical, emotional and social needs as well. We must not be so heavenly minded that we are of no earthly use to each other!

We hear an echo of the experience and words of Jesus as Paul goes on to say, 'At my first defence, no-one came to my support, but everyone deserted me. May it not be held against them.' Friendship keeps its side of the relationship open, even if the other person has broken off communication. In similar, though more extreme circumstances, Jesus had said, 'Father, forgive them, for they do not know what they are doing' (Luke 23:34).

Loyal friendship
Secondly, like the love Paul describes in 1 Corinthians 13, friendship is about loyal support. It's easy to give our support to one another as long as the other person is doing exactly what we want! It's easy to support our house group leader as long as she is leading the group the way we want it led! But as soon as she takes it in a slightly different direction or does something we are not too happy with, our loyalty backs off.

Time and again I have seen churches where this has happened. Influential groups in the church have given loyalty to a pastor, deacon or leader as long as he toes their particular line but woe betide him if what he thinks God is saying doesn't happen to further their own interests! Suddenly they are not the strong friends they seemed to be. Their support is withdrawn.

Paul's call to Timothy and to us is to show a radically different sort of friendship. Paul knew that the pressures facing Timothy were intense; he knew that supporting a man in prison would not make him popular among those Christians in Ephesus who were concerned about what their neighbours might think.

God's call comes to us today through these words of Paul. 'Never mind what other people will think! You – John, Anita, Puddlemarsh-in-the-Hole Church – you be faithful, loyal and committed to your brothers and sisters in Christ, in the good times and in the bad. Make sure that you are like Onesiphorus, that your friendship is real and rich.'

What are friends for?

In the friendships recorded in the Bible we can see a number of ways in which a friend proved crucial to someone's ministry.

To restore perspective

A good friend can help to restore our focus on God when the pressures of life have distorted our perspective. Recent surveys have shown that church ministers suffer from one of the highest levels of stress. Depression and a dogged sense of failure are common visitors.

David, on the run from Saul, knew what this was like. If ever a man was under stress for a prolonged period of time it was him! Knowing that God's plan was for him to become king – David had been anointed king some years earlier – he must have experienced intense frustration while he waited for it to happen. During this anxious, foggy time in David's life, we read that, 'Saul's son Jonathan went to David . . . and helped him to find strength in God.' (1 Samuel 23:16)

When we feel pressured from all sides and don't know which way to turn, it is good to have a friend who will say, 'Slow down; just wait for the Lord to act. He knows what he wants to do with your gifts and he'll see that it gets done in good time.'

To provide practical help

As widows, Ruth and Naomi needed each other. Naomi had the wisdom to know how to survive but Ruth, being younger, had the energy to do the hard work of gleaning in the fields. (see Ruth 2:2)

Paul commented of John Mark that 'he is helpful to me in my ministry' (2 Tim 4:11). Paul had found that the two of them, working together, could accomplish more than either could single-handed. It is good to have a friend who is more experienced than yourself who can help you work out problems that crop up in the course of your ministry.

To give encouragement

Friends can encourage us as we work out our ministries, perhaps pledging support for a bold move or encouraging us to keep going when things get difficult. In the Old Testament Joshua and Caleb encouraged Moses to fulfil his vision for entering the promised land (Numbers 13:30).

Later, living under a king who banned faith in God, Shadrach, Meshach and Abednego stood together in solidarity when threatened with death for their faith (Daniel 3).

When Daniel offered to use his gift of discernment to tell King Nebuchadnezzar what his dream meant, it was to his three friends that he turned for prayer, support and encouragement (Dan 2:17-19).

And when Paul was afraid and despondent, Jesus himself drew near to encourage him: 'the Lord stood at my side and gave me strength' (2 Tim 4:17).

To challenge each other

At one time, Paul felt he had to challenge John Mark's commitment to the missionary work he had been called to do. That was a tough time for Mark but the challenge bore fruit. Paul's whole letter is, in effect, a challenge to Timothy, setting out the standards of ministry and of personal life that God requires.

As Christians today we are under big pressures. We see those whose Christian commitment we once admired now far from

God and it makes us wonder if it is worth our while continuing. When people in our church fellowships say or do things that are less than the best, we easily follow their example. The lowest common denominator is always the most comfortable one to live with. It is all the more important, then, to have friends who will sharpen us up, keep us faithful to our calling and have the temerity to see that we are staying spiritually healthy!

Writing in *Christianity Today* after the fall of a top Christian leader, David Augsburger comments on the need for all Christians to have close friends to whom they are accountable:

> Accountability, puzzling as the concept is in the modern situation, is the mark of maturity in discipleship. It is not optional, nor a mere by-product. It is essential, central and definitive of life in the community of the Spirit.[6]

When someone fails and his Christian life begins to fall apart we find it much easier to back off from him and withhold the loyalty and love which we once gave him when he walked with God. It is as if we feel he is dirty or unclean and we don't want to be contaminated by contact with him. But why should our friendship and loyalty be conditional on people behaving in a certain way? Are we more concerned about their wellbeing or about our 'purity'?

It is important that we do not 'dump' our friends when they fail or do something of which we do not approve. If our message of forgiveness through Jesus is to mean anything we need to love those who fail, caring for them and bringing them back to full fellowship with Christ. In the body of Christ there must be a passionate commitment to one another that goes beyond the ordinary into the extraordinary.

How can we develop the sort of friendship that will be helpful in our ministries and in our Christian walk in general? There are three areas that we need to think about:

- *Ongoing friendship*. We need to give ourselves time to relax! One of the best ways of relaxing is to spend time in the company of friends who like the same sort of recreation – going to the cinema, eating, arguing about current issues, playing squash, or whatever. It is important that we stay the sort of people with whom others can relax and let their hair down, and that we are able to drop 'professionalism' and formality when we are with them. It is also important to maintain friendships with people outside the church fellowship; it is surprisingly easy to let such friendships get choked out by church activities and 'Christian busyness'.

    It is crucial to know that your friends are your friends because you are you, not because of what you do or for what you can give them. Without this sort of confidence in others, friendship can turn into simply another sort of test that adds to stress and tension. The best way to ensure that your friends do think of you this way is, of course, to be that sort of friend to them!

- *Crisis friendship*. Over the course of our lives it is only with a handful of people that we develop really strong friendships that stand the tests of time and distance. These are precious friends to have. They are the sort who will not give up on you even if everyone else does. If they were to discover that you were tragically, cultivating an extra-marital relationship or embezzling church funds, these friends would certainly challenge you – but they would also continue to love you. It is important to make ourselves accountable to such people, perhaps organising get-togethers with them every couple of months or so and giving each other the freedom to ask probing questions about our lives and the way we are using our gifts.

• *Support group friendship.*   Support groups are small groups of people who share a common task or goal and who meet regularly for mutual prayer support, encouragement and sharing. It is particularly important to belong to such a group if you are in any 'front-line' Christian ministry – any sort of evangelistic, teaching or pastoral work. Ministers' 'fraternals' rarely, in my experience, do the work of a support group. Their concern is usually more with business matters, especially the business of running the fraternal! If you find yourself in this situation, don't be afraid to admit your need of a greater depth of sharing and support and begin to sound out others who may be interested in forming such a group with you.

7

Growing the Gift of Preaching

Atheistic governments can't stifle it, philosophers can't ignore it, theologians can't argue it away. *Nothing* can rob the gospel of its truth or of its power to change lives and point people to the gospel.

Because the gospel will never be out of date or made obsolete by something better, it is exciting to be called like Timothy to the ministry of proclaiming it to others. But it can also be daunting! What does this particular ministry involve and how can we grow our gifts for it?

As an apostle, Paul had the unique task of explaining to the first Christians exactly what it was Jesus had done. He taught them in such a way that they could pass on the message of the gospel to all subsequent generations: '. . . of this gospel I was appointed a herald and an apostle and a teacher' (2 Timothy 1:11). Since Paul's day, God has called other people with gifts for communication to continue the task of passing it on and of making sure that people understood what they hear. This was the commission that Paul gave to Timothy:

> What you heard from me, keep as the pattern of sound teaching, with faith and love in Christ Jesus. Guard the good deposit that was entrusted to you – guard it with the help of the Holy Spirit who lives in us.
>
> *2 Timothy 1:13-14*

Paul had invested his teaching and a great deal of his life in Timothy. In this way he had deposited the gospel into his care.

Preach truth

It is very tempting to preach about almost anything so long as it interests people. At the beginning of the twenty-first century, materialism and self-fulfilment have become two key concerns; any preaching which offers wealth, personal fulfilment and happiness as part of the Christian package is likely to attract followers in large numbers. There is a growing interest in a gospel which basically says, 'God exists to make me happy.' But God's specific command to Timothy was to 'preach the word'. This may not always be the same as preaching what people want to hear:

> In the presence of God and of Christ Jesus, who will judge the living and the dead, and in view of his appearing and his kingdom, I give you this charge: Preach the Word; be prepared in season and out of season; correct, rebuke and encourage – with great patience and careful instruction. For the time will come when men will not put up with sound doctrine. Instead, to suit their own desires, they will gather around them a great number of teachers to say what their itching ears want to hear. They will turn their ears away from the truth and turn aside to myths. But you, keep your head in all situations, endure hardship, do the work of an evangelist, discharge all the duties of your ministry.
>
> *2 Timothy 4:1-5*

Paul's charge to Timothy could not have been more serious. It is something like a court scene. When someone is called to give evidence in court, she has to place one hand on the Bible or the

Scripture of her religion and say, 'I swear by Almighty God that the evidence I give shall be the truth, the whole truth and nothing but the truth.' It is as if Paul here has one hand on the Old Testament Scriptures to indicate that God is witness to the truth of what he is going on to write. Paul charges Timothy with a heavy responsibility: to make sure that people know what God has done in Christ, to bring them into his kingdom and to teach them how to live in a way that honours God.

The task is urgent: when Christ comes back it will be in judgment – both on how faithfully we have carried out his ministry and on the response of those who have heard it. I can imagine Timothy thinking, in his less spiritual moments, 'Oh, Jesus isn't going to come back *now*, not just yet, not while I'm a young pastor! Maybe at the end of my ministry he will; but here? Now? Surely not!'

Once when Jan and I were in the States we flew from Lubbock, Texas, to Wichita, Kansas – about six hundred miles. I'd never been to Wichita before and knew only two people there out of its five hundred thousand inhabitants. We taxied in and the couple met us at the airport. Before long, Janet was resting in our hosts' home and I was in the local Christian book shop! While we were there, my host was called away on his pager and I was left alone to wander around the shop thinking how great it was to be six thousand miles away from home, knowing no one!

Just then, someone tapped me on the shoulder and said, 'Steve Gaukroger, isn't it?' 'Pardon?' was the only thing I could think of saying as I turned to see who it was. The stranger standing there told me that, about a year earlier and six hundred miles away, he had been present at the wedding of Janet's sister, which I had conducted. I was absolutely amazed! All Jan could say when I told her was, 'Good job you were behaving yourself, then, wasn't it?!'

There was no way I could have met someone there who knew me – but I did! Sometimes we need to be jolted out of our complacency by the reminder that Jesus could arrive at any moment and challenge all that we are doing. The living God *will* one day speak to us face to face. In view of that, we need to soak our lives in the work of God and preach it powerfully and effectively. We must tell people exactly what it teaches and dare not let them have any doubts about its requirements or its promises. At the same time, our work, homes and worship need to be alive and rich with God's presence *now*.

Preach to change lives

The aim of preaching is to help people bring their lives more fully under God's control, whether those people are already committed to Christ, are in the church but not really living out their faith, have distanced themselves from the church or have not yet been reached for Christ. Paul gives Timothy a number of principles to live by in his work as a preacher, teacher and pastor.

Correct, rebuke and encourage

'*Correcting*' means to channel people's thinking; it is about teaching. Timothy was to be a road sign to right thinking, showing drivers which streets were one-way, how to get from the by-pass onto the motorway or which way to go round the roundabout. Paul warned him that members of his congregation would wander off into all kinds of heresies. Timothy was to correct them, guiding them back onto the path, putting up road signs which said, 'No entry', 'Turn right here', 'Go round this way'.

'Show them the way to go,' is Paul's commission. Without this kind of ministry today, many vulnerable Christians, particularly young people, will end up as Moonies, Mormons or Jehovah's Witnesses. The fringes of Christianity are fertile fields for the cults. People are attracted to them because of their strong personal relationships, their overwhelming expressions of love and care, and their one-on-one discipleship. We need to be giving very clear, specific teaching so that people can discern truth from error. And this teaching needs to be backed up by the warmth of our fellowship. This needs to be deep and genuine if the loneliness and isolation felt by many today are to be met with the love of Christ.

'*Rebuke*' is another thing that Paul charges Timothy to do. This has to do with behaviour, rather than teaching: 'Timothy, there will be people whose behaviour doesn't tie up with God's word and what it says. Don't be frightened to rebuke them; not, of course, in a spirit of anger or as if you were dealing with a little child. Simply be clear about what kind of behaviour is wrong.' Perhaps someone has a tendency to gossip or is refusing to speak to another member of the church family, or is skilfully deceiving the tax man! People need to know where God and his church stand on these issues. We must lovingly and gently tell them.

'*Encourage*.' The preaching ministry has sometimes got itself a bad name because of a heavy-handed, guilt-inducing emphasis on 'oughts': 'Be nice to your wife. Be a good neighbour. Get out there witnessing! Be kind, be loving, pray more, study the Bible harder!' The vast majority of people in our congregations will already have a keen sense of their own failures and further reminder of them will simply drive them further from the saving grace of Christ. In her book, *Searching for Lost Coins*[7], Ann Loades quotes a poem called *You are not enough*, written by an American college student. She introduces it like this:

After father, mother, husband and children have all told her why whatever she does for them is not enough, we have:

> It is not enough
> said her pastor
> that you
>> teach the second graders
>> change the cloths and candles
>> kneel prostrate at the altar
> as long as there are starving children in the
> world
> you must
> not eat
> without guilt.

Receiving encouragement is an essential part of Christian growth. It is important to assure people that God has already fully accepted them. In his sight we are already images of Christ, possessing every quality necessary to be God's children.

Church leaders are by no means immune from this feeling of being inadequate, of not doing enough. I have led a number of leadership training seminars over the last few years and am convinced that much of what people need is not 'know how' but simple encouragement. I am amazed at the number of church leaders who will come to me at the end of these training weeks and say, 'If it hadn't been for this week I was thinking of resigning from my church commitments.'

People at the very brink of leaving the ministry can be encouraged and re-enthused by something as simple as a note I once received from a deacon in the church. All it said was, 'I just wanted to say that I really appreciate all your love and support.' Encouragement can make all the difference.

Teach with patience and care

A church that affects its community is one that is built up over many years 'with great patience and careful instruction.' As individuals draw on the Holy Spirit's power and are renewed in him, and as they come to emotional and mental maturity, the church is strengthened.

Careful instruction and great patience are necessary because there will come a time, says Paul, when people won't come to hear preaching from the Bible but will go from event to event and from teacher to teacher looking for the latest formula for instant success in the Christian life.

I meet them at events like Spring Harvest. I call them 'Spring Harvest Groupies'. They go to celebration events up and down the country – Spring Harvest is only one of them. But when you sit down and ask them what is happening in the place where they live and worship, you sometimes find that they're not even going to church! They're thrilled by the worship and the atmosphere of a great 'celebration' event but are not making their faith count where it hurts in the experience of their day-to-day life.

It is marvellously exhilarating to be at the big conferences but the main point of going is to learn from those we hear there and to bring the heart of what they say back into the groundwork of our church fellowships. If their teaching doesn't work in your local community, it doesn't work! Something can sound very powerful in the emotionally-charged atmosphere of a big meeting but it might be pretty useless in the nitty-gritty of daily work and life.

I have also been saddened to see people following all the different fads and fashions of Christian leadership. In the early 1970s when 'renewal' came on the scene, people went to hear Christian leaders speak about the Holy Spirit. When that became a bit passé they wandered on to 'healing'. 'Signs and wonders'

was the next thing but now it is not quite so high on the agenda.
As that fades people are on the look-out for the next rising star, as
if we can just drop one thing and pick up another, never letting
any of them really change our souls. Our task, as was Timothy's,
is to draw such people back into a whole-hearted commitment
to the body of Christ.

In any community you will find another group of people –
'born again' Christians who are no longer worshipping with a
church fellowship and who do not intend to. If you ask why, you
will discover that something happened in their lives in the past
and they feel the church acted in response to it in a hurtful or
inappropriate way. Sometimes the cause of hurt is really quite
trivial, or there may have been no way the pastor or other members
of the church could have known about it anyway:

Pastor and Doctor

Mrs Huff is up the miff tree,
On a seat fixed good and firm;
And she'd like to tell the pastor
A few things to make him squirm.

Mrs Huff was sick abed, sir,
Yes, sir, sick abed a week!
And the pastor didn't call, sir,
Never even took a peek.

When I asked her if the doctor
Called to see her she said, 'Sure.'
And she looked as if she thought I
Needed some good mental cure.

> Then I asked her how the doctor
>   Knew that sickness laid her low.
> And she said that she had called him
>   On the phone and told him so.
>
> Now the doctor gets his bill paid
>   With a nicely written cheque;
> But the pastor, for not knowing,
>   Simply gets it in the neck.
>   *(Author Unknown)*

Often, of course, the fault does lie with the church: someone made an insensitive remark or failed to follow up what was obviously a cry for help. But some people haven't worshipped with other Christians for three, five, even twenty years because of some dispute over a building project or because they can't find a church that exactly fits their needs. They are denying the body the chance to be helped and encouraged by their gifts and abilities and are denying themselves the chance to grow in God by being a part of his people. It is our task to go out and find them, to call them back and to seek to heal the wounds.

Be consistent

If we are to teach God's truth and if those who hear are to live it, there needs to be consistency on both sides.

The word of God has to be preached and lived 'in season and out of season.' Other translations render this as 'whether the time is right or not' (Good News Bible). As a pastor I have to preach God's word when I feel like it and when I don't; when I am supported and praised and when I am criticized.

If you are one of those people who are significantly affected by your moods, you will know how difficult this impartial consistency is! If you are feeling discouraged, getting over the flu or have problems at home, preparing a sermon can be a real struggle. The last thing you want to do is face the church at all, let alone lead them in worship. At times like these, we need to remember that Jesus is Lord, not our feelings. The test of a pastor's ministry is not whether he or she can preach the word occasionally but whether, day by day and week by week, he or she can minister faithfully, whatever the pressure.

The principle applies to all Christians. We need to be consistent and faithful in our Christian living – in our home life, at work and in the tasks we take on at church. Some people have a history of doing one job after another for the life of the church, full of enthusiasm to start with but sticking at it only for a month or two. Consistency is the key to Christian ministry and one of the marks of Christian maturity is going on ministering through the good times and the bad ones. There is no 'closed season' on it!

There is a geyser in Yellowstone Park in America called 'Old Faithful'. It erupts every sixty-one minutes. That's pretty consistent for an old geyser! Others are far more spectacular, erupting once a month – if you are lucky. But, of course, you have to stand there for a month to be sure of seeing them! 'Old Faithful' is not that spectacular but you know that if you arrive at the site you will not have to wait more than sixty-one minutes to see it.

Be committed to growth

'Do the work of an evangelist' is Paul's next command. But in explaining this, notice that he doesn't say to Timothy, 'Try to find out whether you're gifted as an evangelist.' He says, 'Make sure your people know that it is right to tell others about Jesus – *and make it happen!*' In other words, 'Find the evangelistic gifts in the fellowship', not 'Be out every evening knocking at people's doors and giving them tracts.'

As pastors we can become so concerned about maintenance that we forget the concept of mission. How many people in your church fellowship are involved with 'looking after the saints' and how many are reaching out to those who do not yet know Jesus? If we added up our figures, we would probably find that there are thousands of people engaged in maintaining the Body – in pastoral care, singing in the choir, making coffee – and hardly any in the task of evangelism. Let's reverse that trend and commit ourselves to seeing God's church grow.

It was William Temple who said, 'The church is the only institution that exists for the benefit of its non-members.' The trouble is that we are under a lot of pressure today to be linked only with people who are like us – people who dress the same way, who live in the same sort of houses, who speak the same way, who spend their money on the same sort of things and send their children to the same sort of school. And this pressure carries over into church life. Even if those from outside our social grouping join the church, the temptation is always to make them become like us, rather than like Christ.

The commission Jesus left his followers was to win the world for him. A church that is not growing numerically is probably not being faithful to that commission. It is sometimes said in defence of static churches that we are not called to be successful but to be faithful. But, if we are being faithful we will, in general, be successful in terms of numerical growth, so it is right to aim for this. It is also crucial to set specific goals for growth. As it has been pointed out on many a car sticker: 'Aim at nothing and you are sure to hit it!'

There are situations, of course, where sociological factors make growth very hard but these are relatively rare. William Carey, for instance, a Baptist missionary who went to India in 1793, was there seven years before baptizing his first convert. But the problems that hampered the work of Carey and those other first missionaries to India were ones linked with culture shock and the physical rigours of adapting to a totally different climate and way of life. Today, we can draw on many studies of church growth and on insights into presenting the gospel across barriers of culture and language to help us bring people into the kingdom. And it is worth noting that, despite all the setbacks and difficulties he faced, William Carey's watchword was always, 'Attempt great things for God. Expect great things from God.'

Preach to yourself

Paul's letter to Timothy is shot through with reminders that everything he tells other people must first be tested on himself, like a doctor taking his own medicine or a cook sitting down to eat with the staff in the canteen. If Timothy expected his church members to live the truth, he himself had to handle the Bible with integrity. If they were to become Christ-like in character he, too, was to 'avoid godless chatter' and quarrelling. If he expected them to demonstrate holiness he, too, was to 'flee the evil desires of youth.' When we point at others we should take note that three fingers are pointing back at us!

I often find myself convicted by my own preaching! Presenting others with God's requirements, all the while knowing how far short I myself fall of reaching them, brings a tremendous sense of guilt with it. But, in our personal living and in our thinking, we need constantly to be on our guard. As Paul warned Timothy in his first letter to him, 'Watch your life and doctrine closely.' What we teach and how we live go hand-in-hand and each has an effect on the other. It may be that Paul had Demas in mind when he wrote that warning to Timothy. His story is one that should make us stop and think about how firm our commitment is both to right living and right doctrine.

The Demas experience

Demas is mentioned only three times in the Bible, but those three mentions give us a potted life history of a leading member of Paul's 'ministry team' that is devastating.

In Philemon 24 Paul refers to Demas as one of his team of 'fellow-workers', along with Mark, Aristarchus and Luke. He is obviously working hard alongside Paul, who is imprisoned in Ephesus, to bring the kingdom of God to the people of that city and to strengthen the newly-established church there.

At the end of his letter to the Christians in Colossae Paul mentions him again – but it is only a passing reference. He speaks about Tychicus, 'a dear brother, a faithful minister and a fellow-servant in the Lord'; about Aristarchus, Mark and Justus who 'have proved a comfort to me'; about Epaphras, who 'is always wrestling in prayer for you'; our 'dear friend' Luke – 'and Demas.' Demas is still around, but there is a hint that his spiritual passion is cooling.

Then, in 2 Timothy 4:10 we read, 'Demas, because he loved this world, has deserted me.'

These three references give us a picture of a person sliding away from God. In any church, and among any group of ministers, there may be people at all three stages of the 'Demas experience'. Some are giving all they are to God, wanting to love him, be faithful to him and to work with him. Others have known what it is like to feel that way but now feel something of an empty shell. There may be others who are still there, doing the job for the sake of appearances, but have actually stopped walking with God.

There is a wealth of sadness in Paul's comment on Demas. He feels it keenly as a great desertion. His words echo something of the sadness that Jesus felt at the desertions of Judas and Peter – the two people who, in their different ways, probably hurt Jesus more than anyone else. Peter had not only been part of the twelve but part of the three, the intimate circle with whom Jesus had shared his heart.

Peter, Judas and Demas give us hard-hitting reminders that even those in the so-called 'inner circle of faith' are not immune to the appeal of the world and the temptations of Satan to draw us away from the heart of God. In 1 Corinthians 10:12 Paul put it like this, 'So, if you think you are standing firm, be careful that you don't fall!'

Often, being in pastoral ministry keeps us well aware of the possibility of falling into the same trap as Demas, as we have the task of trying to prevent it happening in others. In fact, our problem can be more that of thinking we're not likely to fare any better! But Paul opened his letter by encouraging Timothy to be faithful and he concludes it by showing that it is possible to be so, as we shall see in the next chapter.

8

Held By God

I have fought the good fight, I have finished the race, I have kept the faith. Now there is in store for me the crown of righteousness, which the Lord, the righteous Judge, will award to me on that day – and not only to me, but also to all who have longed for his appearing.   *2 Timothy 4:7-8*

Taking a picture from the Olympic Games Paul says, 'I prepared. I trained. I ran. What's more, I've now finished the race and God is going to give me the gold medal for my performance. I have kept the faith and am going to hear God's, 'Well done!'"

Paul's claim sounds almost arrogant to us. How can we find the confidence to keep growing and using our gift with the sort of certainty and joyful hope that Paul seemed to have? We need to look more closely at the grounds for his confidence.

A loving heavenly Father

When our oldest daughter was about two years old we had a little 'game'. I would say to her, 'Stand on your head, Bethany!' And she would get down and put her head on the floor. Then I'd say, 'Now lift your hands up.' So she would be there, with her head and feet on the floor and her arms out wide. Brilliant! Wonderful stuff! And then I'd ask, 'Are you all right?', and try to slip out of the room while she wasn't looking. But the second I stopped paying attention or wandered off, she would yell, 'Daddy, look! Daddy, look!' So I'd make a big show of her because she was trying to please me. She didn't really *want* to stand on her head!

Most of us, if we are honest, let our lives be dominated by trying to please people. Perhaps it is our wife or husband we want to please – if only because it leads to a quiet life! It may be the boss at work, the neighbours who don't like our garden looking so scruffy or people at church who expect us to be more Christ-like than we really are. We can feel driven by their expectations and believe that the only way to a peaceful life is to comply with their spoken or unspoken demands. In addition, most us want to be well thought of, respected and looked up to and some of us will do the equivalent of standing on our heads to make sure that we are!

But the good news of the gospel is that we *don't need* to. Ultimately, the only person whom it is important to please is God. And he is our loving heavenly Father who accepts us already just as we are. We need never lose confidence that he loves us, no matter what we do. When we let the reality of this sink into us it will take away all the self-doubts, the anxiety that we cannot do the job to which God has called us, and the feelings of worthlessness. As our Father and Creator who continues to work in us, God never doubts our abilities, potential and value.

A God who upholds

There are times when we feel very much aware of our inability to keep up our Christian ministry and witness in our own strength. Paul may have been able to win the fight, run the race and keep the faith but are we made of the same stuff as Paul? Paul was someone special, anyway – or so we think. We can understand that God would persevere with him but is he really going to do the same for me?

Time and again we realize we have botched things up; our eyes were not on serving God but on some other goal. But in the middle of all our failures and struggles, temptations and pressures,

God invites us to come to him and say, 'Lord, I've fallen again but I really do want to be faithful and consistent in my walk with you.' And he will pick us up and set us on the track again.

Think about it. He is a God of second, third and ninety-fifth chances. He is *even more determined than you are* that you should serve him faithfully and well in the ministry he's given you, and that you should find your greatest fulfilment in doing so. If you ever have doubts about that, think over what he has already done for you and, with Paul, ask yourself,

> If God is for us, who can be against us? He who did not spare his own Son, but gave him up for us all – how will he not also, along with him, graciously give us all things?
>
> *Romans 8:31-32*

As we step out in faith, *he* will provide all the faith and perseverance we need to carry out all that he asks us to do. And, when we have done so, we will hear the great 'Well done!' from the King of the universe. That's an exciting prospect!

> ... the Lord stood at my side and gave me strength, so that through me the message might be fully proclaimed and all the Gentiles might hear it. And I was delivered from the lion's mouth. The Lord will rescue me from every evil attack and will bring me safely to his heavenly kingdom. To him be glory for ever and ever. Amen.
>
> *2 Timothy 4:17-18*

IDENTIFYING YOUR GIFTS

Read the following points and give yourself a mark out of 5 for each. If you give yourself 5 it will be one of your very strong points. If you give yourself 0 or 1 it will be one of your very weak points.

Then transfer the marks that you give yourself to the appropriate squares in the chart. The number in each square corresponds to the point number in the list below.

__ 1   I am very good at listening.

__ 2   I enjoy explaining things to others from the Bible.

__ 3   I love preaching or talking about Jesus to a congregation or group.

__ 4   I am often used to bring others to Christ.

__ 5   I enjoy administrative work.

__ 6   I feel a deep, caring love for those who are ill, and feel a call to help them get well.

__ 7   I am handy at most things and adaptable.

__ 8   I am deeply concerned about the world and social affairs.

__ 9   I am usually looked to for a lead.

__ 10   I make helpful relationships with others easily.

___ 11   Others are helped when I teach them things.

___ 12   I love the study and work in preparing a message.

___ 13   God has given me a great love for others and a
          longing to win them for him.

___ 14   I can organize well, clearly and efficiently.

___ 15   Others find my presence soothing and healing.

___ 16   I like helping other people.

___ 17   I am active in service in the community.

___ 18   In a group I am often elected chairperson or leader.

___ 19   I can encourage others and help bear burdens.

___ 20   I love study and finding the facts.

___ 21   People tell me that they find my sermons a blessing.

___ 22   I find my life is full of opportunities to witness to
          Christ.

___ 23   I love doing office work and do it thoroughly.

___ 24   I have sometimes laid hands on the sick and they
          have been helped.

___ 25   I am a practical type.

__ 26   I am very aware of the needs of society today and feel called to do something about them.

__ 27   When leading something I put a lot of preparation into it.

__ 28   I really care about other people.

__ 29   I have patience in helping others understand Christian things.

__ 30   I feel a clear call to preach.

__ 31   I love to talk to others about Jesus.

__ 32   I am painstaking about details in organisation.

__ 33   I spend time praying with and for sick people.

__ 34   I spend much time helping others in practical ways.

__ 35   I feel God is at work in the world today and I must work along with him there.

__ 36   I am good at delegating work to others in a team setting.

Add up the totals along each line and place them in the lettered box at the end of the column.

1	10	19	28	A
2	11	20	29	B
3	12	21	30	C
4	13	22	31	D
5	14	23	32	E
6	15	24	33	F
7	16	25	34	G
8	17	26	35	H
9	18	27	36	I

If your highest total is in column:

A your gift is pastoral

B " " " teaching

C " " " preaching

D " " " evangelism

E " " " administration

F " " " healing

G " " " giving practical help

H " " " service to society

I " " " leadership

A and F (pastoral and healing gifts) are primarily the 'caring' gifts.
B, C and D (teaching, preaching and evangelism) are primarily the 'thinking and talking' gifts.
E, G, H and I (administration, giving practical help, service to society and leadership) are primarily the 'doing' gifts.

It is easy to mislead yourself in this sort of exercise; we are not always fully aware of our own strengths. So, besides filling it in yourself, it may be helpful to give a copy of the questionnaire to four of your closest friends and ask them to fill it in for you (i.e., changing each of the statements to 'he/she', 'he is/she is' etc) as honestly as possible. Don't show them your marks until after you have theirs.

NOTES

Chapter 3

1 David Watson, *Discipleship*. London: Hodder and Stoughton, 1989.

2 John Stott, *The Message of 2 Timothy: Guard the Gospel*. Leicester: IVP, 1984.

Chapter 4

3 Commentaries, Bible Dictionaries and Concordances are the basic books you will need for this library. You will also find it helpful to build up a collection of books that explain: how to interpret the different types of literature in the Bible (e.g. *Unlock the Bible*, by Stephen Motyer), how to tackle Bible study (e.g. *Get more from your Bible*, by Brian Abshire), how to lead and facilitate small groups (e.g. *Good things come in small groups*, by various authors; *Growing Christians in small groups*, by John Mallison. All of these are published by Scripture Union.

4 William Barclay, *Timothy, Titus and Philemon* from the Daily Study Bible. Edinburgh: The Saint Andrew Press.

Chapter 5

5 Christians differ over their views of what will happen at the end times. The concept of an idyllic period of one thousand years derives from Revelation 20:6. Pre-millennialists are those who believe he will return after it. A-millennialists believe that the reference to one thousand years should be taken symbolically, not literally.

Chapter 6

6 David Augsburger, *Christianity Today*, 20 November 1987.

Chapter 7

7 Ann Loades, *Searching for Lost Coins*. London: SPCK, 1987.

8 The gift-identification questionnaire was devised by Lewis Misselbrook.